Will Shortz Presents
The Monster Book of

KENKEN®

KenKen®: Logic Puzzles That Make You Smarter!

Will Shortz Presents KenKen Easiest, Volume 1
Will Shortz Presents KenKen Easy, Volume 2
Will Shortz Presents KenKen Easy to Hard, Volume 3
Will Shortz Presents The Little Gift Book of KenKen
Will Shortz Presents Crazy for KenKen Easiest
Will Shortz Presents Crazy for KenKen Easy
Will Shortz Presents Crazy for KenKen Easy to Hard
Will Shortz Presents KenKen for the Seaside
Will Shortz Presents KenKen for Your Coffee Break
Will Shortz Presents KenKen for Stress Relief
Will Shortz Presents Tame KenKen
Will Shortz Presents Wild KenKen
Will Shortz Presents Ferocious KenKen
Will Shortz Presents The Ultimate KenKen Omnibus
Will Shortz Presents KenKen for Your Vacation
The New York Times Will Shortz Presents
Easy to Hard KenKen
The New York Times Will Shortz Presents
Challenging KenKen
The New York Times Will Shortz Presents
Diabolical KenKen
Will Shortz Presents The Little Pink Book of KenKen
Will Shortz Presents The Big, Bad Book of KenKen

KenKen for Kids

Will Shortz Presents I Can KenKen! Volume 1
Will Shortz Presents I Can KenKen! Volume 2
Will Shortz Presents I Can KenKen! Volume 3

WILL SHORTZ PRESENTS THE MONSTER BOOK OF KENKEN®

300 EASY TO HARD LOGIC PUZZLES THAT MAKE YOU SMARTER

TETSUYA MIYAMOTO

INTRODUCTION BY WILL SHORTZ

ST. MARTIN'S GRIFFIN
NEW YORK

The puzzles in this volume have previously appeared in *Will Shortz Presents The Puzzle Doctor: KenKen Fever; Will Shortz Presents KenKen for Stress Relief; Will Shortz Presents KenKen for Your Coffee Break; Will Shortz Presents The Little Pink Book of KenKen;* and *The New York Times Will Shortz Presents Diabolical KenKen.*

www.stmartins.com

ISBN 978-0-312-65433-7

10 9 8 7 6 5 4

Will Shortz Presents
The Monster Book of

KENKEN®

Introduction

If you consider all the world's greatest puzzle varieties, the ones that have inspired crazes over the years—crosswords, jigsaw puzzles, tangrams, sudoku, etc.—they have several properties in common. They . . .

- Are simple to learn
- Have great depth
- Are variable in difficulty, from easy to hard
- Are mentally soothing and pleasing
- Have some unique feature that makes them different from everything else and instantly addictive

By these standards, a new puzzle called KenKen, the subject of the book you're holding, has the potential to become one of the world's greats.

KenKen is Japanese for "square wisdom" or "cleverness squared." The rules are simple: Fill the grid with digits so as not to repeat a digit in any row or column (as in sudoku) and so the digits within each heavily outlined group of boxes combine to make the arithmetic result indicated.

The simplest KenKen puzzles start with 3×3 boxes and use only addition. Harder examples have larger grids and more arithmetic operations.

KenKen was invented in 2003 by Tetsuya Miyamoto, a Japanese math instructor, as a means to help his students learn arithmetic and develop logical thinking. Tetsuya's education method is unusual. Put simply, he doesn't teach. His philosophy is to make the tools of learning available to students and then let them progress on their own.

Tetsuya's most popular learning tool has been KenKen, which his students spend hours doing and find more engaging than TV and video games.

It's true that KenKen has great capacity for educating and building the mind. But first and foremost it's a puzzle to be enjoyed. It is to numbers what the crossword puzzle is to words.

So turn the page and begin. . . .

—Will Shortz

How to Solve KenKen

KenKen is a logic puzzle with simple rules:

- Fill the grid with digits so as not to repeat a digit in any row or column.
- Digits within each heavily outlined group of squares, called a cage, must combine to make the arithmetic result indicated.
- A 3×3–square puzzle will use the digits from 1 to 3, a 4×4–square puzzle will use the digits from 1 to 4, etc.

Solving a KenKen puzzle involves pure logic and mathematics. No guesswork is needed. Every puzzle has a unique solution.

In this volume of KenKen, the puzzles use all four arithmetic operations—addition, subtraction, multiplication, and division—in the following manner:

- In a cage marked with a plus sign, the given number will be the sum of the digits you enter in the squares.
- In a cage marked with a minus sign, the given number will be the difference between the digits you enter in the squares (the lower digit subtracted from the higher one).
- In a cage marked with a multiplication sign, the given number will be the product of the digits you enter in the squares.
- In a cage marked with a division sign, the given number will be the quotient of the digits you enter in the squares.

To start, fill in any digits in 1×1 sections—in this puzzle, the 4 in the fourth row. These are literally no-brainers.

48×		3+		4−
	8+	10×	4+	
3−				2÷
	4+		4	
7+			15×	

Take the 5×5–square example on this page.

To start, fill in any digits in 1×1 sections—in this puzzle, the 4 in the fourth row. These are literally no-brainers.

Next, look for sections whose given numbers are either high or low, or that involve distinctive combinations of digits, since these are often the easiest to solve. For example, the L-shaped group in the upper left has a product of 48. The only combination of three digits from 1 to 5 that multiplies to 48 is 3, 4, and 4. Since the two 4s can't appear in the same row or column, they must appear at the ends of the L. The 3 goes between them.

Now look at the pair of squares in the first row with a sum of 3. The only two digits that add up to 3 are 1 and 2. We don't know their order yet, but this information can still be useful.

Sometimes, the next step in solving a KenKen puzzle is to ignore the given numbers and use sudoku-like logic to avoid repeating a digit in a row or column. For example, now that 1, 2, 3, and 4 have been used or are slated for use in the first row, the remaining square (at the end of the row) must be a 5. Then the digit below the 5 must be a 1 for this pair of squares to have a difference of 4.

Next, consider the pair of squares in the third column with a product of 10. The only two digits from 1 to 5 that have a product of 10 are 2 and 5. We don't know their order yet. However, the digit in the square above them, which we previously identified as either a 1 or a 2, must be 1, so as not to repeat a 2 in this column. The 2 that accompanies the 1 goes to its right.

Continuing in this way, using these and other techniques left for you to discover, you can work your way around the grid, filling in the rest of the squares. The complete solution is shown on the following page.

48× 3	4	3+ 1	2	4− 5
4	8+ 5	10× 2	4+ 3	1
3− 2	3	5	1	2÷ 4
5	4+ 1	3	4 4	2
7+ 1	2	4	15× 5	3

Additional Tips

- In advanced KenKen puzzles, as you've seen, cages can have more than two squares. It's okay for a cage to repeat a digit—as long as the digit is not repeated in a row or column.
- Cages with more than two squares will always involve addition or multiplication. Subtraction and division occur only in cages with exactly two squares.
- Remember, in doing KenKen, you never have to guess. Every puzzle can be solved by using step-by-step logic. Keep going, and soon you'll be a KenKen master!

SEARCHING FOR MORE KENKEN®?

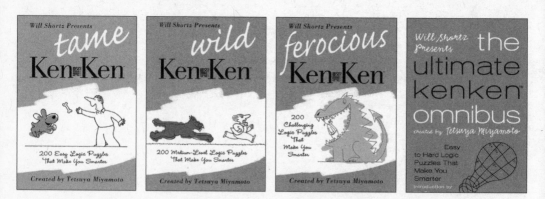
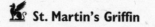

Light and Easy +/−/×/÷ 1

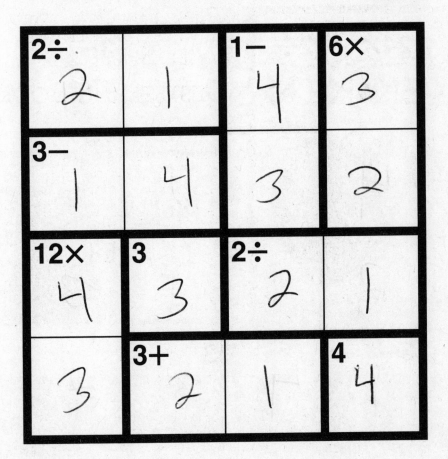

2÷ 2	1	1− 4	6× 3
3− 1	4	3	2
12× 4	3 3	2÷ 2	1
3	3+ 2	1	4 4

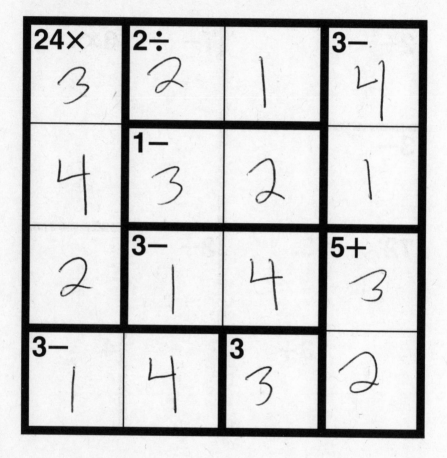

24× 3	2÷ 2	1	3− 4
4	1− 3	2	1
2	3− 1	4	5+ 3
3− 1	4	3 3	2

Light and Easy +/−/×/÷ 3

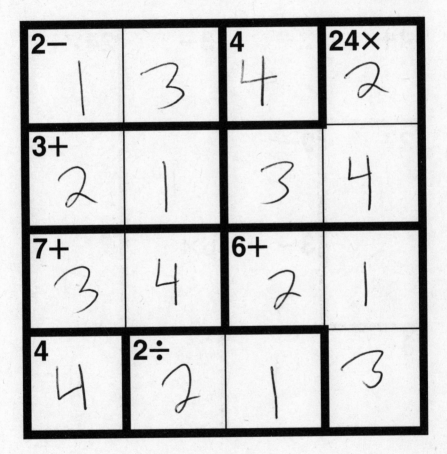

2−		4	24×
1	3	4	2
3+ 2	1	3	4
7+ 3	4	**6+** 2	1
4 4	**2÷** 2	1	3

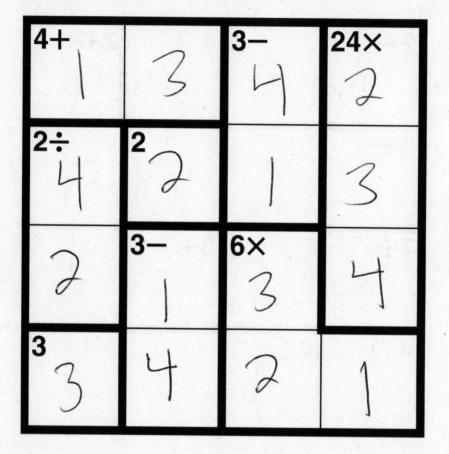

4+ 1	3	3− 4	24× 2
2÷ 4	2 2	1	3
2	3− 1	6× 3	4
3 3	4	2	1

Light and Easy +/−/×/÷   5

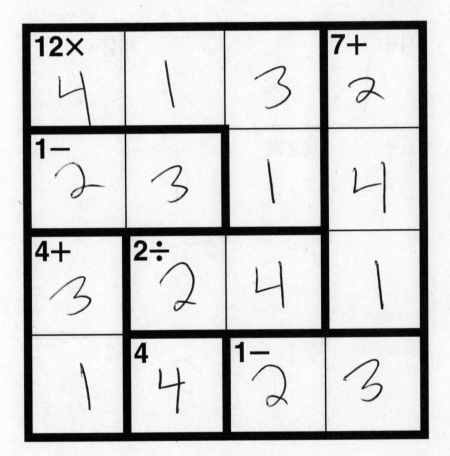

12× 4	1	3	7+ 2
1− 2	3	1	4
4+ 3	2÷ 2	4	1
1	4 4	1− 2	3

6 Light and Easy +/−/×/÷

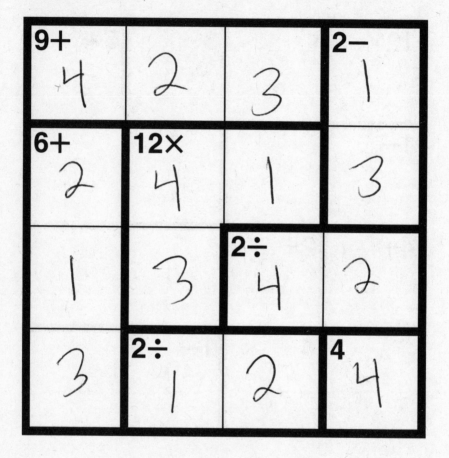

9+ 4	2	3	2− 1
6+ 2	12× 4	1	3
1	3	2÷ 4	2
3	2÷ 1	2	4 4

Light and Easy +/−/×/÷   **7**

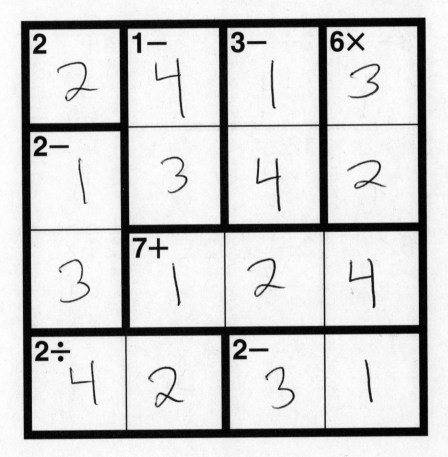

2 2	1− 4	3− 1	6× 3
2− 1	3	4	2
3	7+ 1	2	4
2÷ 4	2	2− 3	1

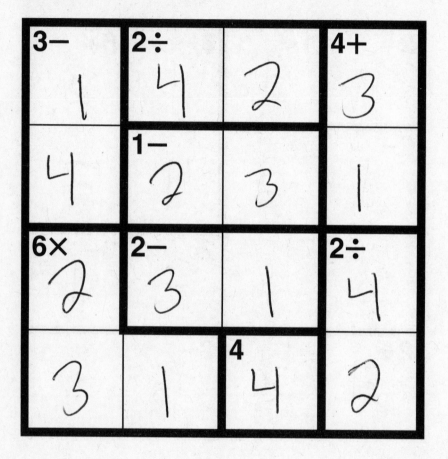

3− 1	2÷ 4	2	4+ 3
4	1− 2	3	1
6× 2	2− 3	1	2÷ 4
3	1	4 4	2

Light and Easy +/−/×/÷   9

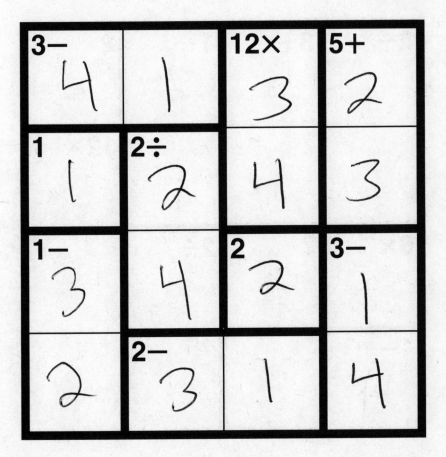

3− 4	1	12× 3	5+ 2
1 1	2÷ 2	4	3
1− 3	4	2 2	3− 1
2	2− 3	1	4

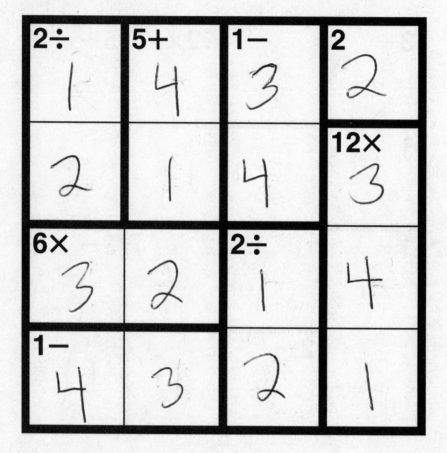

2÷	5+	1−	2
1	4	3	2
2	1	4	12× 3
6× 3	2	2÷ 1	4
1− 4	3	2	1

Light and Easy +/−/×/÷   11

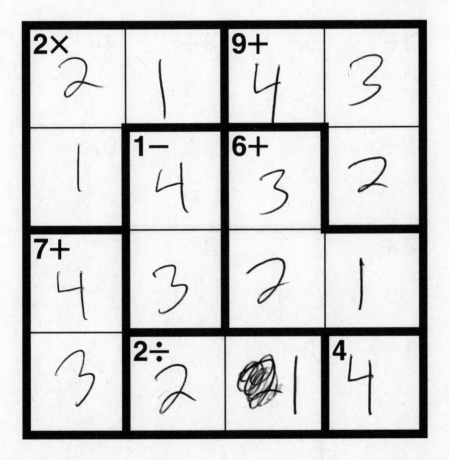

2× 2	1	9+ 4	3
1	1− 4	6+ 3	2
7+ 4	3	2	1
3	2÷ 2	1	4 4

12 Light and Easy +/−/×/÷

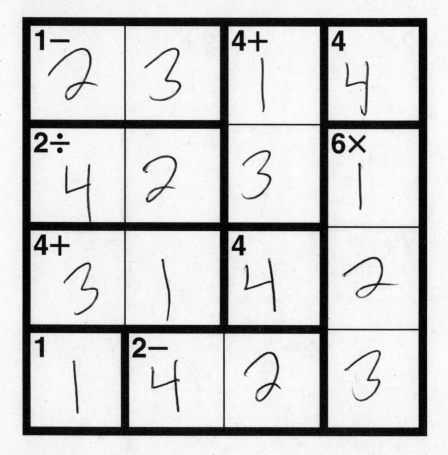

1− 2	3	4+ 1	4 4
2÷ 4	2	3	6× 1
4+ 3	1	4 4	2
1 1	2− 4	2	3

Light and Easy +/−/×/÷ 13

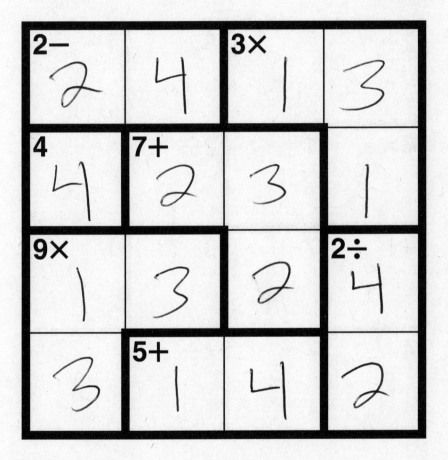

14 Light and Easy +/−/×/÷

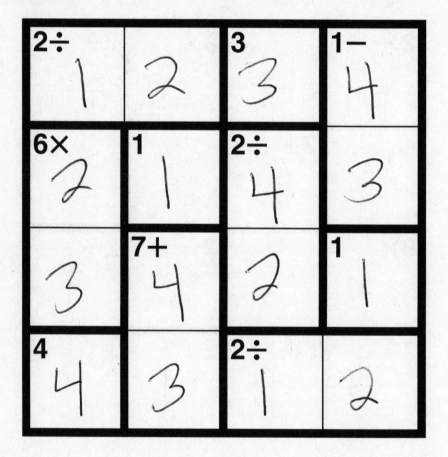

2÷ 1	2	3 3	1− 4
6× 2	1 1	2÷ 4	3
3	7+ 4	2	1 1
4 4	3	2÷ 1	2

Light and Easy +/−/×/÷ 15

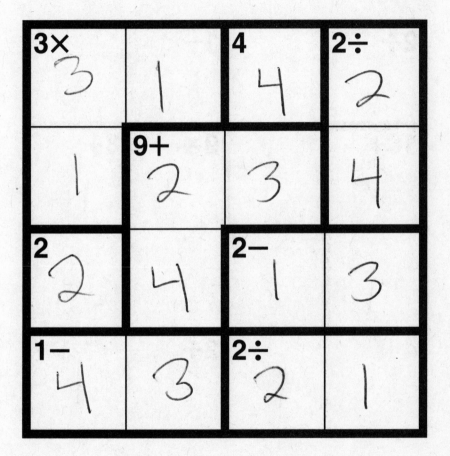

16 Light and Easy +/−/×/÷

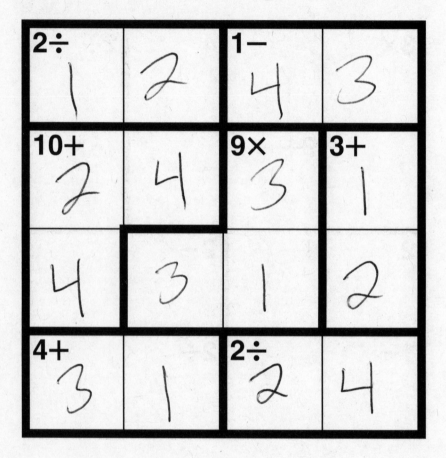

2÷		1−	
1	2	4	3
10+ 2	4	**9×** 3	**3+** 1
4	3	1	2
4+ 3	1	**2÷** 2	4

Light and Easy +/−/×/÷   17

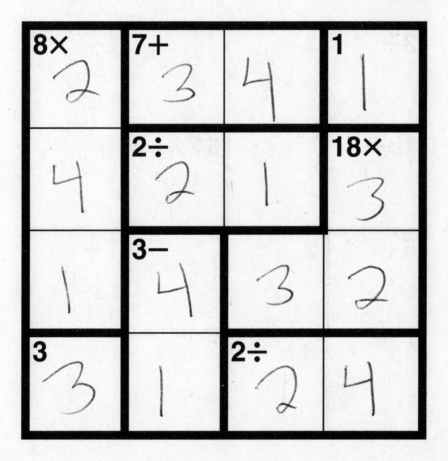

8× 2	7+ 3	4	1 1
4	2÷ 2	1	18× 3
1	3− 4	3	2
3 3	1	2÷ 2	4

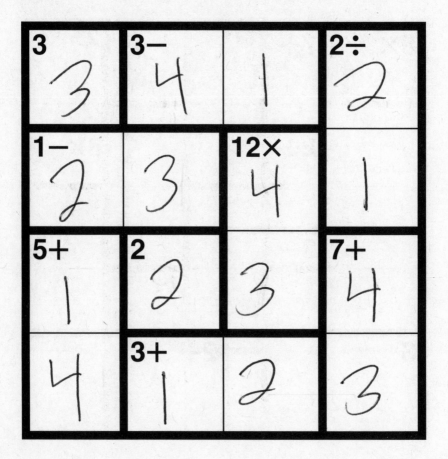

3 3	3− 4	1	2÷ 2
1− 2	3	12× 4	1
5+ 1	2 2	3	7+ 4
4	3+ 1	2	3

Light and Easy +/−/×/÷ 19

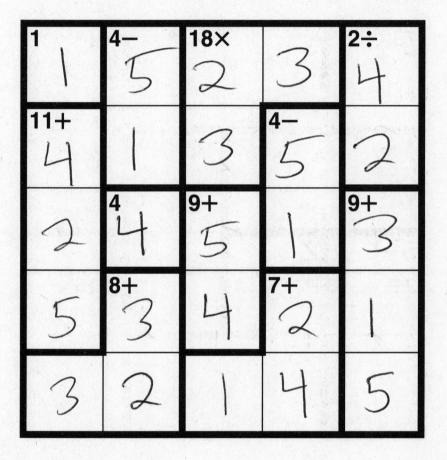

1 1	4− 5	18× 2	3	2÷ 4
11+ 4	1	3	4− 5	2
2	4 4	9+ 5	1	9+ 3
5	8+ 3	4	7+ 2	1
3	2	1	4	5

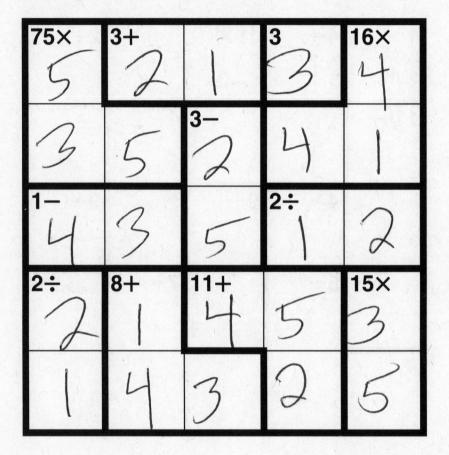

75×	3+		3	16×
5	2	1	3	4
3	5	3− 2	4	1
1− 4	3	5	2÷ 1	2
2÷ 2	8+ 1	11+ 4	5	15× 3
1	4	3	2	5

Light and Easy +/−/×/÷ 21

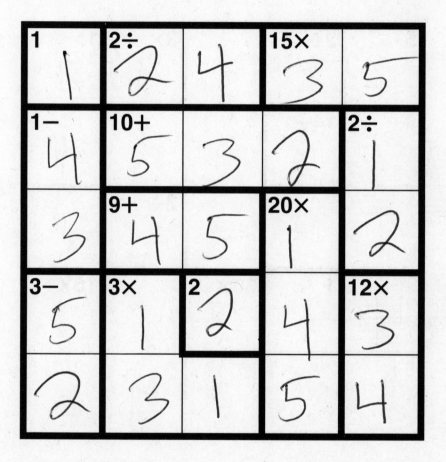

1	2÷		15×	
1	2	4	3	5
1−	10+			2÷
4	5	3	2	1
	9+		20×	
3	4	5	1	2
3−	3×	2		12×
5	1	2	4	3
2	3	1	5	4

22 Light and Easy +/−/×/÷

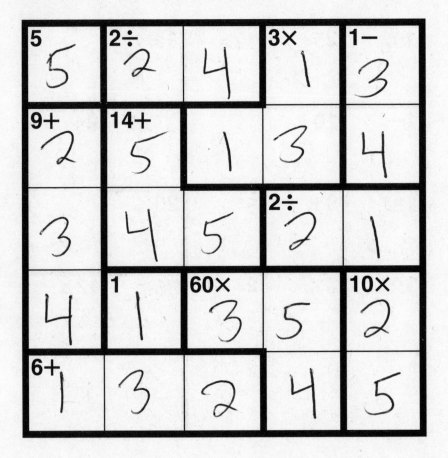

5 5	**2÷** 2	4	**3×** 1	**1−** 3
9+ 2	**14+** 5	1	3	4
3	4	5	**2÷** 2	1
4	**1** 1	**60×** 3	5	**10×** 2
6+ 1	3	2	4	5

Light and Easy +/−/×/÷   23

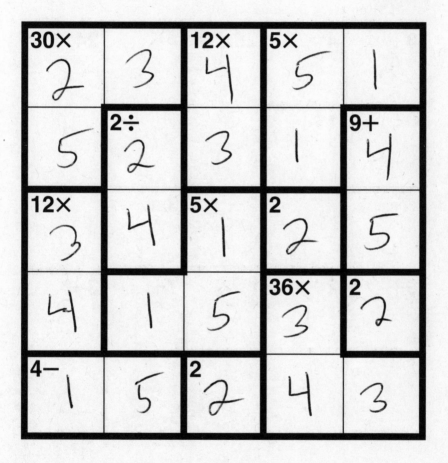

30×		12×	5×	
2	3	4	5	1
5	2÷ 2	3	1	9+ 4
12× 3	4	5× 1	2 2	5
4	1	5	36× 3	2 2
4− 1	5	2 2	4	3

24 Light and Easy +/−/×/÷

3+	4	25×		24×
	11+			
		2−	3−	
9+	2÷		7+	3−

Light and Easy +/−/×/÷ 25

3−	12×	2÷	5×	
				12+
3+		2−		
1−	25×		2÷	
			1−	

26 Light and Easy +/−/×/÷

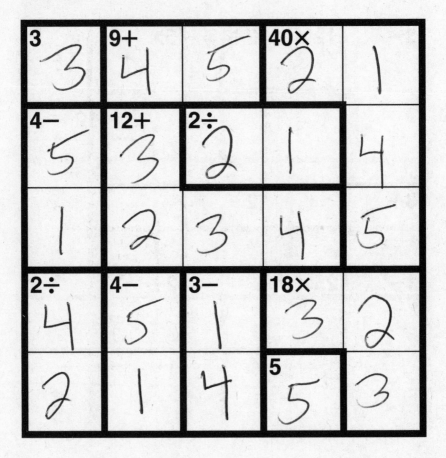

3 3	9+ 4	5	40× 2	1
4− 5	12+ 3	2÷ 2	1	4
1	2	3	4	5
2÷ 4	4− 5	3− 1	18× 3	2
2	1	4	5 5	3

Light and Easy +/−/×/÷   27

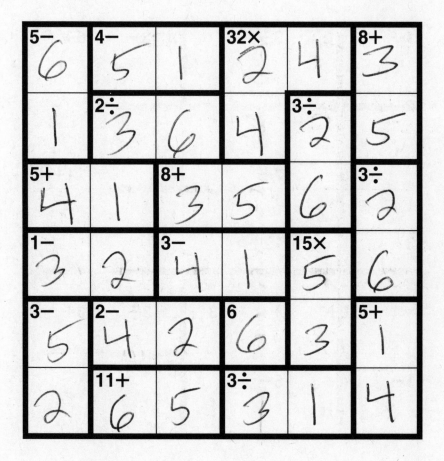

5− 6	4− 5	1	32× 2	4	8+ 3
1	2÷ 3	6	4	3÷ 2	5
5+ 4	1	8+ 3	5	6	3÷ 2
1− 3	2	3− 4	1	15× 5	6
3− 5	2− 4	2	6 6	3	5+ 1
2	11+ 6	5	3÷ 3	1	4

28 Light and Easy +/−/×/÷

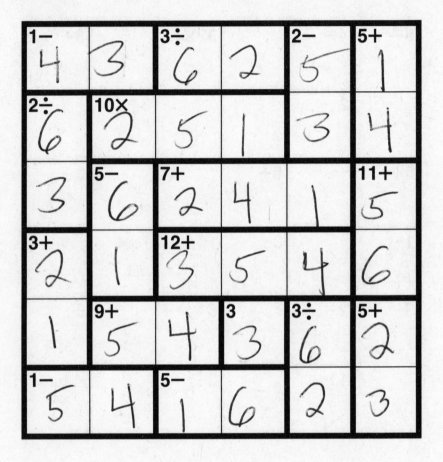

1− 4	3	3÷ 6	2	2− 5	5+ 1
2÷ 6	10× 2	5	1	3	4
3	5− 6	7+ 2	4	1	11+ 5
3+ 2	1	12+ 3	5	4	6
1	9+ 5	4	3 3	3÷ 6	5+ 2
1− 5	4	5− 1	6	2	3

Light and Easy +/−/×/÷ 29

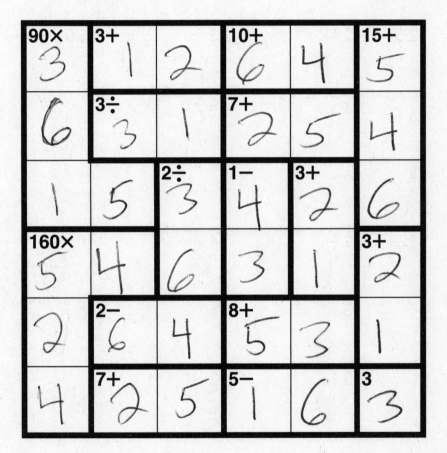

90× 3	3+ 1	2	10+ 6	4	15+ 5
6	3÷ 3	1	7+ 2	5	4
1	5	2÷ 3	1− 4	3+ 2	6
160× 5	4	6	3	1	3+ 2
2	2− 6	4	8+ 5	3	1
4	7+ 2	5	5− 1	6	3 3

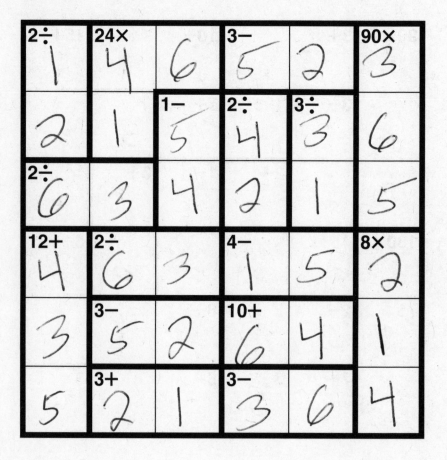

2÷ 1	24× 4	6	3− 5	2	90× 3
2	1	1− 5	2÷ 4	3÷ 3	6
2÷ 6	3	4	2	1	5
12+ 4	2÷ 6	3	4− 1	5	8× 2
3	3− 5	2	10+ 6	4	1
5	3+ 2	1	3− 3	6	4

Light and Easy +/−/×/÷ 31

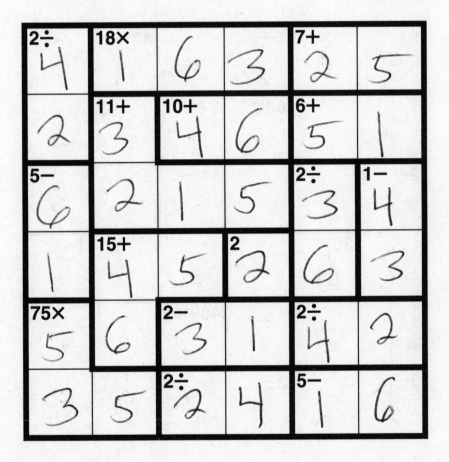

2÷ 4	18× 1	6	3	7+ 2	5
2	11+ 3	10+ 4	6	6+ 5	1
5− 6	2	1	5	2÷ 3	1− 4
1	15+ 4	5	2 2	6	3
75× 5	6	2− 3	1	2÷ 4	2
3	5	2÷ 2	4	5− 1	6

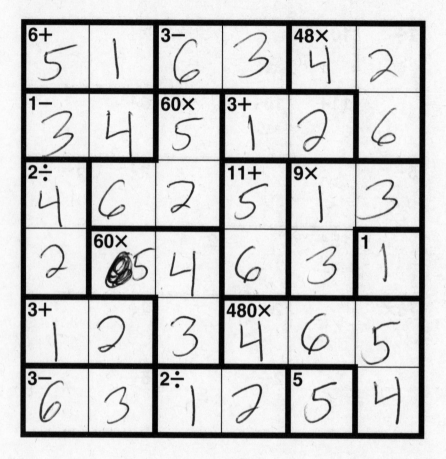

6+ 5	1	3− 6	3	48× 4	2
1− 3	4	60× 5	3+ 1	2	6
2÷ 4	6	2	11+ 5	9× 1	3
2	60× 5	4	6	3	1 1
3+ 1	2	3	480× 4	6	5
3− 6	3	2÷ 1	2	5 5	4

Light and Easy +/−/×/÷

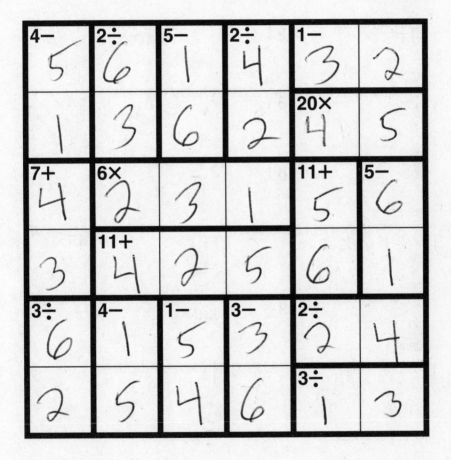

4− 5	2÷ 6	5− 1	2÷ 4	1− 3	2
1	3	6	2	20× 4	5
7+ 4	6× 2	3	1	11+ 5	5− 6
3	11+ 4	2	5	6	1
3÷ 6	4− 1	1− 5	3− 3	2÷ 2	4
2	5	4	6	3÷ 1	3

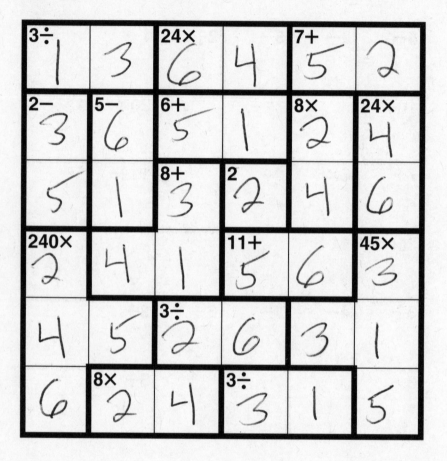

3÷ 1	3	24× 6	4	7+ 5	2
2− 3	5− 6	6+ 5	1	8× 2	24× 4
5	1	8+ 3	2 2	4	6
240× 2	4	1	11+ 5	6	45× 3
4	5	3÷ 2	6	3	1
6	8× 2	4	3÷ 3	1	5

Light and Easy +/−/×/÷   35

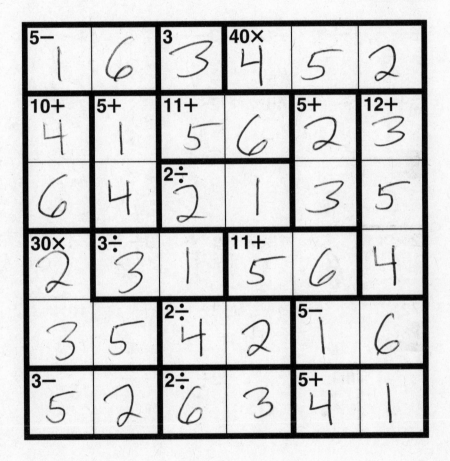

5−		3	40×		
1	6	3	4	5	2
10+	**5+**	**11+**		**5+**	**12+**
4	1	5	6	2	3
6	4	**2÷** 2	1	3	5
30× 2	**3÷** 3	1	**11+** 5	6	4
3	5	**2÷** 4	2	**5−** 1	6
3− 5	2	**2÷** 6	3	**5+** 4	1

36 Light and Easy +/−/×/÷

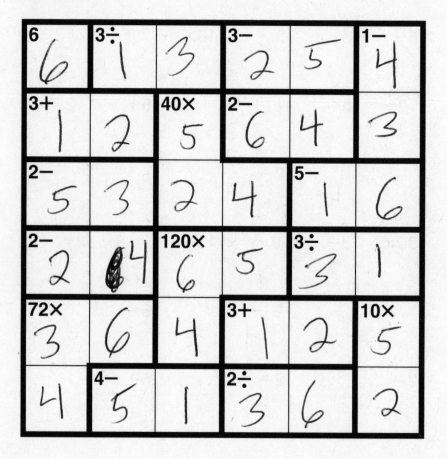

6 6	3÷ 1	3	3− 2	5	1− 4
3+ 1	2	40× 5	2− 6	4	3
2− 5	3	2	4	5− 1	6
2− 2	4	120× 6	5	3÷ 3	1
72× 3	6	4	3+ 1	2	10× 5
4	4− 5	1	2÷ 3	6	2

Light and Easy +/−/×/÷ 37

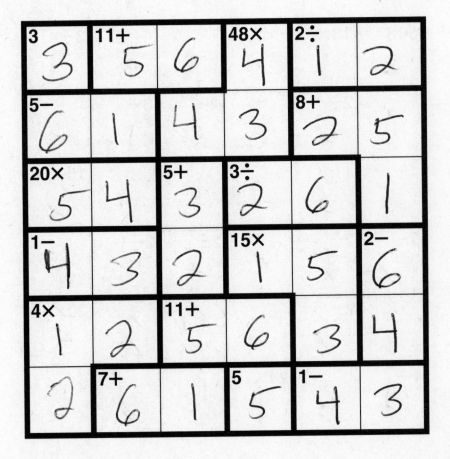

3 3	**11+** 5	6	**48×** 4	**2÷** 1	2
5− 6	1	4	3	**8+** 2	5
20× 5	4	**5+** 3	**3÷** 2	6	1
1− 4	3	2	**15×** 1	5	**2−** 6
4× 1	2	**11+** 5	6	3	4
2	**7+** 6	1	**5** 5	**1−** 4	3

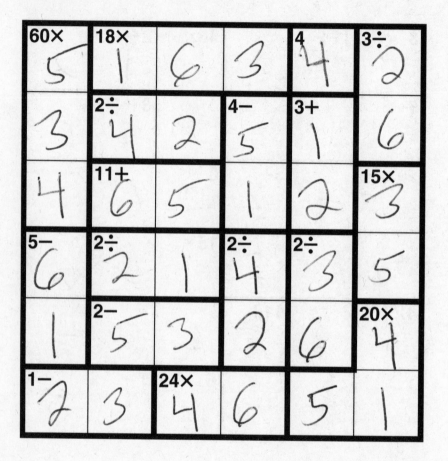

60× 5	18× 1	6	3	4 4	3÷ 2
3	2÷ 4	2	4− 5	3+ 1	6
4	11+ 6	5	1	2	15× 3
5− 6	2÷ 2	1	2÷ 4	2÷ 3	5
1	2− 5	3	2	6	20× 4
1− 2	3	24× 4	6	5	1

Light and Easy +/−/×/÷ 39

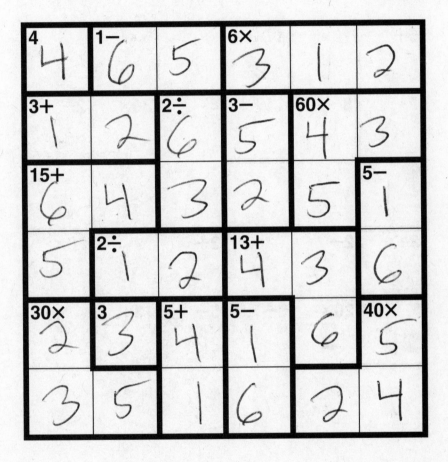

4 4	1− 6	5	6× 3	1	2
3+ 1	2	2÷ 6	3− 5	60× 4	3
15+ 6	4	3	2	5	5− 1
5	2÷ 1	2	13+ 4	3	6
30× 2	3 3	5+ 4	5− 1	6	40× 5
3	5	1	6	2	4

40 Light and Easy +/−/×/÷

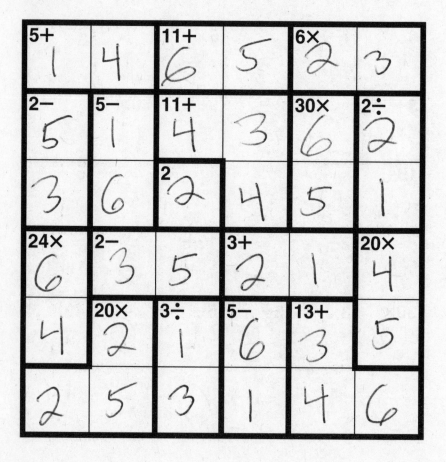

5+		11+		6×	
1	4	6	5	2	3
2− 5	**5−** 1	**11+** 4	3	**30×** 6	**2÷** 2
3	6	**2** 2	4	5	1
24× 6	**2−** 3	5	**3+** 2	1	**20×** 4
4	**20×** 2	**3÷** 1	**5−** 6	**13+** 3	5
2	5	3	1	4	6

Light and Easy +/−/×/÷ 41

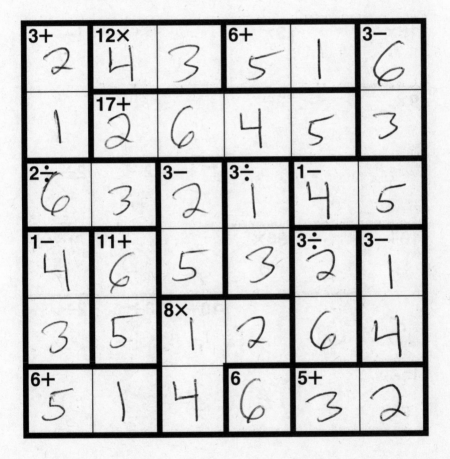

3+ 2	12× 4	3	6+ 5	1	3− 6
1	17+ 2	6	4	5	3
2÷ 6	3	3− 2	3÷ 1	1− 4	5
1− 4	11+ 6	5	3	3÷ 2	3− 1
3	5	8× 1	2	6	4
6+ 5	1	4	6 6	5+ 3	2

42 Light and Easy +/−/×/÷

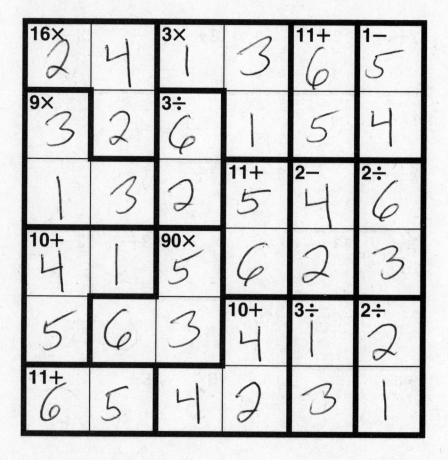

16× 2	4	3× 1	3	11+ 6	1− 5
9× 3	2	3÷ 6	1	5	4
1	3	2	11+ 5	2− 4	2÷ 6
10+ 4	1	90× 5	6	2	3
5	6	3	10+ 4	3÷ 1	2÷ 2
11+ 6	5	4	2	3	1

Light and Easy +/−/×/÷ 43

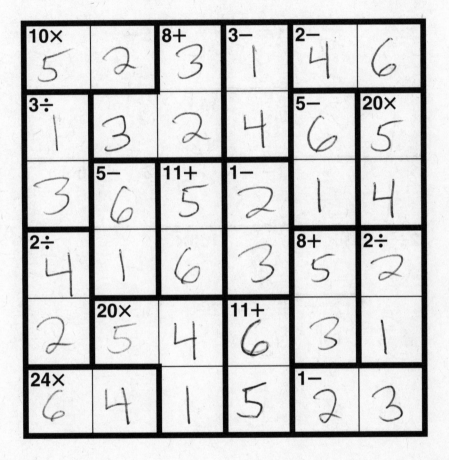

10× 5	2	8+ 3	3− 1	2− 4	6
3÷ 1	3	2	4	5− 6	20× 5
3	5− 6	11+ 5	1− 2	1	4
2÷ 4	1	6	3	8+ 5	2÷ 2
2	20× 5	4	11+ 6	3	1
24× 6	4	1	5	1− 2	3

44 Light and Easy +/−/×/÷

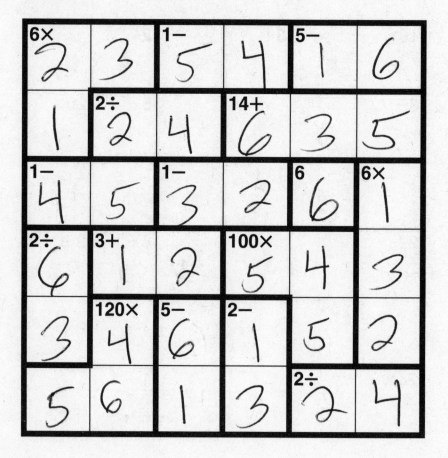

6× 2	3	1− 5	4	5− 1	6
1	2÷ 2	4	14+ 6	3	5
1− 4	5	1− 3	2	6 6	6× 1
2÷ 6	3+ 1	2	100× 5	4	3
3	120× 4	5− 6	2− 1	5	2
5	6	1	3	2÷ 2	4

Light and Easy +/−/×/÷ 45

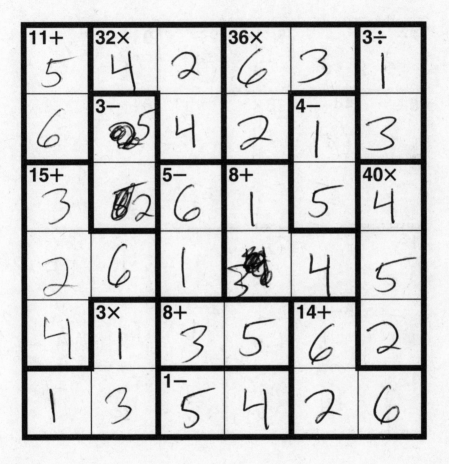

11+	32×		36×		3÷
5	4	2	6	3	1
6	3− 5	4	2	4− 1	3
15+ 3	2	5− 6	8+ 1	5	40× 4
2	6	1	3	4	5
4	3× 1	8+ 3	5	14+ 6	2
1	3	1− 5	4	2	6

46 Light and Easy +/−/×/÷

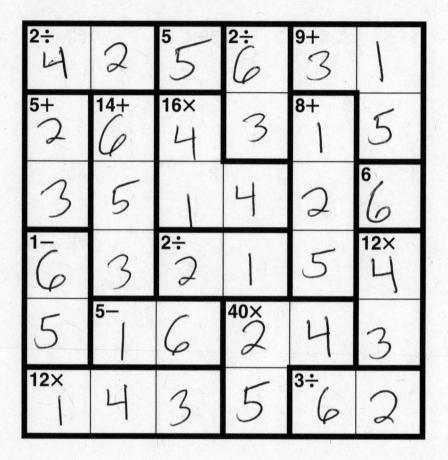

2÷ 4	2	5 5	2÷ 6	9+ 3	1
5+ 2	14+ 6	16× 4	3	8+ 1	5
3	5	1	4	2	6 6
1− 6	3	2÷ 2	1	5	12× 4
5	5− 1	6	40× 2	4	3
12× 1	4	3	5	3÷ 6	2

Light and Easy +/−/×/÷ 47

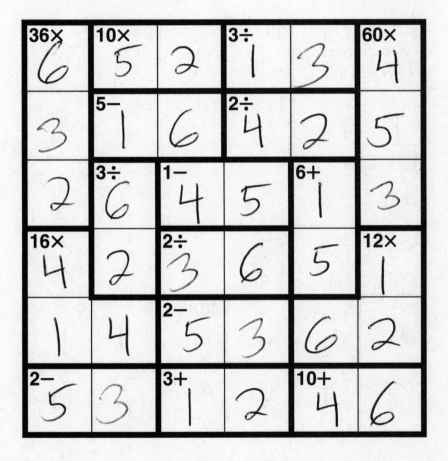

36× 6	10× 5	2	3÷ 1	3	60× 4
3	5− 1	6	2÷ 4	2	5
2	3÷ 6	1− 4	5	6+ 1	3
16× 4	2	2÷ 3	6	5	12× 1
1	4	2− 5	3	6	2
2− 5	3	3+ 1	2	10+ 4	6

48 Light and Easy +/−/×/÷

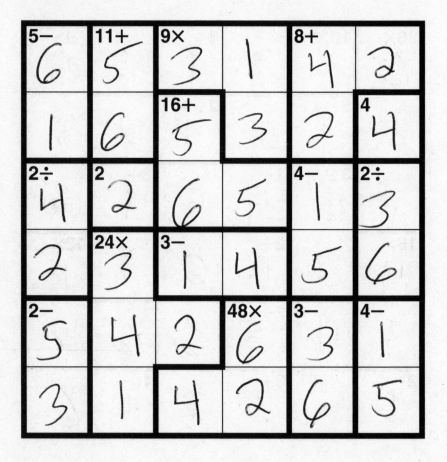

5− 6	11+ 5	9× 3	1	8+ 4	2
1	6	16+ 5	3	2	4 4
2÷ 4	2 2	6	5	4− 1	2÷ 3
2	24× 3	3− 1	4	5	6
2− 5	4	2	48× 6	3− 3	4− 1
3	1	4	2	6	5

Light and Easy +/−/×/÷ 49

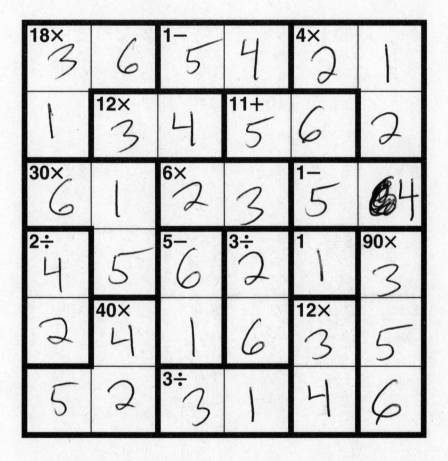

18× 3	6	1− 5	4	4× 2	1
1	12× 3	4	11+ 5	6	2
30× 6	1	6× 2	3	1− 5	4
2÷ 4	5	5− 6	3÷ 2	1 1	90× 3
2	40× 4	1	6	12× 3	5
5	2	3÷ 3	1	4	6

50 Light and Easy +/−/×/÷

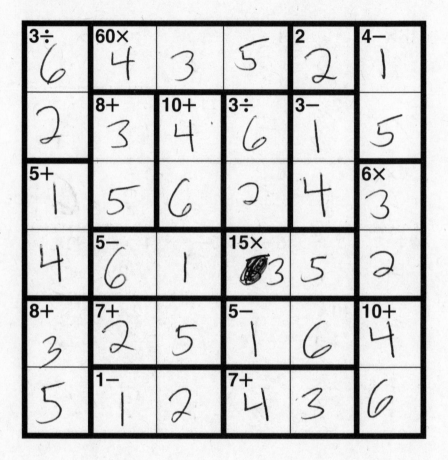

3÷ 6	60× 4	3	5	2 2	4− 1
2	8+ 3	10+ 4	3÷ 6	3− 1	5
5+ 1	5	6	2	4	6× 3
4	5− 6	1	15× 3	5	2
8+ 3	7+ 2	5	5− 1	6	10+ 4
5	1− 1	2	7+ 4	3	6

Light and Easy +/−/×/÷ **51**

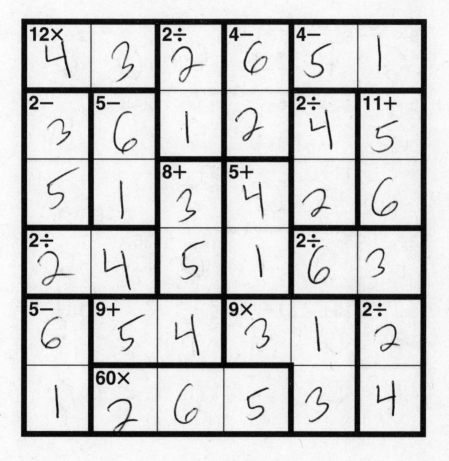

12× 4	3	2÷ 2	4− 6	4− 5	1
2− 3	5− 6	1	2	2÷ 4	11+ 5
5	1	8+ 3	5+ 4	2	6
2÷ 2	4	5	1	2÷ 6	3
5− 6	9+ 5	4	9× 3	1	2÷ 2
1	60× 2	6	5	3	4

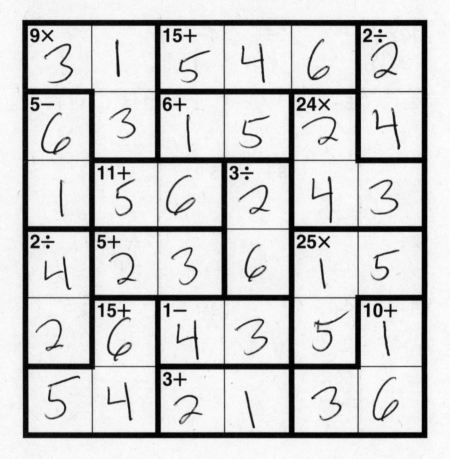

9× 3	1	**15+** 5	4	6	**2÷** 2
5− 6	3	**6+** 1	5	**24×** 2	4
1	**11+** 5	6	**3÷** 2	4	3
2÷ 4	**5+** 2	3	6	**25×** 1	5
2	**15+** 6	**1−** 4	3	5	**10+** 1
5	4	**3+** 2	1	3	6

Light and Easy +/−/×/÷ 53

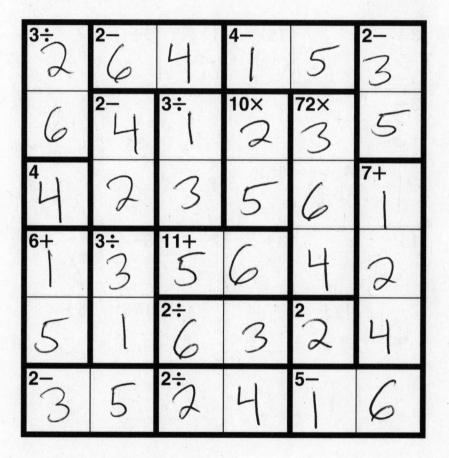

3÷ 2	2− 6	4	4− 1	5	2− 3
6	2− 4	3÷ 1	10× 2	72× 3	5
4 4	2	3	5	6	7+ 1
6+ 1	3÷ 3	11+ 5	6	4	2
5	1	2÷ 6	3	2 2	4
2− 3	5	2÷ 2	4	5− 1	6

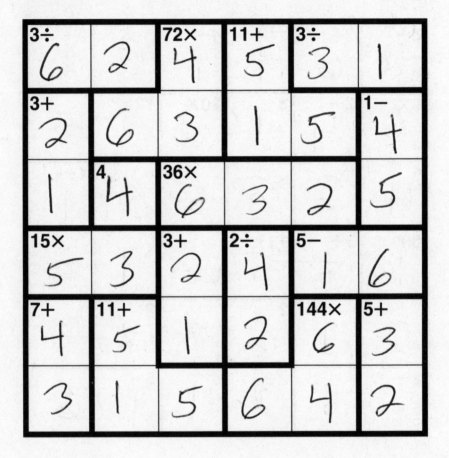

3÷ 6	2	72× 4	11+ 5	3÷ 3	1
3+ 2	6	3	1	5	1− 4
1	4⁴ 4	36× 6	3	2	5
15× 5	3	3+ 2	2÷ 4	5− 1	6
7+ 4	11+ 5	1	2	144× 6	5+ 3
3	1	5	6	4	2

Light and Easy +/−/×/÷ 55

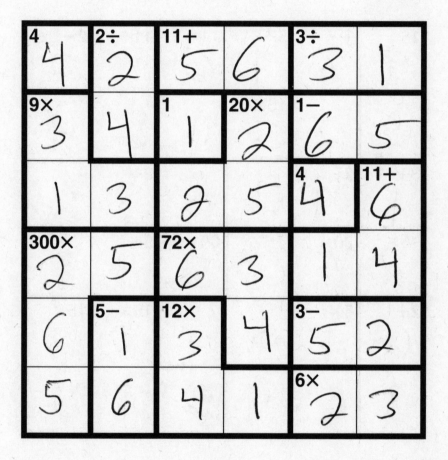

4 **4**	2÷ **2**	11+ **5**	**6**	3÷ **3**	**1**
9× **3**	**4**	1 **1**	20× **2**	1− **6**	**5**
1	**3**	**2**	**5**	4 **4**	11+ **6**
300× **2**	**5**	72× **6**	**3**	**1**	**4**
6	5− **1**	12× **3**	**4**	3− **5**	**2**
5	**6**	**4**	**1**	6× **2**	**3**

56 Light and Easy +/−/×/÷

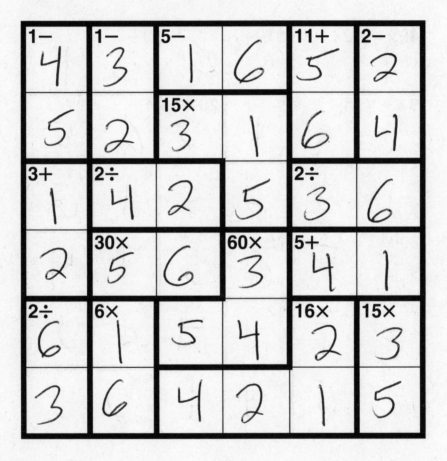

1−	1−	5−		11+	2−
4	3	1	6	5	2
		15×			
5	2	3	1	6	4
3+	2÷			2÷	
1	4	2	5	3	6
	30×		60×	5+	
2	5	6	3	4	1
2÷	6×			16×	15×
6	1	5	4	2	3
3	6	4	2	1	5

Light and Easy +/−/×/÷ 57

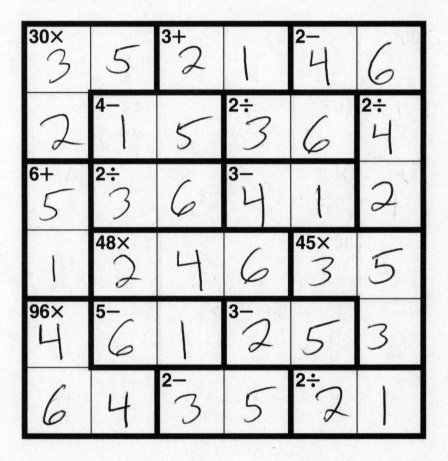

30× 3	5	3+ 2	1	2− 4	6
2	4− 1	5	2÷ 3	6	2÷ 4
6+ 5	2÷ 3	6	3− 4	1	2
1	48× 2	4	6	45× 3	5
96× 4	5− 6	1	3− 2	5	3
6	4	2− 3	5	2÷ 2	1

58 Light and Easy +/−/×/÷

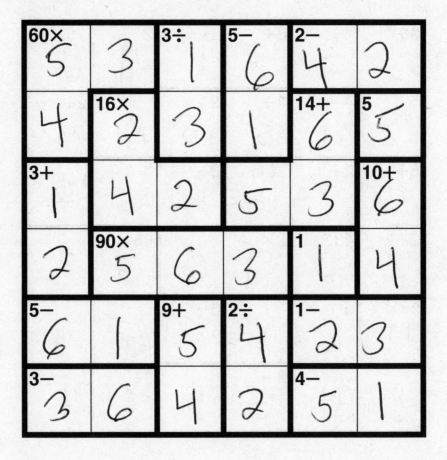

60× 5	3	3÷ 1	5− 6	2− 4	2
4	16× 2	3	1	14+ 6	5 5
3+ 1	4	2	5	3	10+ 6
2	90× 5	6	3	1 1	4
5− 6	1	9+ 5	2÷ 4	1− 2	3
3− 3	6	4	2	4− 5	1

Light and Easy +/−/×/÷ 59

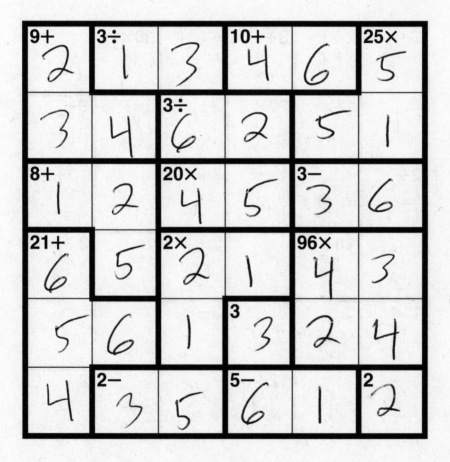

9+ 2	3÷ 1	3	10+ 4	6	25× 5
3	4	3÷ 6	2	5	1
8+ 1	2	20× 4	5	3− 3	6
21+ 6	5	2× 2	1	96× 4	3
5	6	1	3 3	2	4
4	2− 3	5	5− 6	1	2 2

60 Light and Easy +/−/×/÷

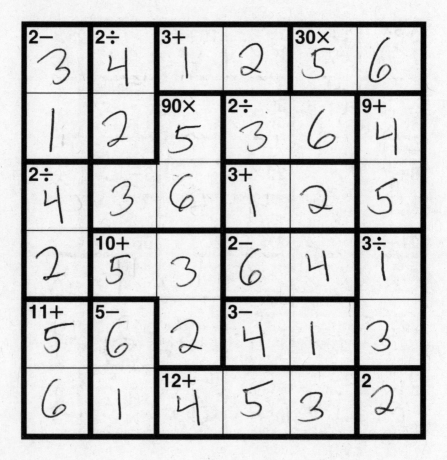

2−	2÷	3+		30×	
3	4	1	2	5	6
1	2	90×	2÷	6	9+
		5	3		4
2÷	3	6	3+	2	5
4			1		
2	10+	3	2−	4	3÷
	5		6		1
11+	5−	2	3−	1	3
5	6		4		
6	1	12+	5	3	2
		4			2

Light and Easy +/−/×/÷ | 61

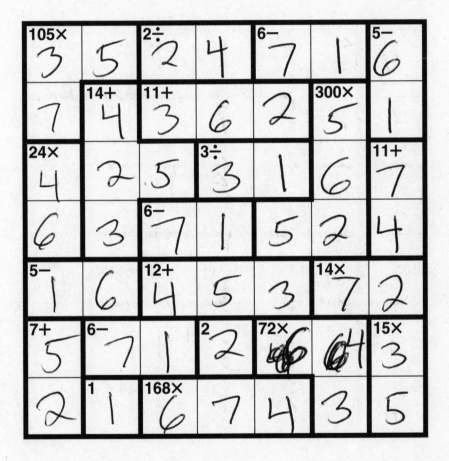

105×		2÷		6−		5−
3	5	2	4	7	1	6
7	14+ 4	11+ 3	6	2	300× 5	1
24× 4	2	5	3÷ 3	1	6	11+ 7
6	3	6− 7	1	5	2	4
5− 1	6	12+ 4	5	3	14× 7	2
7+ 5	6− 7	1	2 2	72× 6	4	15× 3
2	1 1	168× 6	7	4	3	5

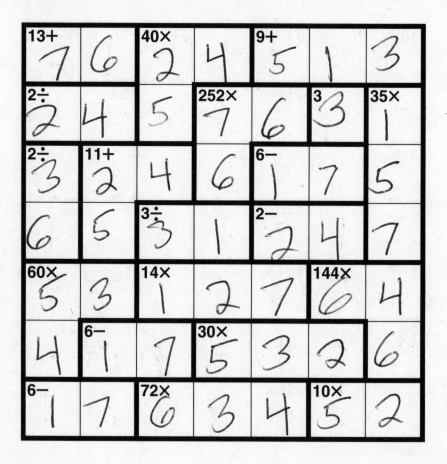

13+		40×		9+		
7	6	2	4	5	1	3
2÷			**252×**		**3**	**35×**
2	4	5	7	6	3	1
2÷	**11+**			**6−**		
3	2	4	6	1	7	5
6	5	**3÷** 3	1	**2−** 2	4	7
60×		**14×**			**144×**	
5	3	1	2	7	6	4
4	**6−** 1	7	**30×** 5	3	2	6
6− 1	7	**72×** 6	3	4	**10×** 5	2

Light and Easy +/−/×/÷   63

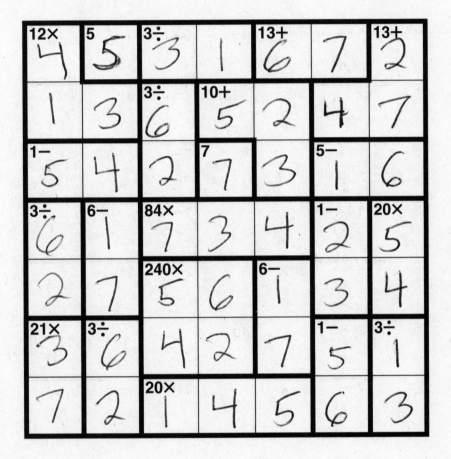

12× 4	5 5	3÷ 3	1	13+ 6	7	13+ 2
1	3	3÷ 6	10+ 5	2	4	7
1− 5	4	2	7 7	3	5− 1	6
3÷ 6	6− 1	84× 7	3	4	1− 2	20× 5
2	7	240× 5	6	6− 1	3	4
21× 3	3÷ 6	4	2	7	1− 5	3÷ 1
7	2	20× 1	4	5	6	3

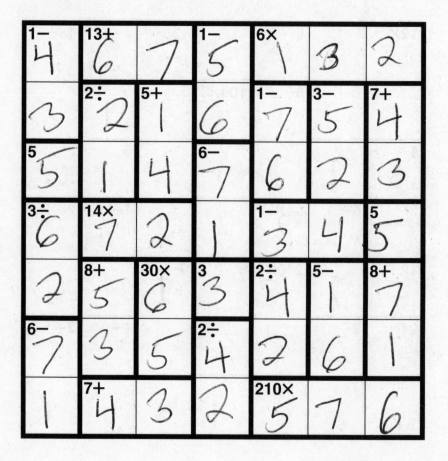

1− 4	13+ 6	7	1− 5	6× 1	3	2
3	2÷ 2	5+ 1	6	1− 7	3− 5	7+ 4
5 5	1	4	6− 7	6	2	3
3÷ 6	14× 7	2	1	1− 3	4	5 5
2	8+ 5	30× 6	3 3	2÷ 4	5− 1	8+ 7
6− 7	3	5	2÷ 4	2	6	1
1	7+ 4	3	2	210× 5	7	6

Light and Easy +/−/×/÷ **65**

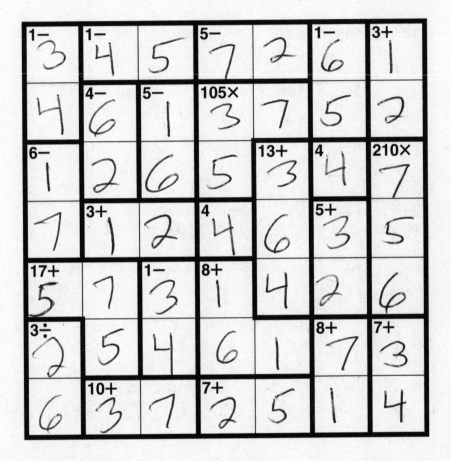

1−3	1−4	5	5−7	2	1−6	3+1
4	4−6	5−1	105×3	7	5	2
6−1	2	6	5	13+3	4 4	210×7
7	3+1	2	4 4	6	5+3	5
17+5	7	1−3	8+1	4	2	6
3÷2	5	4	6	1	8+7	7+3
6	10+3	7	7+2	5	1	4

66 Light and Easy +/−/×/÷

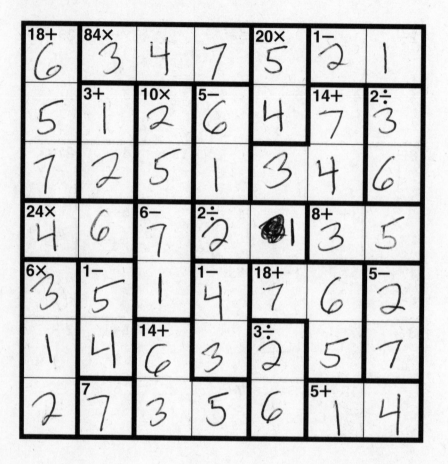

18+ 6	84× 3	4	7	20× 5	1− 2	1
5	3+ 1	10× 2	5− 6	4	14+ 7	2÷ 3
7	2	5	1	3	4	6
24× 4	6	6− 7	2÷ 2	1	8+ 3	5
6× 3	1− 5	1	1− 4	18+ 7	6	5− 2
1	4	14+ 6	3	3÷ 2	5	7
2	7 7	3	5	6	5+ 1	4

Light and Easy +/−/×/÷ 67

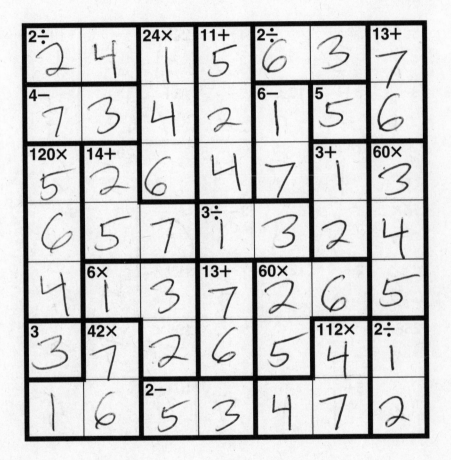

2÷ 2	4	24× 1	11+ 5	2÷ 6	3	13+ 7
4− 7	3	4	2	6− 1	5 5	6
120× 5	14+ 2	6	4	7	3+ 1	60× 3
6	5	7	3÷ 1	3	2	4
4	6× 1	3	13+ 7	60× 2	6	5
3 3	42× 7	2	6	5	112× 4	2÷ 1
1	6	2− 5	3	4	7	2

68 Light and Easy +/−/×/÷

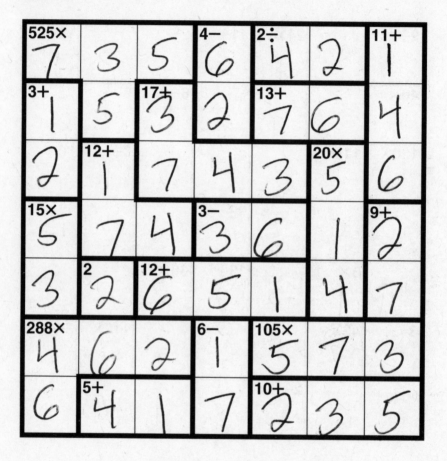

525× 7	3	5	4− 6	2÷ 4	2	11+ 1
3+ 1	5	17+ 3	2	13+ 7	6	4
2	12+ 1	7	4	3	20× 5	6
15× 5	7	4	3− 3	6	1	9+ 2
3	2 2	12+ 6	5	1	4	7
288× 4	6	2	6− 1	105× 5	7	3
6	5+ 4	1	7	10+ 2	3	5

Light and Easy +/−/×/÷ 69

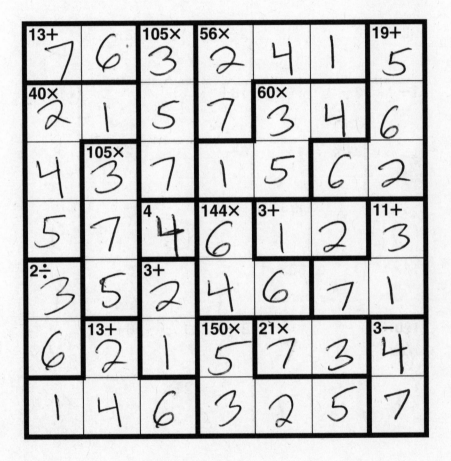

13+ 7	6	105× 3	56× 2	4	1	19+ 5
40× 2	1	5	7	60× 3	4	6
4	105× 3	7	1	5	6	2
5	7	4 4	144× 6	3+ 1	2	11+ 3
2÷ 3	5	3+ 2	4	6	7	1
6	13+ 2	1	150× 5	21× 7	3	3− 4
1	4	6	3	2	5	7

70 Light and Easy +/−/×/÷

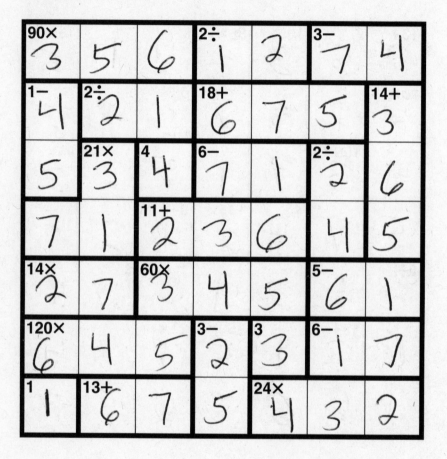

90×			2÷		3−	
3	5	6	1	2	7	4
1−	2÷		18+			14+
4	2	1	6	7	5	3
	21×	4	6−		2÷	
5	3	4	7	1	2	6
		11+				
7	1	2	3	6	4	5
14×		60×			5−	
2	7	3	4	5	6	1
120×			3−	3	6−	
6	4	5	2	3	1	7
1	13+			24×		
1	6	7	5	4	3	2

Light and Easy +/−/×/÷ 71

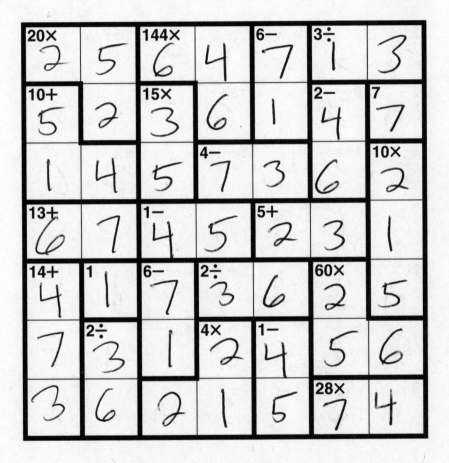

20× 2	5	144× 6	4	6− 7	3÷ 1	3
10+ 5	2	15× 3	6	1	2− 4	7 7
1	4	5	4− 7	3	6	10× 2
13+ 6	7	1− 4	5	5+ 2	3	1
14+ 4	1 1	6− 7	2÷ 3	6	60× 2	5
7	2÷ 3	1	4× 2	1− 4	5	6
3	6	2	1	5	28× 7	4

72 Light and Easy +/−/×/÷

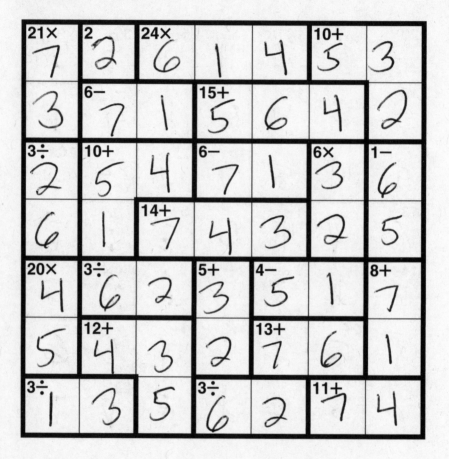

21× 7	2 2	24× 6	1	4	10+ 5	3
3	6− 7	1	15+ 5	6	4	2
3÷ 2	10+ 5	4	6− 7	1	6× 3	1− 6
6	1	14+ 7	4	3	2	5
20× 4	3÷ 6	2	5+ 3	4− 5	1	8+ 7
5	12+ 4	3	2	13+ 7	6	1
3÷ 1	3	5	3÷ 6	2	11+ 7	4

Light and Easy +/−/×/÷   73

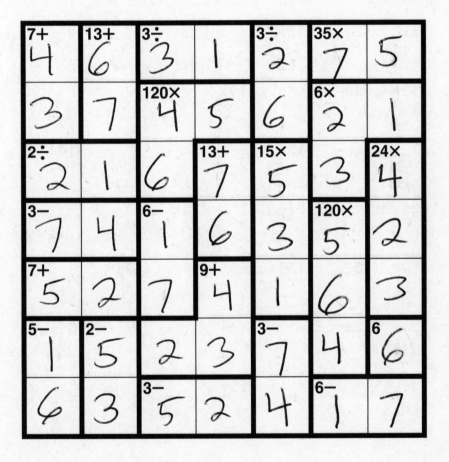

7+ 4	13+ 6	3÷ 3	1	3÷ 2	35× 7	5
3	7	120× 4	5	6	6× 2	1
2÷ 2	1	6	13+ 7	15× 5	3	24× 4
3− 7	4	6− 1	6	3	120× 5	2
7+ 5	2	7	9+ 4	1	6	3
5− 1	2− 5	2	3	3− 7	4	6 6
6	3	3− 5	2	4	6− 1	7

74 Light and Easy +/−/×/÷

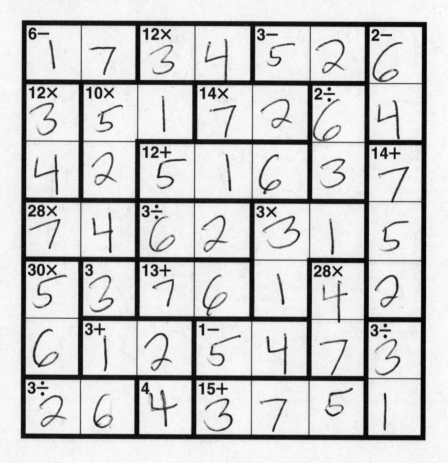

6− 1	7	12× 3	4	3− 5	2	2− 6
12× 3	10× 5	1	14× 7	2	2÷ 6	4
4	2	12+ 5	1	6	3	14+ 7
28× 7	4	3÷ 6	2	3× 3	1	5
30× 5	3 3	13+ 7	6	1	28× 4	2
6	3+ 1	2	1− 5	4	7	3÷ 3
3÷ 2	6	4 4	15+ 3	7	5	1

Light and Easy +/−/×/÷ 75

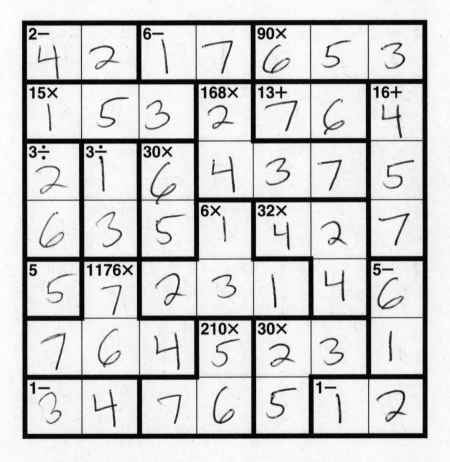

2− 4	2	6− 1	7	90× 6	5	3
15× 1	5	3	168× 2	13+ 7	6	16+ 4
3÷ 2	3÷ 1	30× 6	4	3	7	5
6	3	5	6× 1	32× 4	2	7
5 5	1176× 7	2	3	1	4	5− 6
7	6	4	210× 5	30× 2	3	1
1− 3	4	7	6	5	1− 1	2

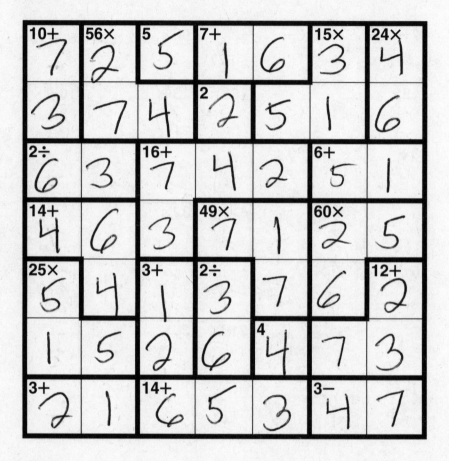

10+ 7	56× 2	5 5	7+ 1	6	15× 3	24× 4
3	7	4	2² 2	5	1	6
2÷ 6	3	16+ 7	4	2	6+ 5	1
14+ 4	6	3	49× 7	1	60× 2	5
25× 5	4	3+ 1	2÷ 3	7	6	12+ 2
1	5	2	6	4⁴ 4	7	3
3+ 2	1	14+ 6	5	3	3− 4	7

Light and Easy +/−/×/÷   77

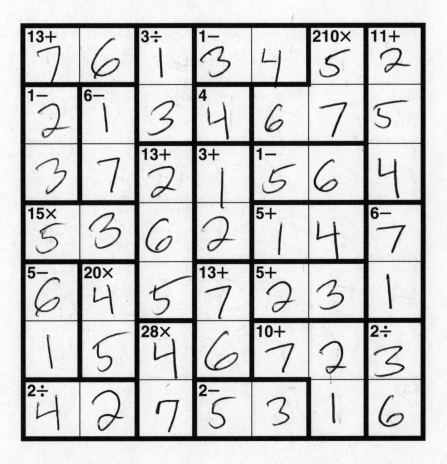

13+ 7	6	3÷ 1	1− 3	4	210× 5	11+ 2
1− 2	6− 1	3	4 4	6	7	5
3	7	13+ 2	3+ 1	1− 5	6	4
15× 5	3	6	2	5+ 1	4	6− 7
5− 6	20× 4	5	13+ 7	5+ 2	3	1
1	5	28× 4	6	10+ 7	2	2÷ 3
2÷ 4	2	7	2− 5	3	1	6

78 Light and Easy +/−/×/÷

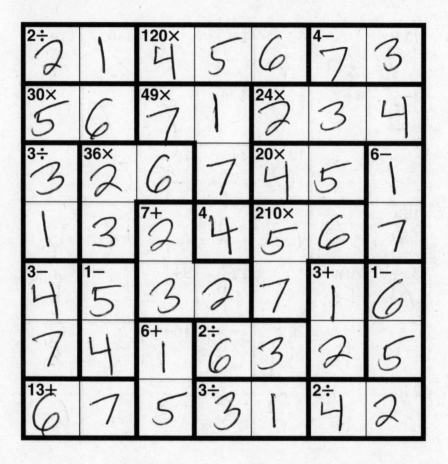

2÷ 2	1	120× 4	5	6	4− 7	3
30× 5	6	49× 7	1	24× 2	3	4
3÷ 3	36× 2	6	7	20× 4	5	6− 1
1	3	7+ 2	4 4	210× 5	6	7
3− 4	1− 5	3	2	7	3+ 1	1− 6
7	4	6+ 1	2÷ 6	3	2	5
13± 6	7	5	3÷ 3	1	2÷ 4	2

Light and Easy +/−/×/÷

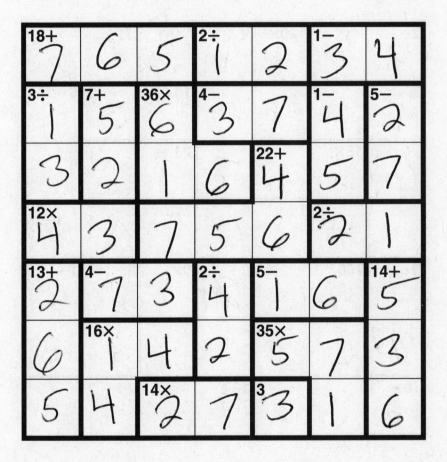

18+ 7	6	5	2÷ 1	2	1− 3	4
3÷ 1	7+ 5	36× 6	4− 3	7	1− 4	5− 2
3	2	1	6	22+ 4	5	7
12× 4	3	7	5	6	2÷ 2	1
13+ 2	4− 7	3	2÷ 4	5− 1	6	14+ 5
6	16× 1	4	2	35× 5	7	3
5	4	14× 2	7	3 3	1	6

80 Light and Easy +/−/×/÷

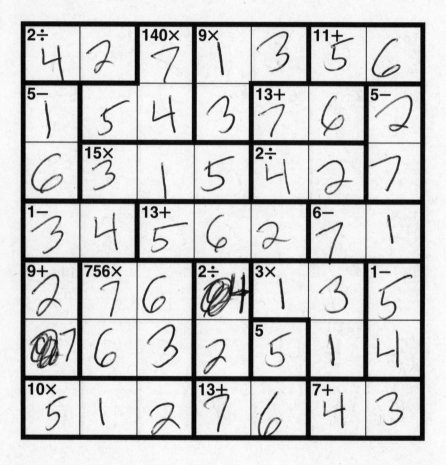

2÷		140×	9×		11+	
4	2	7	1	3	5	6
5−				13+		5−
1	5	4	3	7	6	2
	15×			2÷		
6	3	1	5	4	2	7
1−		13+			6−	
3	4	5	6	2	7	1
9+	756×		2÷	3×		1−
2	7	6	4	1	3	5
7	6	3	2	5	1	4
10×			13±		7+	
5	1	2	7	6	4	3

Light and Easy +/−/×/÷

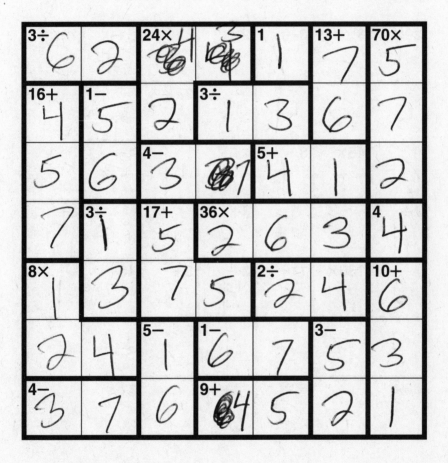

3÷ 6	2	**24×**	**3** 1	**13+** 7	**70×** 5
16+ 4	**1−** 5	2	**3÷** 1	3	6	7
5	6	**4−** 3	**7**	**5+** 4	1	2
7	**3÷** 1	**17+** 5	**36×** 2	6	3	**4** 4
8× 1	3	7	5	**2÷** 2	4	**10+** 6
2	4	**5−** 1	**1−** 6	7	**3−** 5	3
4− 3	7	6	**9+** 4	5	2	1

30× 1	8× 4	3− 7	2− 5	6 6	3+ 2	11+ 3
5	2	4	3	28× 7	1	6
6	45× 3	6− 1	7	4	1− 5	2
2÷ 4	5	3	3+ 2	1	6	8+ 7
2	126× 6	11+ 5	3− 4	5+ 3	16+ 7	1
3	7	6	1	2	4	5
6− 7	1	60× 2	6	5	12× 3	4

Light and Easy +/−/×/÷ 83

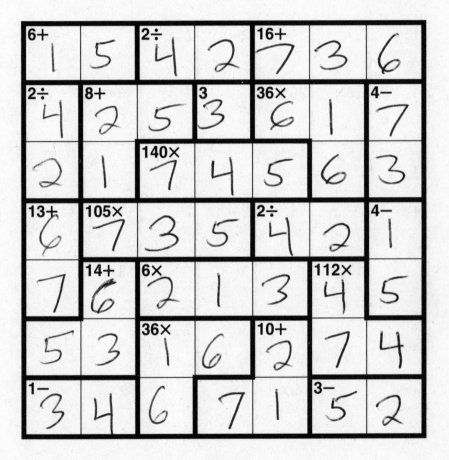

6+ 1	5	2÷ 4	2	16+ 7	3	6
2÷ 4	8+ 2	5	3 3	36× 6	1	4− 7
2	1	140× 7	4	5	6	3
13+ 6	105× 7	3	5	2÷ 4	2	4− 1
7	14+ 6	6× 2	1	3	112× 4	5
5	3	36× 1	6	10+ 2	7	4
1− 3	4	6	7	1	3− 5	2

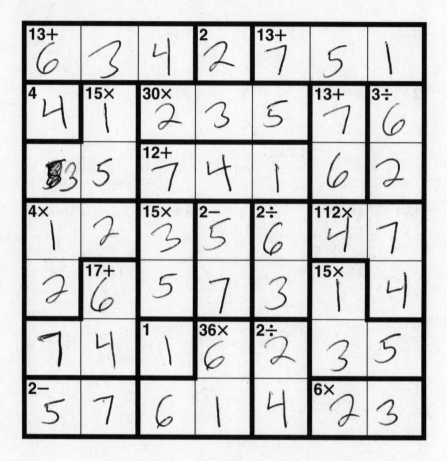

13+ 6	3	4	2 2	13+ 7	5	1
4 4	15× 1	30× 2	3	5	13+ 7	3÷ 6
3	5	12+ 7	4	1	6	2
4× 1	2	15× 3	2− 5	2÷ 6	112× 4	7
2	17+ 6	5	7	3	15× 1	4
7	4	1 1	36× 6	2÷ 2	3	5
2− 5	7	6	1	4	6× 2	3

Light and Easy +/−/×/÷ 85

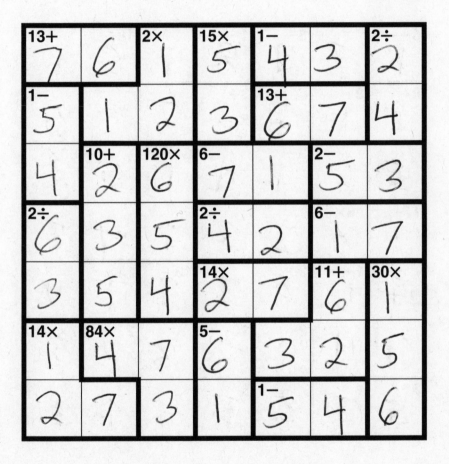

13+ 7	6	2× 1	15× 5	1− 4	3	2÷ 2
1− 5	1	2	3	13+ 6	7	4
4	10+ 2	120× 6	6− 7	1	2− 5	3
2÷ 6	3	5	2÷ 4	2	6− 1	7
3	5	4	14× 2	7	11+ 6	30× 1
14× 1	84× 4	7	5− 6	3	2	5
2	7	3	1	1− 5	4	6

86 Light and Easy +/−/×/÷

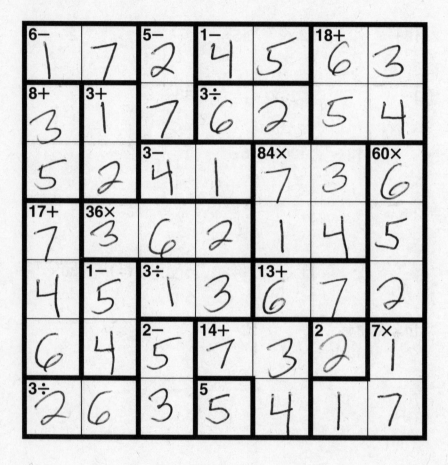

6− 1	7	5− 2	1− 4	5	18+ 6	3
8+ 3	3+ 1	7	3÷ 6	2	5	4
5	2	3− 4	1	84× 7	3	60× 6
17+ 7	36× 3	6	2	1	4	5
4	1− 5	3÷ 1	3	13+ 6	7	2
6	4	2− 5	14+ 7	3	2 2	7× 1
3÷ 2	6	3	5 5	4	1	7

Light and Easy +/−/×/÷ 87

13+		40×			7×	
3−		126×		5		3−
	3÷			4−		
2÷		1−		16+		
4−		2×		108×	1−	
12+					14+	
	168×			3+		

88 Moderate +/−/×/÷

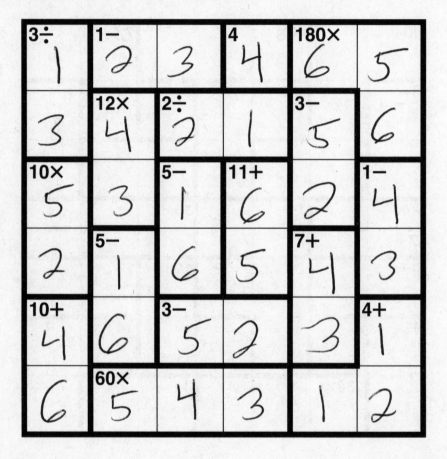

3÷	1−		4	180×	
1	2	3	4	6	5
3	12× 4	2÷ 2	1	3− 5	6
10× 5	3	5− 1	11+ 6	2	1− 4
2	5− 1	6	5	7+ 4	3
10+ 4	6	3− 5	2	3	4+ 1
6	60× 5	4	3	1	2

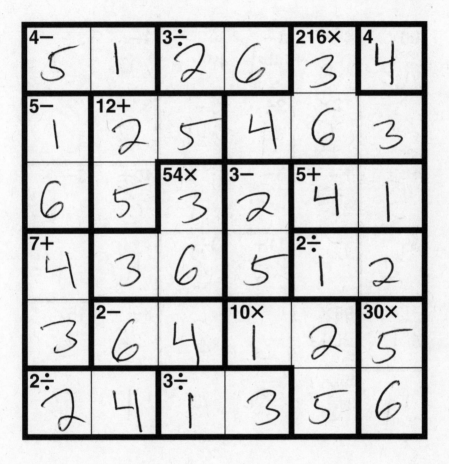

4− 5	1	3÷ 2	6	216× 3	4 4
5− 1	12+ 2	5	4	6	3
6	5	54× 3	3− 2	5+ 4	1
7+ 4	3	6	5	2÷ 1	2
3	2− 6	4	10× 1	2	30× 5
2÷ 2	4	3÷ 1	3	5	6

90 Moderate +/−/×/÷

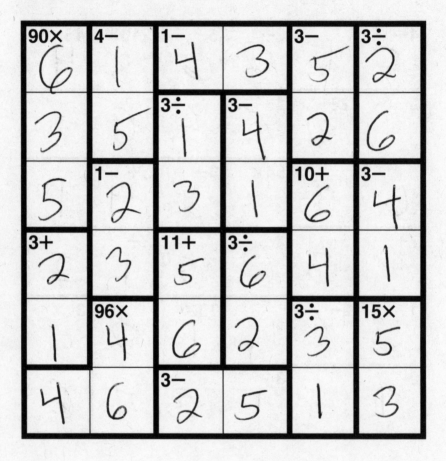

90× 6	4− 1	1− 4	3	3− 5	3÷ 2
3	5	3÷ 1	3− 4	2	6
5	1− 2	3	1	10+ 6	3− 4
3+ 2	3	11+ 5	3÷ 6	4	1
1	96× 4	6	2	3÷ 3	15× 5
4	6	3− 2	5	1	3

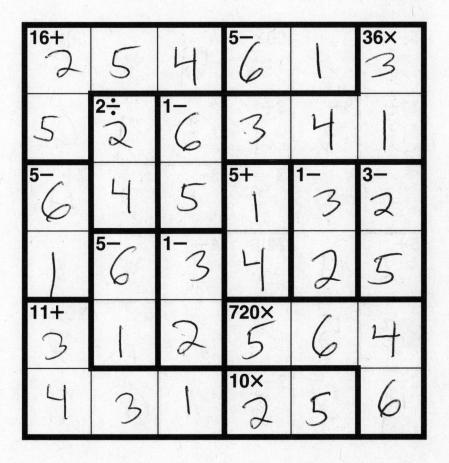

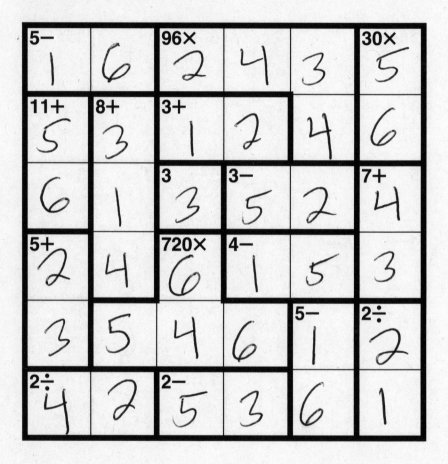

5−		96×			30×
1	6	2	4	3	5
11+ 5	**8+** 3	**3+** 1	2	4	6
6	1	**3** 3	**3−** 5	2	**7+** 4
5+ 2	4	**720×** 6	**4−** 1	5	3
3	5	4	6	**5−** 1	**2÷** 2
2÷ 4	2	**2−** 5	3	6	1

Moderate +/−/×/÷ 93

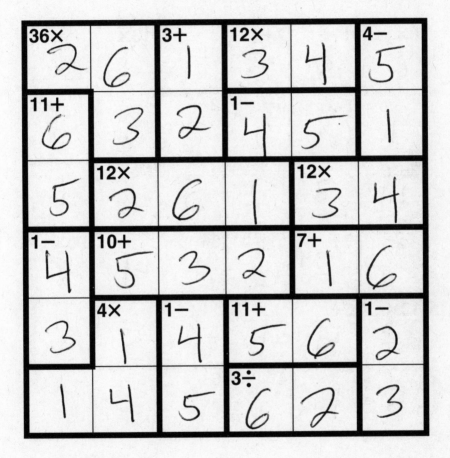

36× 2	6	3+ 1	12× 3	4	4− 5
11+ 6	3	2	1− 4	5	1
5	12× 2	6	1	12× 3	4
1− 4	10+ 5	3	2	7+ 1	6
3	4× 1	1− 4	11+ 5	6	1− 2
1	4	5	3÷ 6	2	3

94 Moderate +/−/×/÷

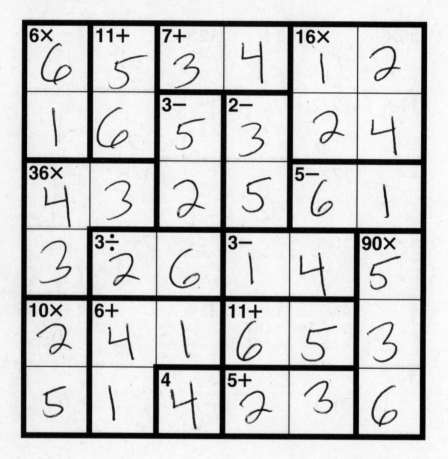

6× 6	11+ 5	7+ 3	4	16× 1	2
1	6	3− 5	2− 3	2	4
36× 4	3	2	5	5− 6	1
3	3÷ 2	6	3− 1	4	90× 5
10× 2	6+ 4	1	11+ 6	5	3
5	1	4 4	5+ 2	3	6

Moderate +/−/×/÷   95

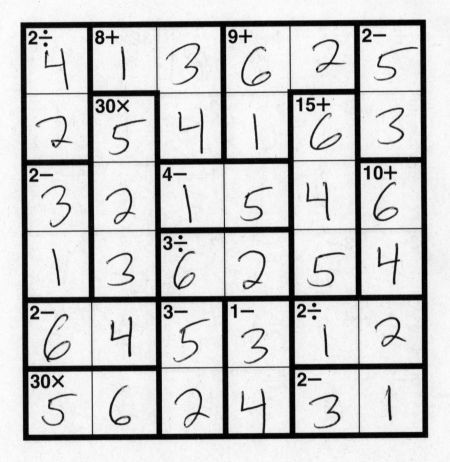

2÷ 4	8+ 1	3	9+ 6	2	2− 5
2	30× 5	4	1	15+ 6	3
2− 3	2	4− 1	5	4	10+ 6
1	3	3÷ 6	2	5	4
2− 6	4	3− 5	1− 3	2÷ 1	2
30× 5	6	2	4	2− 3	1

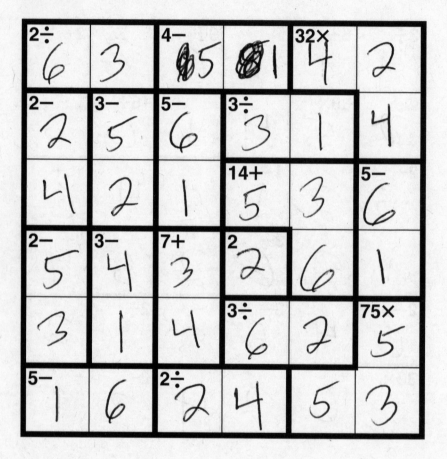

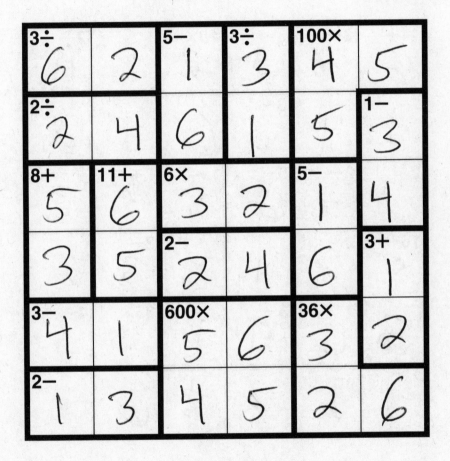

3÷ 6	2	5− 1	3÷ 3	100× 4	5
2÷ 2	4	6	1	5	1− 3
8+ 5	11+ 6	6× 3	2	5− 1	4
3	5	2− 2	4	6	3+ 1
3− 4	1	600× 5	6	36× 3	2
2− 1	3	4	5	2	6

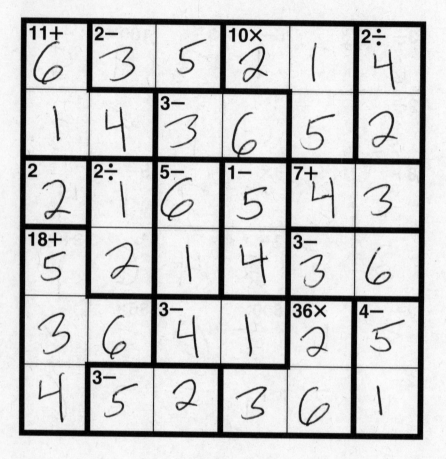

11+ 6	2− 3	5	10× 2	1	2÷ 4
1	4	3− 3	6	5	2
2 2	2÷ 1	5− 6	1− 5	7+ 4	3
18+ 5	2	1	4	3− 3	6
3	6	3− 4	1	36× 2	4− 5
4	3− 5	2	3	6	1

Moderate +/−/×/÷   99

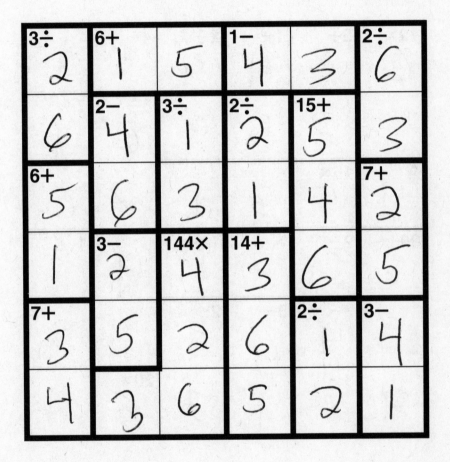

3÷ 2	6+ 1	5	1− 4	3	2÷ 6
6	2− 4	3÷ 1	2÷ 2	15+ 5	3
6+ 5	6	3	1	4	7+ 2
1	3− 2	144× 4	14+ 3	6	5
7+ 3	5	2	6	2÷ 1	3− 4
4	3	6	5	2	1

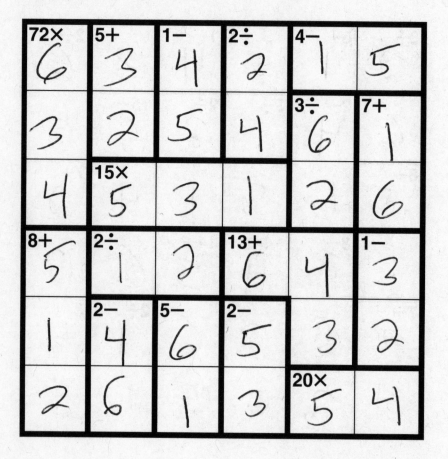

72× 6	5+ 3	1− 4	2÷ 2	4− 1	5
3	2	5	4	3÷ 6	7+ 1
4	15× 5	3	1	2	6
8+ 5	2÷ 1	2	13+ 6	4	1− 3
1	2− 4	5− 6	2− 5	3	2
2	6	1	3	20× 5	4

Moderate +/−/×/÷ 101

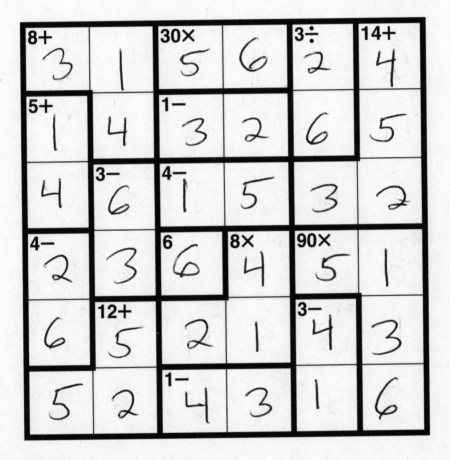

8+ 3	1	30× 5	6	3÷ 2	14+ 4
5+ 1	4	1− 3	2	6	5
4	3− 6	4− 1	5	3	2
4− 2	3	6 6	8× 4	90× 5	1
6	12+ 5	2	1	3− 4	3
5	2	1− 4	3	1	6

102 Moderate +/−/×/÷

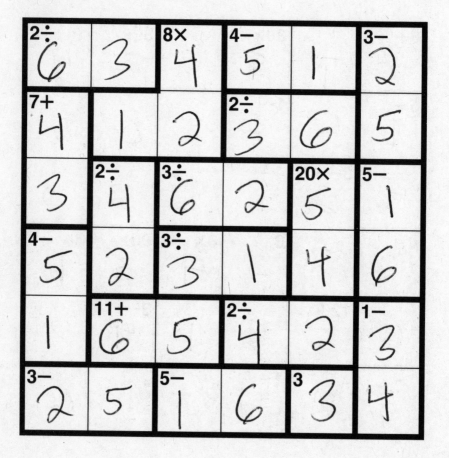

2÷ 6	3	8× 4	4− 5	1	3− 2
7+ 4	1	2	2÷ 3	6	5
3	2÷ 4	3÷ 6	2	20× 5	5− 1
4− 5	2	3÷ 3	1	4	6
1	11+ 6	5	2÷ 4	2	1− 3
3− 2	5	5− 1	6	3 3	4

Moderate +/−/×/÷ 103

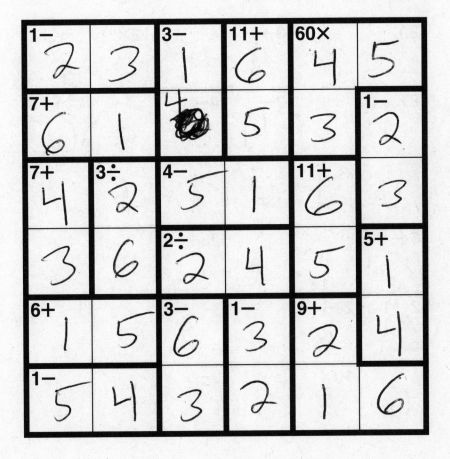

1− 2	3	3− 1	11+ 6	60× 4	5
7+ 6	1	4 ⬤	5	3	1− 2
7+ 4	3÷ 2	4− 5	1	11+ 6	3
3	6	2÷ 2	4	5	5+ 1
6+ 1	5	3− 6	1− 3	9+ 2	4
1− 5	4	3	2	1	6

104 Moderate +/−/×/÷

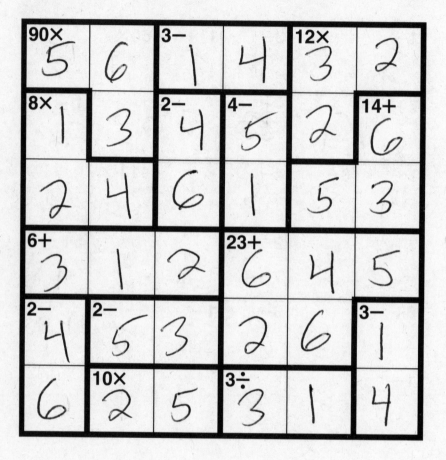

90× 5	6	3− 1	4	12× 3	2
8× 1	3	2− 4	4− 5	2	14+ 6
2	4	6	1	5	3
6+ 3	1	2	23+ 6	4	5
2− 4	2− 5	3	2	6	3− 1
6	10× 2	5	3÷ 3	1	4

Moderate +/−/×/÷ 105

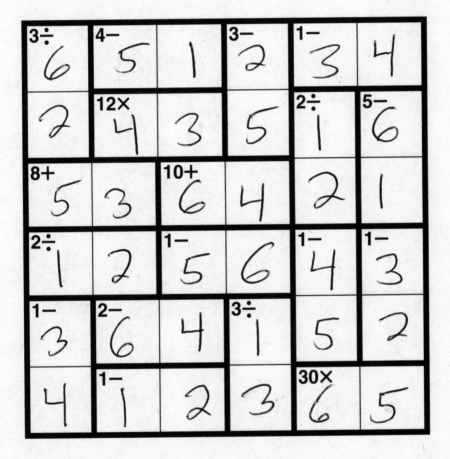

3÷ 6	4− 5	1	3− 2	1− 3	4
2	12× 4	3	5	2÷ 1	5− 6
8+ 5	3	10+ 6	4	2	1
2÷ 1	2	1− 5	6	1− 4	1− 3
1− 3	2− 6	4	3÷ 1	5	2
4	1− 1	2	3	30× 6	5

106 Moderate +/−/×/÷

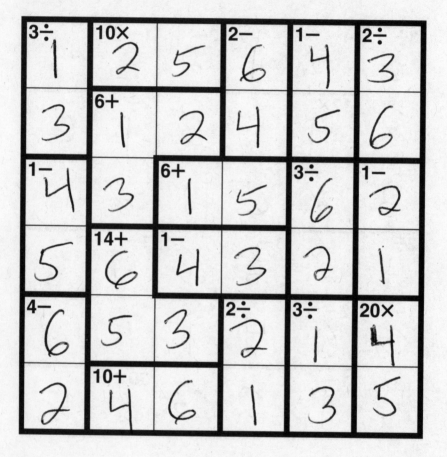

3÷ 1	10× 2	5	2− 6	1− 4	2÷ 3
3	6+ 1	2	4	5	6
1− 4	3	6+ 1	5	3÷ 6	1− 2
5	14+ 6	1− 4	3	2	1
4− 6	5	3	2÷ 2	3÷ 1	20× 4
2	10+ 4	6	1	3	5

Moderate +/−/×/÷ 107

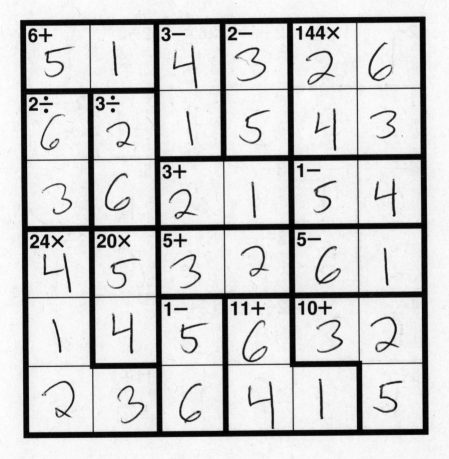

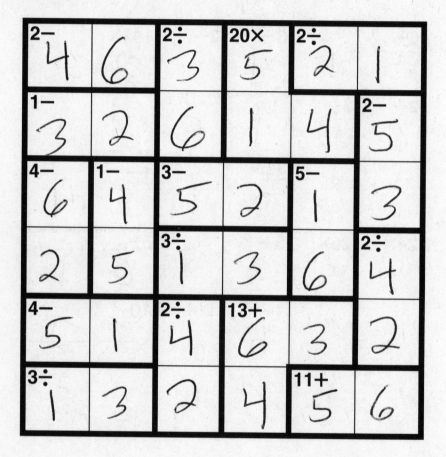

2−4	6	2÷3	20×5	2÷2	1
1−3	2	6	1	4	2−5
4−6	1−4	3−5	2	5−1	3
2	5	3÷1	3	6	2÷4
4−5	1	2÷4	13+6	3	2
3÷1	3	2	4	11+5	6

Moderate +/−/×/÷ 109

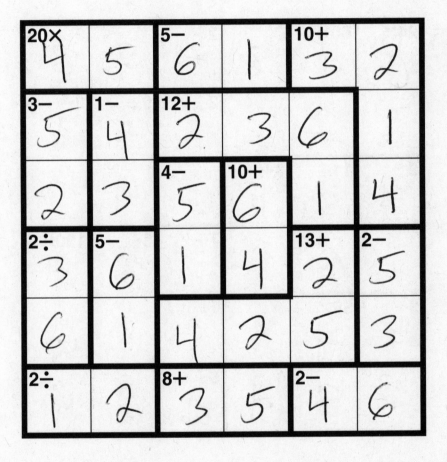

20× 4	5	5− 6	1	10+ 3	2
3− 5	1− 4	12+ 2	3	6	1
2	3	4− 5	10+ 6	1	4
2÷ 3	5− 6	1	4	13+ 2	2− 5
6	1	4	2	5	3
2÷ 1	2	8+ 3	5	2− 4	6

110 Moderate +/−/×/÷

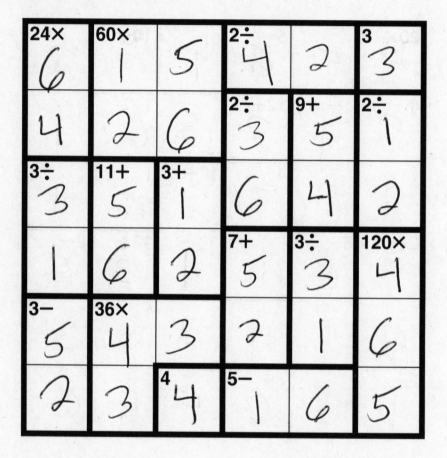

24×	60×		2÷		3
6	1	5	4	2	3
4	2	6	2÷ 3	9+ 5	2÷ 1
3÷ 3	11+ 5	3+ 1	6	4	2
1	6	2	7+ 5	3÷ 3	120× 4
3− 5	36× 4	3	2	1	6
2	3	4 4	5− 1	6	5

Moderate +/−/×/÷ 111

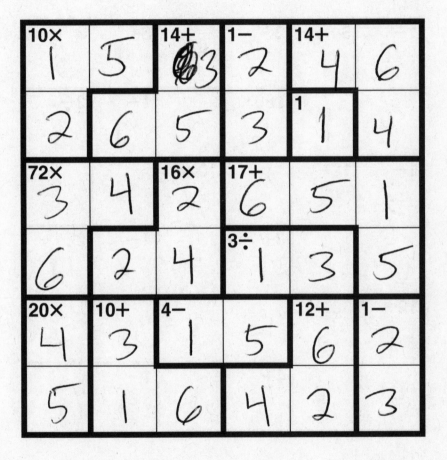

10× 1	5	14+ 3	1− 2	14+ 4	6
2	6	5	3	¹1	4
72× 3	4	16× 2	17+ 6	5	1
6	2	4	3÷ 1	3	5
20× 4	10+ 3	4− 1	5	12+ 6	1− 2
5	1	6	4	2	3

112 Moderate +/−/×/÷

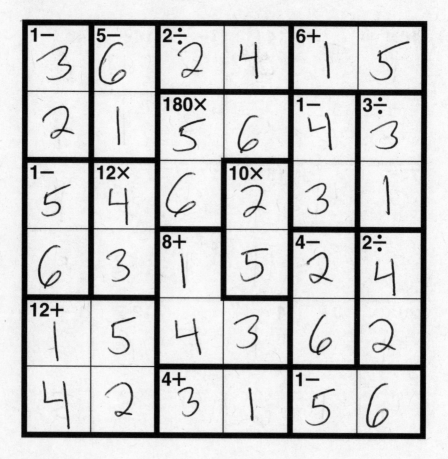

1− 3	5− 6	2÷ 2	4	6+ 1	5
2	1	180× 5	6	1− 4	3÷ 3
1− 5	12× 4	6	10× 2	3	1
6	3	8+ 1	5	4− 2	2÷ 4
12+ 1	5	4	3	6	2
4	2	4+ 3	1	1− 5	6

Moderate +/−/×/÷ 113

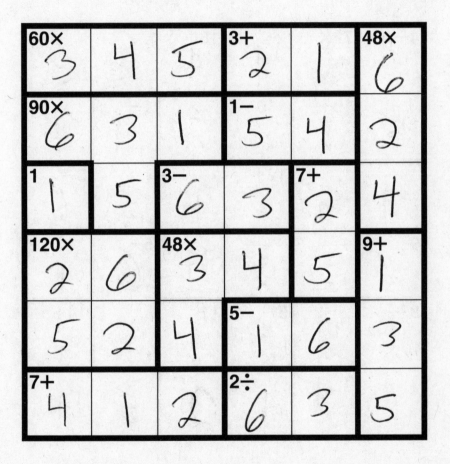

60× 3	4	5	3+ 2	1	48× 6
90× 6	3	1	1− 5	4	2
1 1	5	3− 6	3	7+ 2	4
120× 2	6	48× 3	4	5	9+ 1
5	2	4	5− 1	6	3
7+ 4	1	2	2÷ 6	3	5

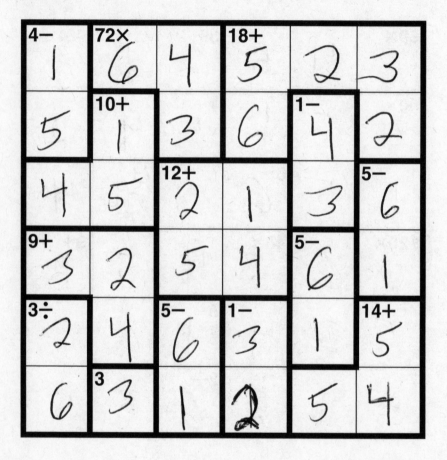

4− 1	72× 6	4	18+ 5	2	3
5	10+ 1	3	6	1− 4	2
4	5	12+ 2	1	3	5− 6
9+ 3	2	5	4	5− 6	1
3÷ 2	4	5− 6	1− 3	1	14+ 5
6	3 3	1	2	5	4

Moderate +/−/×/÷ 115

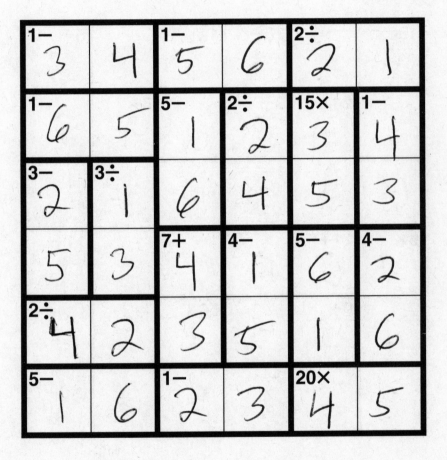

1− 3	4	1− 5	6	2÷ 2	1
1− 6	5	5− 1	2÷ 2	15× 3	1− 4
3− 2	3÷ 1	6	4	5	3
5	3	7+ 4	4− 1	5− 6	4− 2
2÷ 4	2	3	5	1	6
5− 1	6	1− 2	3	20× 4	5

116 Moderate +/−/×/÷

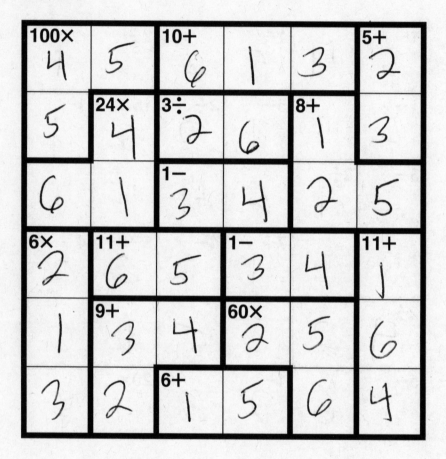

100× 4	5	10+ 6	1	3	5+ 2
5	24× 4	3÷ 2	6	8+ 1	3
6	1	1− 3	4	2	5
6× 2	11+ 6	5	1− 3	4	11+ 1
1	9+ 3	4	60× 2	5	6
3	2	6+ 1	5	6	4

Moderate +/−/×/÷ 117

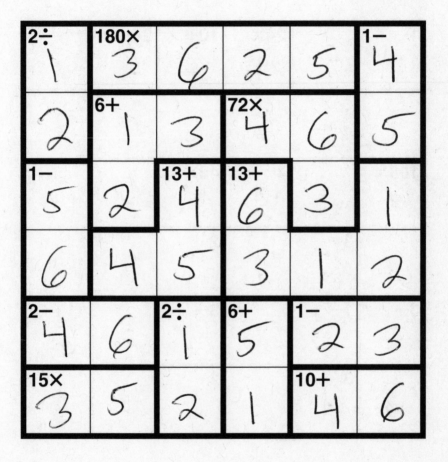

$2\div$ 1	$180\times$ 3	6	2	5	$1-$ 4
2	$6+$ 1	3	$72\times$ 4	6	5
$1-$ 5	2	$13+$ 4	$13+$ 6	3	1
6	4	5	3	1	2
$2-$ 4	6	$2\div$ 1	$6+$ 5	$1-$ 2	3
$15\times$ 3	5	2	1	$10+$ 4	6

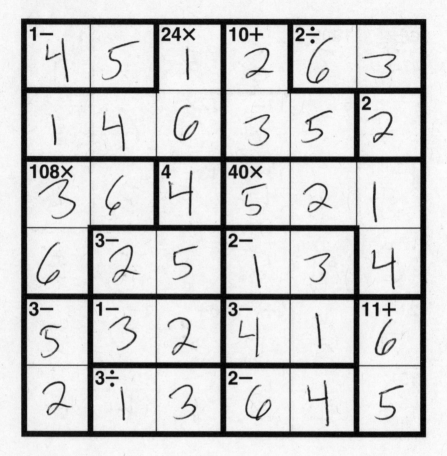

1− 4	5	24× 1	10+ 2	2÷ 6	3
1	4	6	3	5	2² 2
108× 3	6	4⁴ 4	40× 5	2	1
6	3− 2	5	2− 1	3	4
3− 5	1− 3	2	3− 4	1	11+ 6
2	3÷ 1	3	2− 6	4	5

Moderate +/−/×/÷ 119

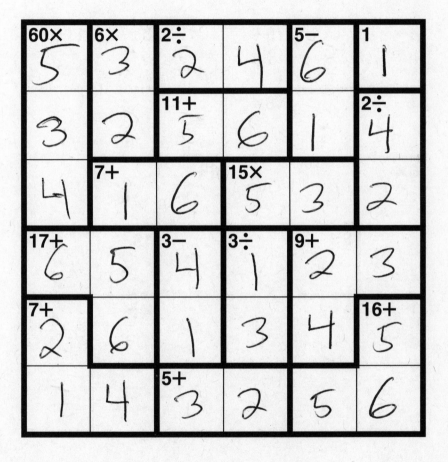

60×	6×	2÷		5−	1
5	3	2	4	6	1
3	2	11+ 5	6	1	2÷ 4
4	7+ 1	6	15× 5	3	2
17+ 6	5	3− 4	3÷ 1	9+ 2	3
7+ 2	6	1	3	4	16+ 5
1	4	5+ 3	2	5	6

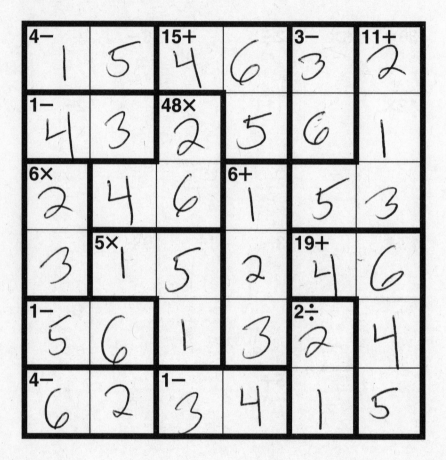

4−		15+		3−	11+
1	5	4	6	3	2
1−		48×			
4	3	2	5	6	1
6×			6+		
2	4	6	1	5	3
	5×			19+	
3	1	5	2	4	6
1−				2÷	
5	6	1	3	2	4
4−		1−			
6	2	3	4	1	5

Moderate +/−/×/÷ 121

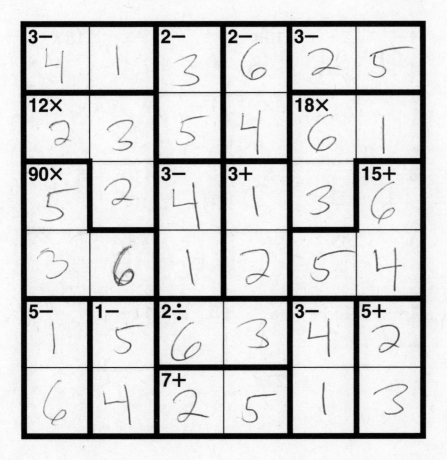

3−		2−	2−	3−	
4	1	3	6	2	5
12×				**18×**	
2	3	5	4	6	1
90×		**3−**	**3+**		**15+**
5	2	4	1	3	6
3	6	1	2	5	4
5−	**1−**	**2÷**		**3−**	**5+**
1	5	6	3	4	2
6	4	**7+** 2	5	1	3

122 Moderate +/−/×/÷

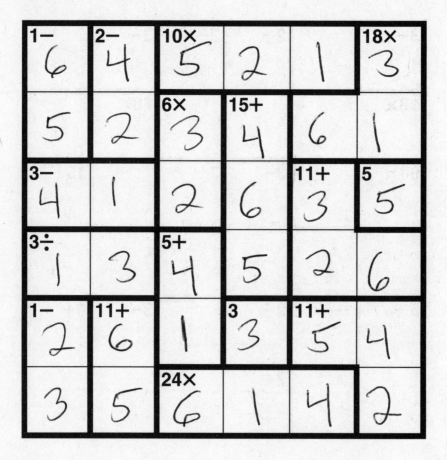

1− 6	**2−** 4	**10×** 5	2	1	**18×** 3
5	2	**6×** 3	**15+** 4	6	1
3− 4	1	2	6	**11+** 3	**5** 5
3÷ 1	3	**5+** 4	5	2	6
1− 2	**11+** 6	1	**3** 3	**11+** 5	4
3	5	**24×** 6	1	4	2

Moderate +/−/×/÷ 123

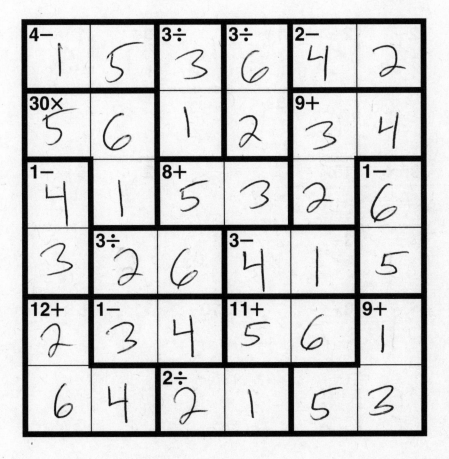

4−		3÷	3÷	2−	
1	5	3	6	4	2
30×				**9+**	
5	6	1	2	3	4
1−		**8+**			**1−**
4	1	5	3	2	6
3	**3÷** 2	6	**3−** 4	1	5
12+ 2	**1−** 3	4	**11+** 5	6	**9+** 1
6	4	**2÷** 2	1	5	3

124 Moderate +/−/×/÷

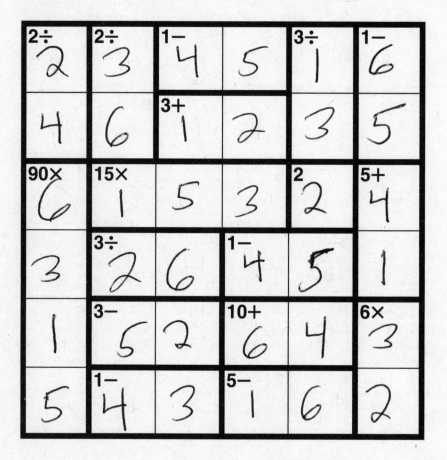

2÷ 2	2÷ 3	1− 4	5	3÷ 1	1− 6
4	6	3+ 1	2	3	5
90× 6	15× 1	5	3	2 2	5+ 4
3	3÷ 2	6	1− 4	5	1
1	3− 5	2	10+ 6	4	6× 3
5	1− 4	3	5− 1	6	2

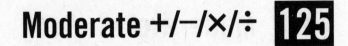
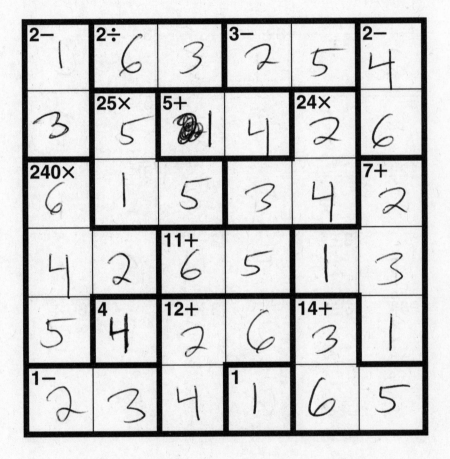

2−1	2÷6	3	3−2	5	2−4
3	25×5	5+1	4	24×2	6
240×6	1	5	3	4	7+2
4	2	11+6	5	1	3
5	4·4	12+2	6	14+3	1
1−2	3	4	1·1	6	5

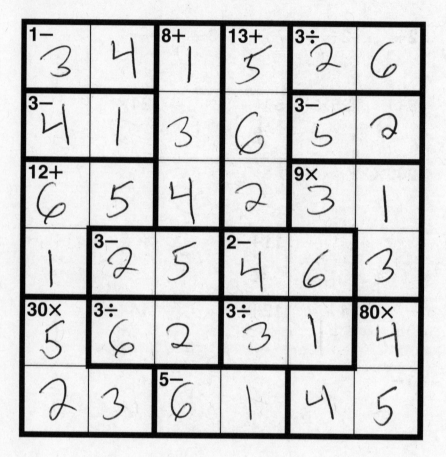

1− 3	4	8+ 1	13+ 5	3÷ 2	6
3− 4	1	3	6	3− 5	2
12+ 6	5	4	2	9× 3	1
1	3− 2	5	2− 4	6	3
30× 5	3÷ 6	2	3÷ 3	1	80× 4
2	3	5− 6	1	4	5

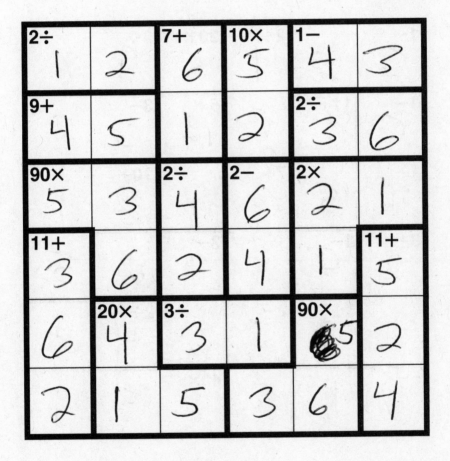

2÷ 1	2	7+ 6	10× 5	1− 4	3
9+ 4	5	1	2	2÷ 3	6
90× 5	3	2÷ 4	2− 6	2× 2	1
11+ 3	6	2	4	1	11+ 5
6	20× 4	3÷ 3	1	90× 5	2
2	1	5	3	6	4

128 Moderate +/−/×/÷

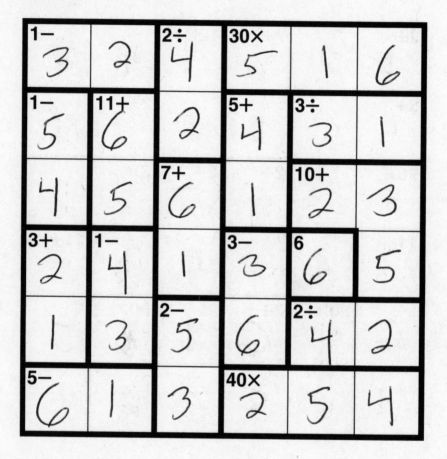

1− 3	2	2÷ 4	30× 5	1	6
1− 5	11+ 6	2	5+ 4	3÷ 3	1
4	5	7+ 6	1	10+ 2	3
3+ 2	1− 4	1	3− 3	6 6	5
1	3	2− 5	6	2÷ 4	2
5− 6	1	3	40× 2	5	4

Moderate +/−/×/÷ 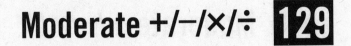 129

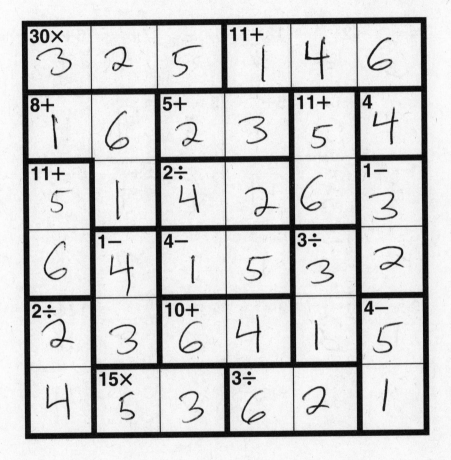

30× 3	2	5	11+ 1	4	6
8+ 1	6	5+ 2	3	11+ 5	4 4
11+ 5	1	2÷ 4	2	6	1− 3
6	1− 4	4− 1	5	3÷ 3	2
2÷ 2	3	10+ 6	4	1	4− 5
4	15× 5	3	3÷ 6	2	1

130 Moderate +/−/×/÷

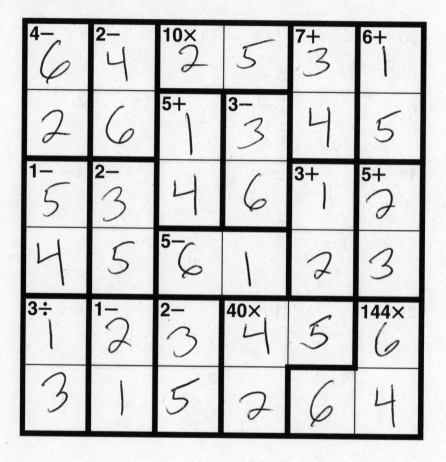

4−	2−	10×		7+	6+
6	4	2	5	3	1
2	6	5+ 1	3− 3	4	5
1− 5	2− 3	4	6	3+ 1	5+ 2
4	5	5− 6	1	2	3
3÷ 1	1− 2	2− 3	40× 4	5	144× 6
3	1	5	2	6	4

Moderate +/−/×/÷ 131

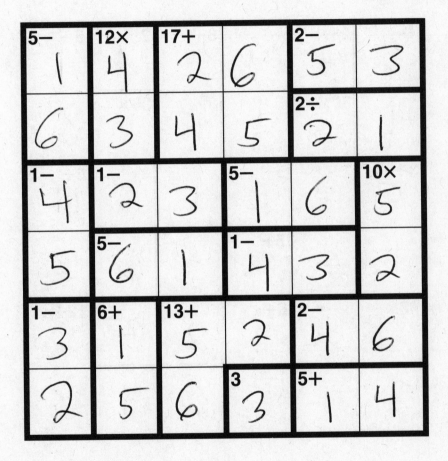

132 Moderate +/−/×/÷

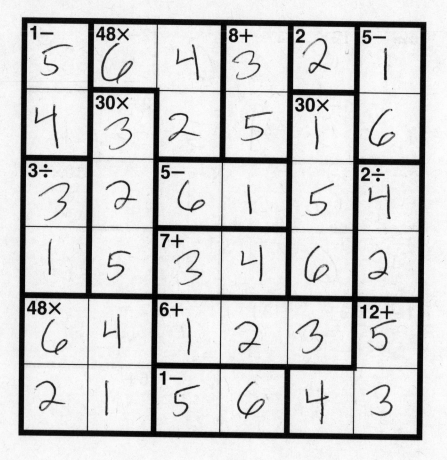

1−	48×		8+	2	5−
5	6	4	3	2	1
4	30× 3	2	5	30× 1	6
3÷ 3	2	5− 6	1	5	2÷ 4
1	5	7+ 3	4	6	2
48× 6	4	6+ 1	2	3	12+ 5
2	1	1− 5	6	4	3

Moderate +/−/×/÷ 133

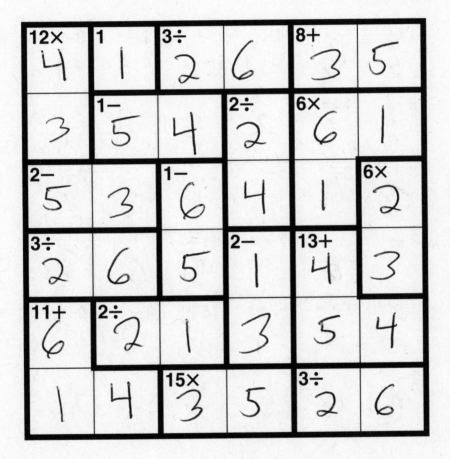

12× 4	**1** 1	**3÷** 2	6	**8+** 3	5
3	**1−** 5	4	**2÷** 2	**6×** 6	1
2− 5	3	**1−** 6	4	1	**6×** 2
3÷ 2	6	5	**2−** 1	**13+** 4	3
11+ 6	**2÷** 2	1	3	5	4
1	4	**15×** 3	5	**3÷** 2	6

134 Moderate +/−/×/÷

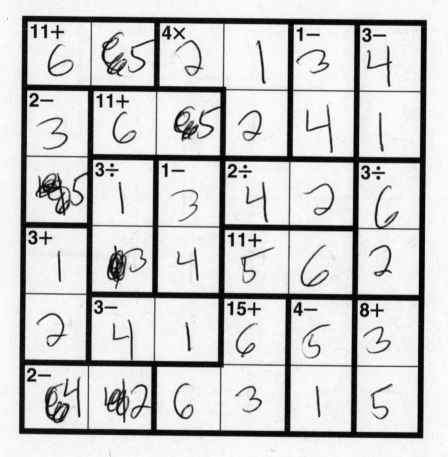

11+ 6	5	4× 2	1	1− 3	3− 4
2− 3	11+ 6	5	2	4	1
5	3÷ 1	1− 3	2÷ 4	2	3÷ 6
3+ 1	3	4	11+ 5	6	2
2	3− 4	1	15+ 6	4− 5	8+ 3
2− 4	2	6	3	1	5

Moderate +/−/×/÷ 135

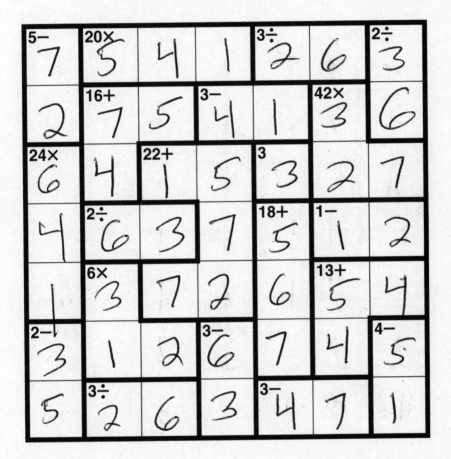

5− 7	20× 5	4	1	3÷ 2	6	2÷ 3
2	16+ 7	5	3− 4	1	42× 3	6
24× 6	4	22+ 1	5	3 3	2	7
4	2÷ 6	3	7	18+ 5	1− 1	2
1	6× 3	7	2	6	13+ 5	4
2− 3	1	2	3− 6	7	4	4− 5
5	3÷ 2	6	3	3− 4	7	1

136 Moderate +/−/×/÷

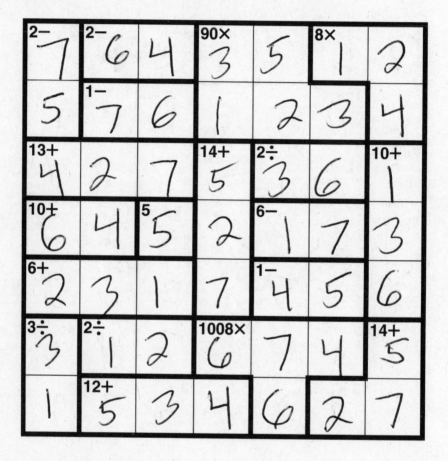

2− 7	**2−** 6	4	**90×** 3	5	**8×** 1	2
5	**1−** 7	6	1	2	3	4
13+ 4	2	7	**14+** 5	**2÷** 3	6	**10+** 1
10+ 6	4	**5** 5	2	**6−** 1	7	3
6+ 2	3	1	7	**1−** 4	5	6
3÷ 3	**2÷** 1	2	**1008×** 6	7	4	**14+** 5
1	**12+** 5	3	4	6	2	7

Moderate +/−/×/÷ 137

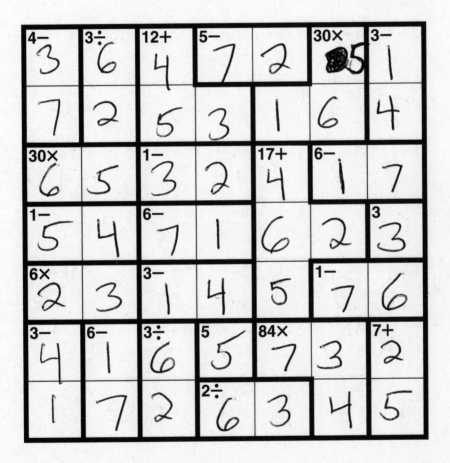

4− 3	3÷ 6	12+ 4	5− 7	2	30× 5	3− 1
7	2	5	3	1	6	4
30× 6	5	1− 3	2	17+ 4	6− 1	7
1− 5	4	6− 7	1	6	2	3 3
6× 2	3	3− 1	4	5	1− 7	6
3− 4	6− 1	3÷ 6	5 5	84× 7	3	7+ 2
1	7	2	2÷ 6	3	4	5

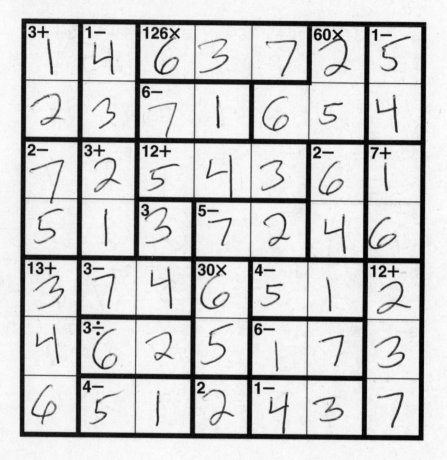

3+ 1	1− 4	126× 6	3	7	60× 2	1− 5
2	3	6− 7	1	6	5	4
2− 7	3+ 2	12+ 5	4	3	2− 6	7+ 1
5	1	3 3	5− 7	2	4	6
13+ 3	3− 7	4	30× 6	4− 5	1	12+ 2
4	3÷ 6	2	5	6− 1	7	3
6	4− 5	1	2 2	1− 4	3	7

Moderate +/−/×/÷ 139

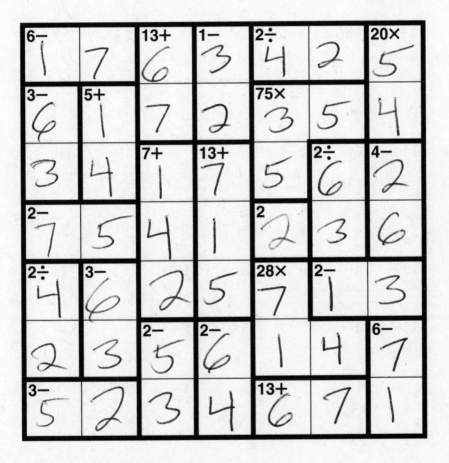

6− 1	7	13+ 6	1− 3	2÷ 4	2	20× 5
3− 6	5+ 1	7	2	75× 3	5	4
3	4	7+ 1	13+ 7	5	2÷ 6	4− 2
2− 7	5	4	1	2 2	3	6
2÷ 4	3− 6	2	5	28× 7	2− 1	3
2	3	2− 5	2− 6	1	4	6− 7
3− 5	2	3	4	13+ 6	7	1

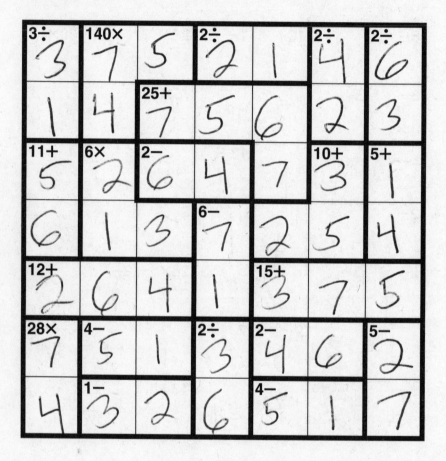

3÷ 3	140× 7	5	2÷ 2	1	2÷ 4	2÷ 6
1	4	25+ 7	5	6	2	3
11+ 5	6× 2	2− 6	4	7	10+ 3	5+ 1
6	1	3	6− 7	2	5	4
12+ 2	6	4	1	15+ 3	7	5
28× 7	4− 5	1	2÷ 3	2− 4	6	5− 2
4	1− 3	2	6	4− 5	1	7

Moderate +/−/×/÷ 141

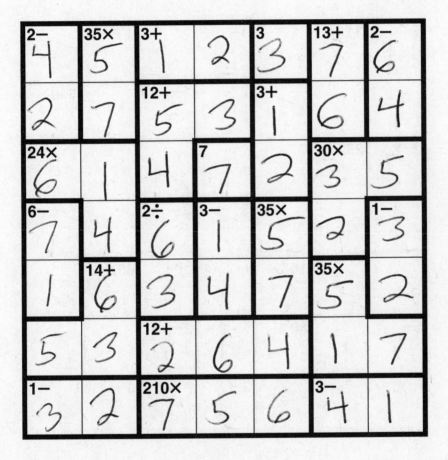

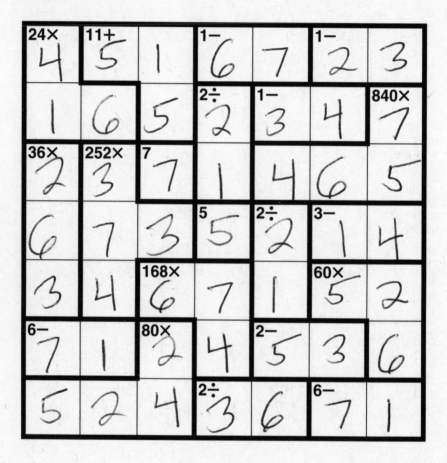

Moderate +/−/×/÷ 143

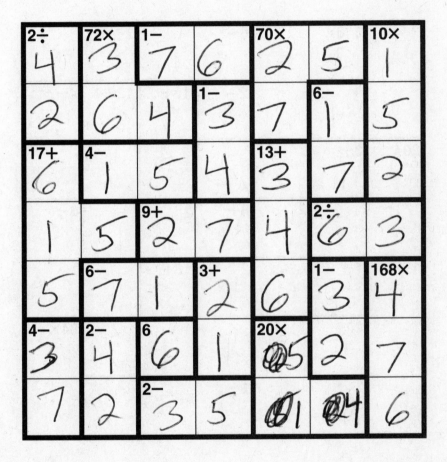

2÷ 4	72× 3	1− 7	6	70× 2	5	10× 1
2	6	4	1− 3	7	6− 1	5
17+ 6	4− 1	5	4	13+ 3	7	2
1	5	9+ 2	7	4	2÷ 6	3
5	6− 7	1	3+ 2	6	1− 3	168× 4
4− 3	2− 4	6 6	1	20× 5	2	7
7	2	2− 3	5	1	4	6

144 Moderate +/−/×/÷

2÷ 4	300× 2	5	6− 7	1	2÷ 6	3
2	4⁴	6	5	15+ 7	120× 3	4− 1
294× 7	3÷ 1	3	6	2	4	5
6	7	2² 2	8+ 3	5	1	3− 4
15× 1	1− 3	4	2² 2	10+ 6	5	7
3	20+ 5	7	1	4	2	84× 6
5	6	1	1− 4	3	7	2

Moderate +/−/×/÷ 145

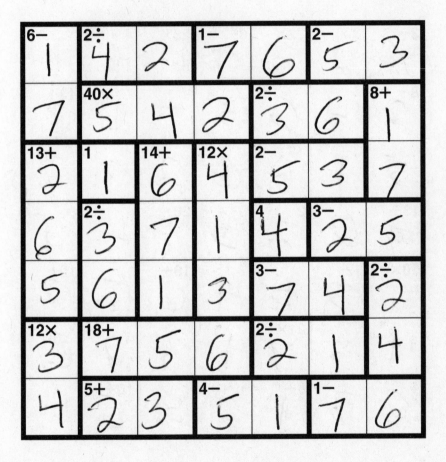

6−	2÷		1−		2−	
1	4	2	7	6	5	3
	40×			2÷		8+
7	5	4	2	3	6	1
13+	1	14+	12×	2−		
2	1	6	4	5	3	7
	2÷			4	3−	
6	3	7	1	4	2	5
				3−		2÷
5	6	1	3	7	4	2
12×	18+			2÷		
3	7	5	6	2	1	4
	5+		4−		1−	
4	2	3	5	1	7	6

146 Moderate +/−/×/÷

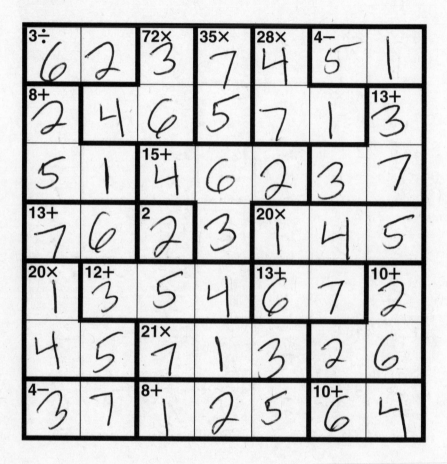

3÷ 6	2	72× 3	35× 7	28× 4	4− 5	1
8+ 2	4	6	5	7	1	13+ 3
5	1	15+ 4	6	2	3	7
13+ 7	6	2 2	3	20× 1	4	5
20× 1	12+ 3	5	4	13+ 6	7	10+ 2
4	5	21× 7	1	3	2	6
4− 3	7	8+ 1	2	5	10+ 6	4

Moderate +/−/×/÷ 147

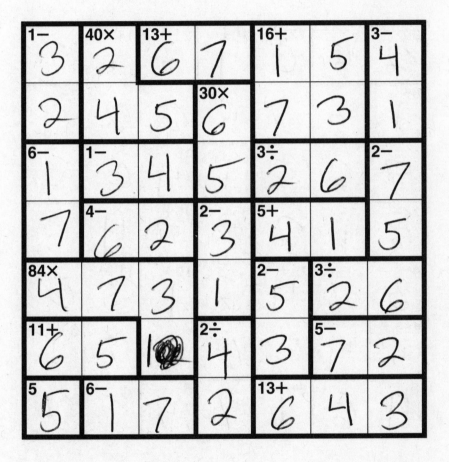

1− 3	40× 2	13+ 6	7	16+ 1	5	3− 4
2	4	5	30× 6	7	3	1
6− 1	1− 3	4	5	3÷ 2	6	2− 7
7	4− 6	2	2− 3	5+ 4	1	5
84× 4	7	3	1	2− 5	3÷ 2	6
11+ 6	5	1	2÷ 4	3	5− 7	2
5 5	6− 1	7	2	13+ 6	4	3

148 Moderate +/−/×/÷

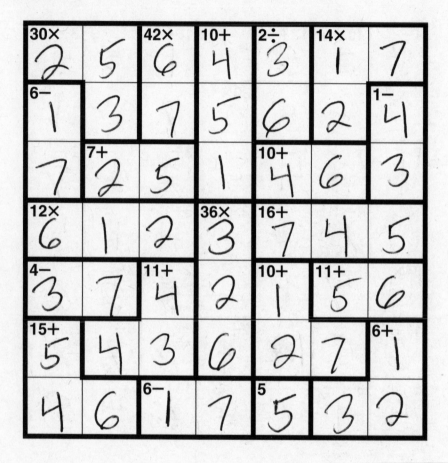

30×		42×	10+	2÷	14×	
2	5	6	4	3	1	7
6−						1−
1	3	7	5	6	2	4
	7+			10+		
7	2	5	1	4	6	3
12×			36×	16+		
6	1	2	3	7	4	5
4−		11+		10+	11+	
3	7	4	2	1	5	6
15+						6+
5	4	3	6	2	7	1
		6−		5		
4	6	1	7	5	3	2

Moderate +/−/×/÷ 149

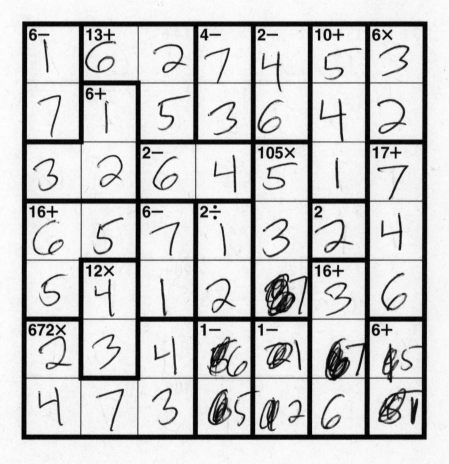

6−	13+		4−	2−	10+	6×
1	6	2	7	4	5	3
7	6+ 1	5	3	6	4	2
3	2	2− 6	4	105× 5	1	17+ 7
16+ 6	5	6− 7	2÷ 1	3	2 2	4
5	12× 4	1	2	7	16+ 3	6
672× 2	3	4	1− 6	1− 1	7	6+ 5
4	7	3	5	2	6	1

150 Moderate +/−/×/÷

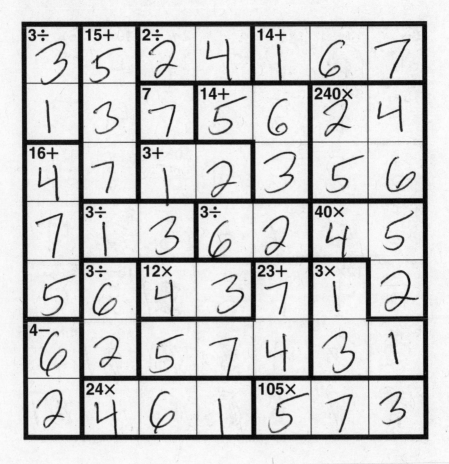

3÷ 3	15+ 5	2÷ 2	4	14+ 1	6	7
1	3	7 7	14+ 5	6	240× 2	4
16+ 4	7	3+ 1	2	3	5	6
7	3÷ 1	3	3÷ 6	2	40× 4	5
5	3÷ 6	12× 4	3	23+ 7	3× 1	2
4− 6	2	5	7	4	3	1
2	24× 4	6	1	105× 5	7	3

Moderate +/−/×/÷ 151

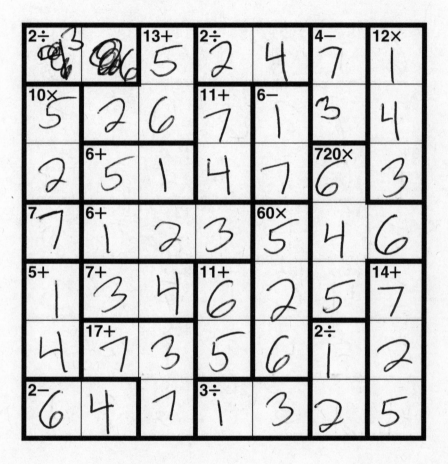

2÷ 3	6	13+ 5	2÷ 2	4	4− 7	12× 1
10× 5	2	6	11+ 7	6− 1	3	4
2	6+ 5	1	4	7	720× 6	3
7 7	6+ 1	2	3	60× 5	4	6
5+ 1	7+ 3	4	11+ 6	2	5	14+ 7
4	17+ 7	3	5	6	2÷ 1	2
2− 6	4	7	3÷ 1	3	2	5

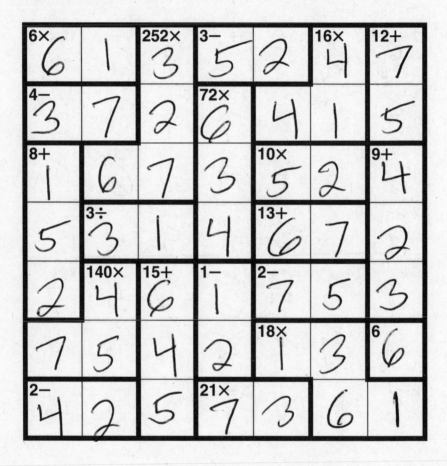

6× 6	1	252× 3	3− 5	2	16× 4	12+ 7
4− 3	7	2	72× 6	4	1	5
8+ 1	6	7	3	10× 5	2	9+ 4
5	3÷ 3	1	4	13+ 6	7	2
2	140× 4	15+ 6	1− 1	2− 7	5	3
7	5	4	2	18× 1	3	6 6
2− 4	2	5	21× 7	3	6	1

Moderate +/−/×/÷ 153

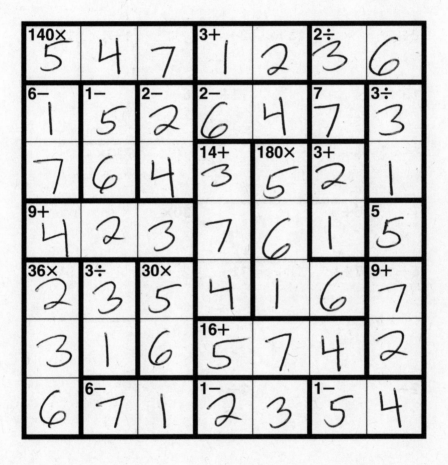

140×			3+		2÷	
5	4	7	1	2	3	6
6−	**1−**	**2−**	**2−**		**7**	**3÷**
1	5	2	6	4	7	3
			14+	**180×**	**3+**	
7	6	4	3	5	2	1
9+						**5**
4	2	3	7	6	1	5
36×	**3÷**	**30×**				**9+**
2	3	5	4	1	6	7
3	1	6	**16+** 5	7	4	2
6	**6−** 7	1	**1−** 2	3	**1−** 5	4

see #151

154 Moderate +/−/×/÷

2÷		13+	2÷		4−	12×
10×			11+	6−		
	6+				720×	
7	6+			60×		
5+	7+		11+			14+
	17+				2÷	
2−			3÷			

Moderate +/−/×/÷ 155

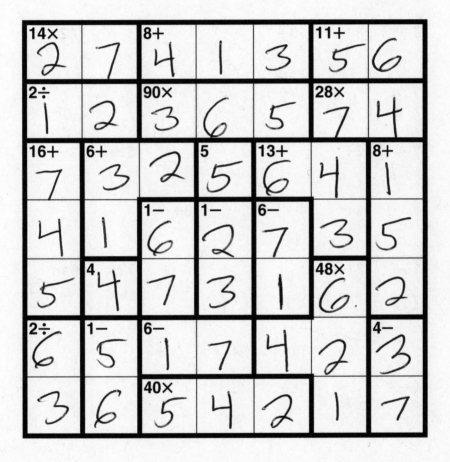

14×		8+			11+	
2	7	4	1	3	5	6
2÷		**90×**			**28×**	
1	2	3	6	5	7	4
16+	**6+**		**5**	**13+**		**8+**
7	3	2	5	6	4	1
4	1	**1−** 6	**1−** 2	**6−** 7	3	5
5	**4** 4	7	3	1	**48×** 6	2
2÷ 6	**1−** 5	**6−** 1	7	4	2	**4−** 3
3	6	**40×** 5	4	2	1	7

156 Moderate +/−/×/÷

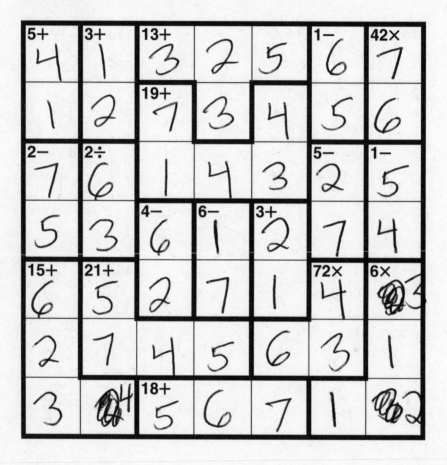

5+ 4	3+ 1	13+ 3	2	5	1− 6	42× 7
1	2	19+ 7	3	4	5	6
2− 7	2÷ 6	1	4	3	5− 2	1− 5
5	3	4− 6	6− 1	3+ 2	7	4
15+ 6	21+ 5	2	7	1	72× 4	6× 3
2	7	4	5	6	3	1
3	4	18+ 5	6	7	1	2

Moderate +/−/×/÷ 157

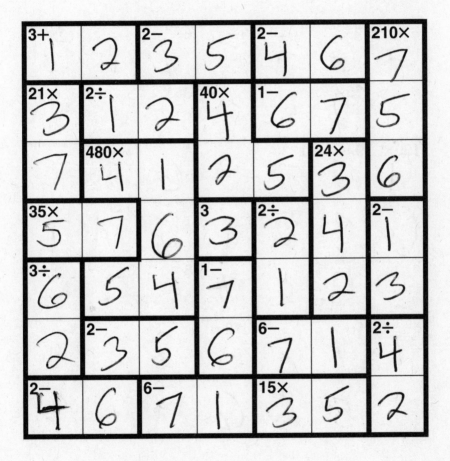

3+ 1	2	2− 3	5	2− 4	6	210× 7
21× 3	2÷ 1	2	40× 4	1− 6	7	5
7	480× 4	1	2	5	24× 3	6
35× 5	7	6	3 3	2÷ 2	4	2− 1
3÷ 6	5	4	1− 7	1	2	3
2	2− 3	5	6	6− 7	1	2÷ 4
2− 4	6	6− 7	1	15× 3	5	2

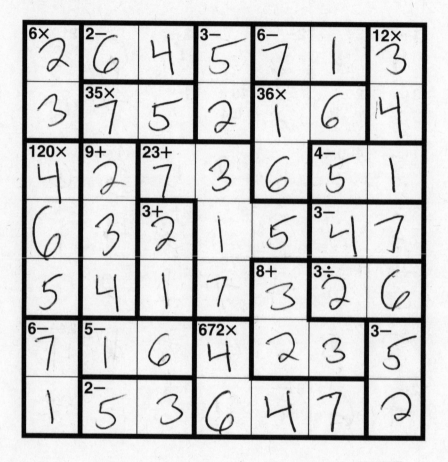

6× 2	2− 6	4	3− 5	6− 7	1	12× 3
3	35× 7	5	2	36× 1	6	4
120× 4	9+ 2	23+ 7	3	6	4− 5	1
6	3	3+ 2	1	5	3− 4	7
5	4	1	7	8+ 3	3÷ 2	6
6− 7	5− 1	6	672× 4	2	3	3− 5
1	2− 5	3	6	4	7	2

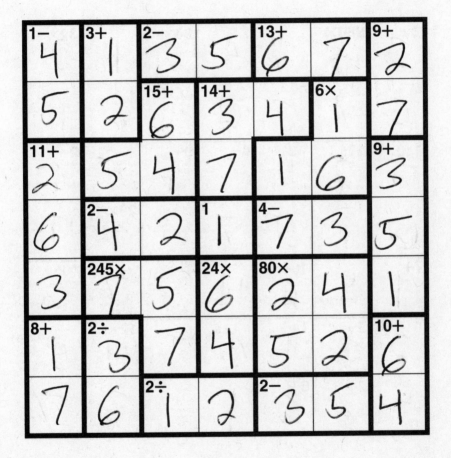

1− 4	3+ 1	2− 3	5	13+ 6	7	9+ 2
5	2	15+ 6	14+ 3	4	6× 1	7
11+ 2	5	4	7	1	6	9+ 3
6	2− 4	2	1 1	4− 7	3	5
3	245× 7	5	24× 6	80× 2	4	1
8+ 1	2÷ 3	7	4	5	2	10+ 6
7	6	2÷ 1	2	2− 3	5	4

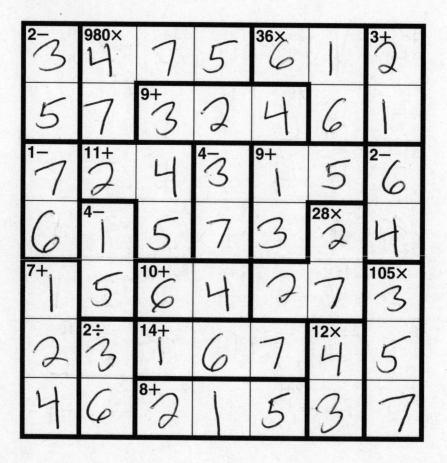

2− 3	980× 4	7	5	36× 6	1	3÷ 2
5	7	9+ 3	2	4	6	1
1− 7	11+ 2	4	4− 3	9+ 1	5	2− 6
6	4− 1	5	7	3	28× 2	4
7+ 1	5	10+ 6	4	2	7	105× 3
2	2÷ 3	14+ 1	6	7	12× 4	5
4	6	8+ 2	1	5	3	7

Moderate +/−/×/÷ 161

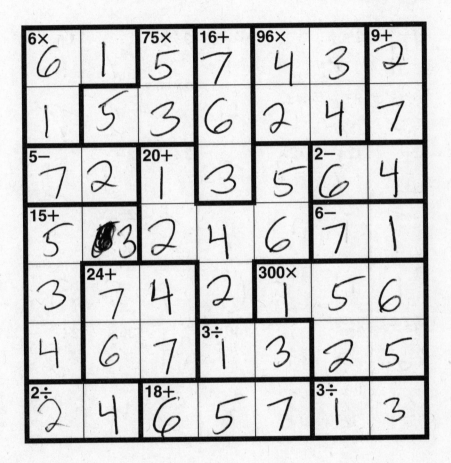

6× 6	1	75× 5	16+ 7	96× 4	3	9+ 2
1	5	3	6	2	4	7
5− 7	2	20+ 1	3	5	2− 6	4
15+ 5	3	2	4	6	6− 7	1
3	24+ 7	4	2	300× 1	5	6
4	6	7	3÷ 1	3	2	5
2÷ 2	4	18+ 6	5	7	3÷ 1	3

162 Moderate +/−/×/÷

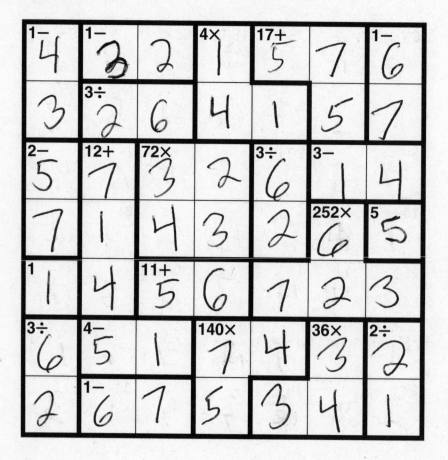

¹⁻4	¹⁻3	2	⁴ˣ1	¹⁷⁺5	7	¹⁻6
3	³÷2	6	4	1	5	7
²⁻5	¹²⁺7	⁷²ˣ3	2	³÷6	³⁻1	4
7	1	4	3	2	²⁵²ˣ6	⁵5
¹1	4	¹¹⁺5	6	7	2	3
³÷6	⁴⁻5	1	¹⁴⁰ˣ7	4	³⁶ˣ3	²÷2
2	¹⁻6	7	5	3	4	1

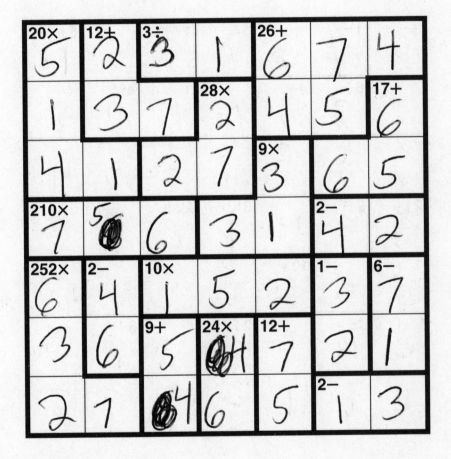

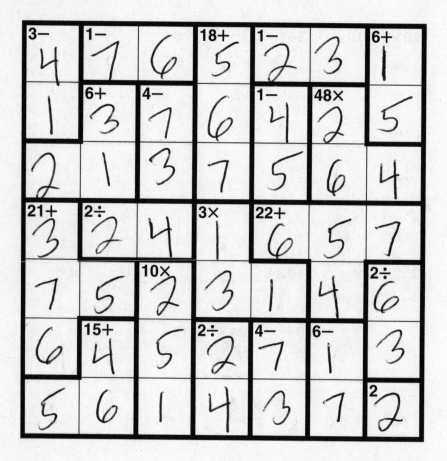

3− 4	1− 7	6	18+ 5	1− 2	3	6+ 1
1	6+ 3	4− 7	6	1− 4	48× 2	5
2	1	3	7	5	6	4
21+ 3	2÷ 2	4	3× 1	22+ 6	5	7
7	5	10× 2	3	1	4	2÷ 6
6	15+ 4	5	2÷ 2	4− 7	6− 1	3
5	6	1	4	3	7	²2

Moderate +/−/×/÷ 165

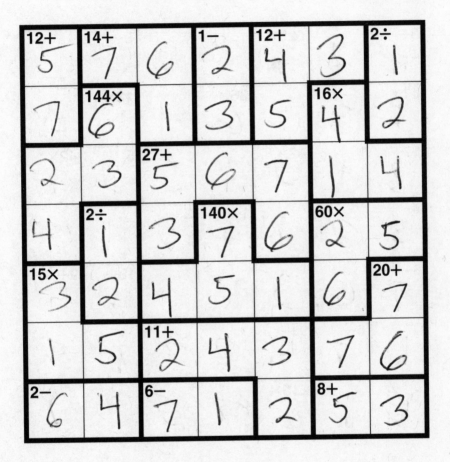

12+ 5	14+ 7	6	1− 2	12+ 4	3	2÷ 1
7	144× 6	1	3	5	16× 4	2
2	3	27+ 5	6	7	1	4
4	2÷ 1	3	140× 7	6	60× 2	5
15× 3	2	4	5	1	6	20+ 7
1	5	11+ 2	4	3	7	6
2− 6	4	6− 7	1	2	8+ 5	3

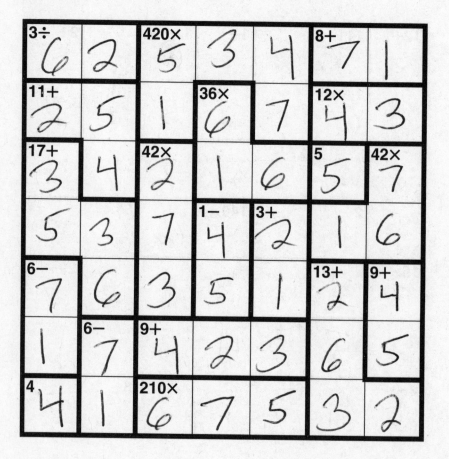

3÷ 6	2	420× 5	3	4	8+ 7	1
11+ 2	5	1	36× 6	7	12× 4	3
17+ 3	4	42× 2	1	6	5 5	42× 7
5	3	7	1− 4	3+ 2	1	6
6− 7	6	3	5	1	13+ 2	9+ 4
1	6− 7	9+ 4	2	3	6	5
4 4	1	210× 6	7	5	3	2

Moderate +/−/×/÷

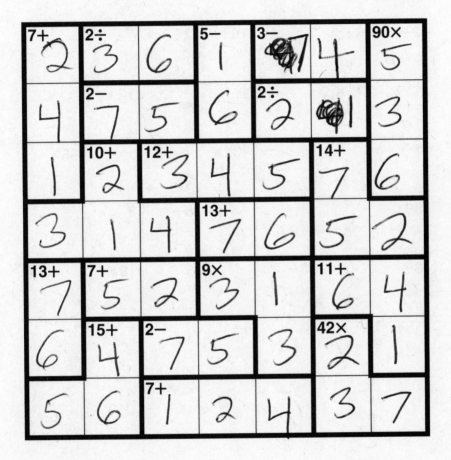

7+ 2	2÷ 3	6	5− 1	3− 7	4	90× 5
4	2− 7	5	6	2÷ 2	1	3
1	10+ 2	12+ 3	4	5	14+ 7	6
3	1	4	13+ 7	6	5	2
13+ 7	7+ 5	2	9× 3	1	11+ 6	4
6	15+ 4	2− 7	5	3	42× 2	1
5	6	7+ 1	2	4	3	7

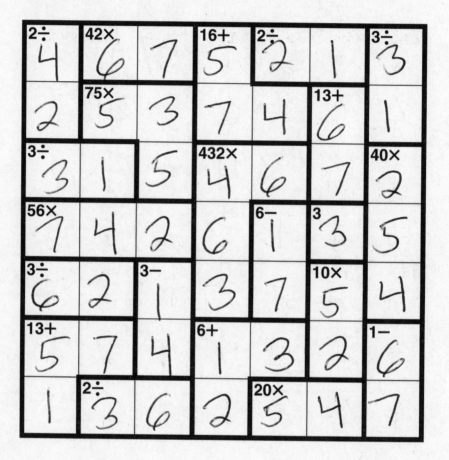

2÷ 4	42× 6	7	16+ 5	2÷ 2	1	3÷ 3
2	75× 5	3	7	4	13+ 6	1
3÷ 3	1	5	432× 4	6	7	40× 2
56× 7	4	2	6	6− 1	3 3	5
3÷ 6	2	3− 1	3	7	10× 5	4
13+ 5	7	4	6+ 1	3	2	1− 6
1	2÷ 3	6	2	20× 5	4	7

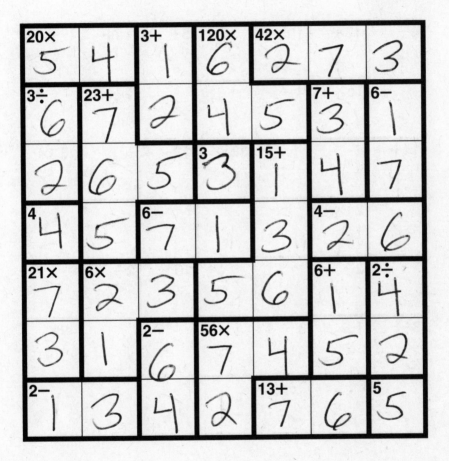

20× 5	4	3+ 1	120× 6	42× 2	7	3
3÷ 6	23+ 7	2	4	5	7+ 3	6− 1
2	6	5	3 3	15+ 1	4	7
4 4	5	6− 7	1	3	4− 2	6
21× 7	6× 2	3	5	6	6+ 1	2÷ 4
3	1	2− 6	56× 7	4	5	2
2− 1	3	4	2	13+ 7	6	5 5

170 Moderate +/−/×/÷

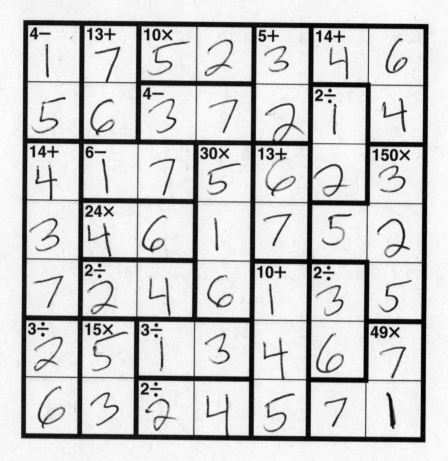

4−	13+	10×		5+	14+	
1	7	5	2	3	4	6
5	6	4−			2÷	
		3	7	2	1	4
14+	6−		30×	13+		150×
4	1	7	5	6	2	3
	24×					
3	4	6	1	7	5	2
	2÷			10+	2÷	
7	2	4	6	1	3	5
3÷	15×	3÷				49×
2	5	1	3	4	6	7
6	3	2÷				
		2	4	5	7	1

Moderate +/−/×/÷ 171

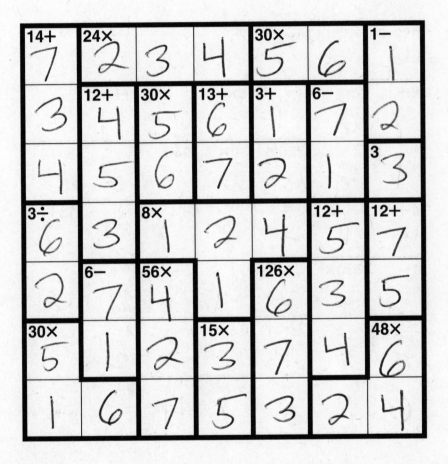

14+ 7	24× 2	3	4	30× 5	6	1− 1
3	12+ 4	30× 5	13+ 6	3+ 1	6− 7	2
4	5	6	7	2	1	3 3
3÷ 6	3	8× 1	2	4	12+ 5	12+ 7
2	6− 7	56× 4	1	126× 6	3	5
30× 5	1	2	15× 3	7	4	48× 6
1	6	7	5	3	2	4

172 Moderate +/−/×/÷

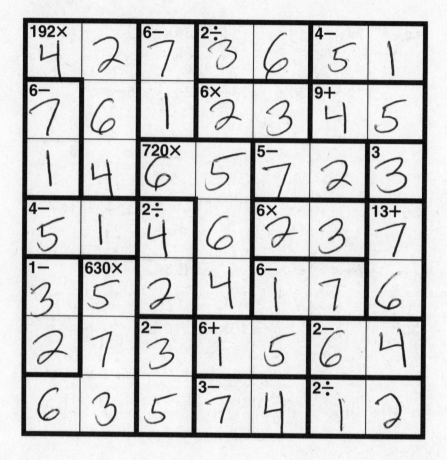

192× 4	2	6− 7	2÷ 3	6	4− 5	1
6− 7	6	1	6× 2	3	9+ 4	5
1	4	720× 6	5	5− 7	2	3 3
4− 5	1	2÷ 4	6	6× 2	3	13+ 7
1− 3	630× 5	2	4	6− 1	7	6
2	7	2− 3	6+ 1	5	2− 6	4
6	3	5	3− 7	4	2÷ 1	2

Moderate +/−/×/÷ 173

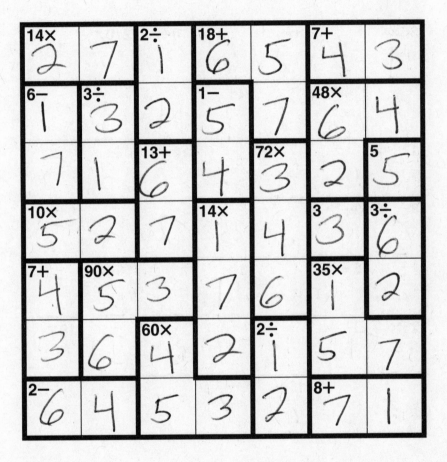

14× 2	7	2÷ 1	18+ 6	5	7+ 4	3
6− 1	3÷ 3	2	1− 5	7	48× 6	4
7	1	13+ 6	4	72× 3	2	5 5
10× 5	2	7	14× 1	4	3 3	3÷ 6
7+ 4	90× 5	3	7	6	35× 1	2
3	6	60× 4	2	2÷ 1	5	7
2− 6	4	5	3	2	8+ 7	1

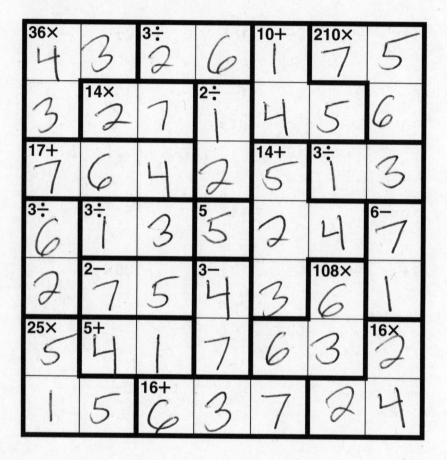

36× 4	3	3÷ 2	6	10+ 1	210× 7	5
3	14× 2	7	2÷ 1	4	5	6
17+ 7	6	4	2	14+ 5	3÷ 1	3
3÷ 6	3÷ 1	3	5 5	2	4	6− 7
2	2− 7	5	3− 4	3	108× 6	1
25× 5	5+ 4	1	7	6	3	16× 2
1	5	16+ 6	3	7	2	4

Moderate +/−/×/÷ 175

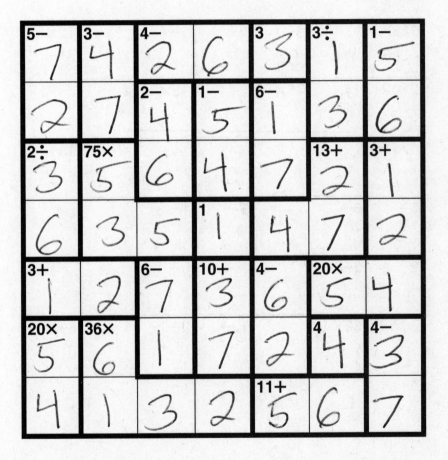

5−7	3−4	4−2	6	3·3	3÷1	1−5
2	7	2−4	1−5	6−1	3	6
2÷3	75×5	6	4	7	13+2	3+1
6	3	5	¹1	4	7	2
3+1	2	6−7	10+3	4−6	20×5	4
20×5	36×6	1	7	2	⁴4	4−3
4	1	3	2	11+5	6	7

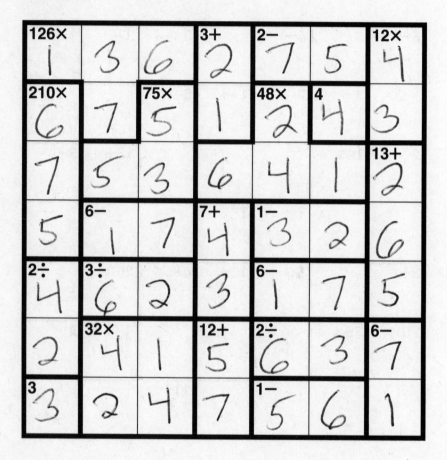

126×			3+	2−		12×
1	3	6	2	7	5	4
210× 6	7	**75×** 5	1	**48×** 2	**4** 4	3
7	5	3	6	4	1	**13+** 2
5	**6−** 1	7	**7+** 4	**1−** 3	2	6
2÷ 4	**3÷** 6	2	3	**6−** 1	7	5
2	**32×** 4	1	**12+** 5	**2÷** 6	3	**6−** 7
3 3	2	4	7	**1−** 5	6	1

Moderate +/−/×/÷ 177

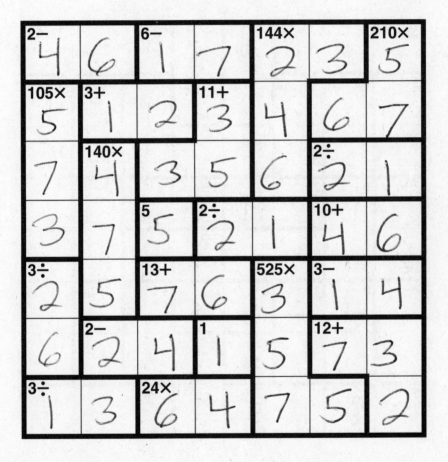

2− 4	6	6− 1	7	144× 2	3	210× 5
105× 5	3+ 1	2	11+ 3	4	6	7
7	140× 4	3	5	6	2÷ 2	1
3	7	5 5	2÷ 2	1	10+ 4	6
3÷ 2	5	13+ 7	6	525× 3	3− 1	4
6	2− 2	4	1 1	5	12+ 7	3
3÷ 1	3	24× 6	4	7	5	2

178 Moderate +/−/×/÷

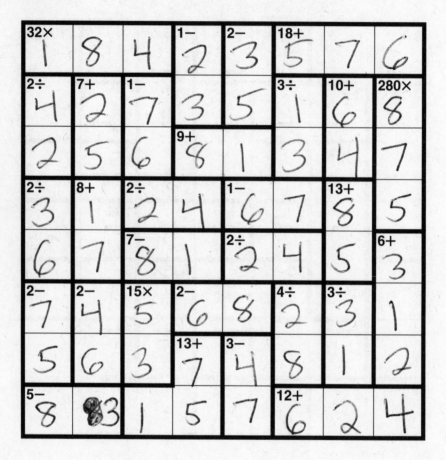

32× 1	8	4	1− 2	2− 3	18+ 5	7	6
2÷ 4	7+ 2	1− 7	3	5	3÷ 1	10+ 6	280× 8
2	5	6	9+ 8	1	3	4	7
2÷ 3	8+ 1	2÷ 2	4	1− 6	7	13+ 8	5
6	7	7− 8	1	2÷ 2	4	5	6+ 3
2− 7	2− 4	15× 5	2− 6	8	4÷ 2	3÷ 3	1
5	6	3	13+ 7	3− 4	8	1	2
5− 8	3	1	5	7	12+ 6	2	4

6 **6**	4− **5**	42×		2÷		112×	10+
3−	**1**		2−				
	17+		21+	3÷		5 **5**	
4−					2−		
	168×		14+		4÷		1680×
13+		2 **2**		30×			
	2−	8+	2−		8+		
				4−			

180 Moderate +/−/×/÷

7−		19+		15+		48×	
2÷		42×			12+		
6+				2÷			1−
15+		3−	12×	256×			
	16+			3÷			1680×
		2÷	60×	7+			
4÷				126×	12+		
7+							

Moderate +/−/×/÷ 181

15+ 7	6− 1	192× 4	8	4− 2	6	1− 5	6+ 3
8	7	3	2	140× 4	5	6	1
15× 5	3	96× 6	24× 4	7	56× 8	1	2
1	2	8	6	4− 5	7	1− 3	4
40× 2	1− 6	5	3÷ 3	1	84× 4	1− 8	7
4	5	2 2	1	36× 6	3	7	240× 8
2÷ 6	2÷ 8	20+ 1	7	3	2	2÷ 4	5
3	4	7	5	9+ 8	1	2	6

182 Moderate +/−/×/÷

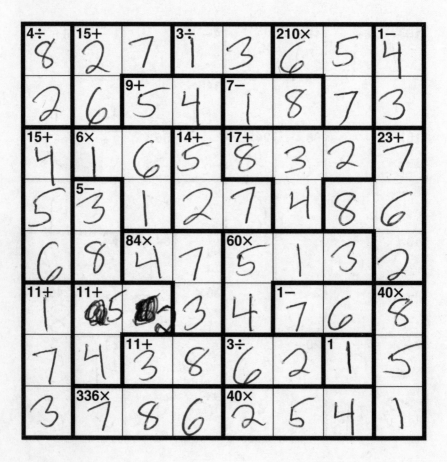

4÷ 8	15+ 2	7	3÷ 1	3	210× 6	5	1− 4
2	6	9+ 5	4	7− 1	8	7	3
15+ 4	6× 1	6	14+ 5	17+ 8	3	2	23+ 7
5	5− 3	1	2	7	4	8	6
6	8	84× 4	7	60× 5	1	3	2
11+ 1	11+ 5 2	3	4	1− 7	6	40× 8
7	4	11+ 3	8	3÷ 6	2	1	5
3	336× 7	8	6	40× 2	5	4	1

Moderate +/−/×/÷ 183

5− 8	3	**1−**		**7+**	**28×**		**9+**
2− 6	**2−**				**9+**		
4	**1−**		**2÷**		**5** 5	**2÷**	
2− 5	**2÷**		**14×**		**36×** 1	6	**3** 3
7	**2÷**		**2−**		6	**2÷**	
3+ 1	**5−**		**15+**			**1−**	
2	**2−**		**40×**		**4−**		**9+**
2÷ 3	6	**6−**			**4÷**		

184 Moderate +/−/×/÷

8+		1−	36×	2−		9+	2÷
5 5							
48×			11+ 5	1	15+		3÷ 3
9+		1−	20+	5	216×		1
2−							2− 7
21+		2÷		3÷			5
23+		4410×				1−	4− 2
				3+			6

Moderate +/−/×/÷ 185

10+			8+	15+		1792×	
2−		2÷					
10×	3−		21+			10+	
		1−		4÷		1−	
7−	5−	1−		1−			7+
		24×	120×				
2−			7+			108×	
17+				1−			

186 Moderate +/−/×/÷

7− **8**	**1**	3÷ **3**	1−		40×		
1−	96×	**1**	420×		1−		32×
		2		1−			
10+		1−		4÷		2−	3−
	22+		7−	6×			
		4		4−		13+	
		1− **8**	2−		14×		
20× **5**	**4**	**7**	5+		15+		

Moderate +/−/×/÷ 187

3−	6−		6+	6−	1−		48×
	2÷				20×		
1−		2−		6−		5+	
3÷		20×	12+		7+	5−	
7−			1−			3−	
2÷		5−	1−	13+	3−	4−	
80×						18+	
		11+		2÷			

188 Moderate +/−/×/÷

2−	42×		1−		4−	4÷	
		6+				3−	
7	15+			7−		10+	7+
5−			1−				
2−		18+	7+		32×	3÷	12+
16×			1				
	32×	280×			2−	3÷	
			8+			13+	

Moderate +/−/×/÷ 189

4−		2÷	2−	6×	11+	21+	8
2−							24×
2−	18+				1−		
	7−		1−			10×	3÷
4−	2÷		4−		40×		
	14+					8+	70×
2÷		1−	1−	15+	2÷		
4−							

190 Moderate +/−/×/÷

26+	1−		56×	8×		6×	
	13+				16+	6+	7+
	10+		16+				
				2÷	3÷	21+	
24×	20×	6−					280×
		13+		21+			
			15×	15+			
	4÷					13+	

4−	3÷		24×		3−		6−
	2÷		15+	35×	4÷		
56×	24×				24×		
		1−			2÷	4÷	
35×			1−	3÷		7−	
2÷	1	23+			14×	60×	
	64×		7−			14+	
				1−			

192 Moderate +/−/×/÷

60×		784×			8−		10+
240×		17+		7−	48×		72×
							27+
36×			3+	2−		17+	
8−	2−			12×		8+	
	2÷		17+			2−	
17+		16×		16+	9×	19+	
	17+		24+				24×
				13+			

Moderate +/−/×/÷ 193

1−		17+		30×		56×	
16+	25×		24×	4÷		22+	3−
				1568×	3		
90×	22+	11+			8−	22+	
					1−		
		5×		3−	1080×		
8×		21+	3÷				40×
			2÷		25+		
3−		3−					

194 Moderate +/−/×/÷

336×	10+		100×	5−	144×	8−		4×
36×	4÷		14+			14+		20+
	3÷		13+			5−		
	3÷		12+			35×		
32×		22+			4÷		12+	
	100×	7−	23+			7−	49×	
			37+					
4−							2−	

4−	13+	84×			120×		7−	
		15+		8−		6×		3÷
15+					315×			
6+			19+	20×			19+	70×
5	7−			3÷		60×		
84×				5−				
20+			9+	9+				2÷
8−	30×				18+	4−		
		19+					4−	

196 Moderate +/−/×/÷

5−	2−	35×			17+		36×	
		2−		315×		192×		
17+	1−		1−				3+	224×
	3240×		12+	11+	162×			
20×		2				4−		
						35×	19+	3÷
	21×		17+		48×			
2÷	3÷	2÷						405×
		19+			1−			

Moderate +/−/×/÷ 197

14+		2×	144×			31+		280×
			4−		5−			
23+		39+	8−	3−	30×			
1						19+		
24+			7	1−			4−	
			2÷	4÷	2−	6×		
						70×		17+
14+	128×		11+		432×			
						8−		

198 Moderate +/−/×/÷

4÷		12+		450×	6−		8−	11+
15+						630×		
1−	54×	8	11+					3÷
				2−		5−		
90×	49×	2÷		5−		8	1−	
			3024×	5−		1−		6−
	3÷				3+		28+	
2÷		140×		3×				3−
3−					2÷			

Moderate +/−/×/÷ 199

288×		16+		2÷		7	5×
4−	1−	14+					
10+		672×	2÷	7−		23+	
	3−			189×	12+	17+	
8−	10×		1				
	29+		5−				13+
	2÷			1−			
9+		60×	24+			23+	
12+				5−			

210×		15+		189×		8−		1−
	5−	1−			2−		17+	
8−			14+	180×				24+
	13+				15×	5−		
5		22+				4÷		
5−		19+		24×		3÷		
	17+	3+				15+		
9+			49×	13+	11+			25+

Moderate +/−/×/÷ 201

48×		1−	24+	10+	15+	4−	16+	
1−								
	288×	8−				14+	12+	
		84×						
7×	18+		19+			16×		486×
			6+	60×				
7+	54×			15+		13+		3−
	7+					54×		
3÷		16+			8−		24×	

202 Challenging +/−/×/÷

2÷		8+		48×	3+	180×		
4	270×	5−	7+			80×		
				4−		17+		4÷
	3+	2÷	17+		15×	210×		
14×			180×			8		24×
	16+	17+	6+		48×			
17+				9+	2÷		6−	
		12+			9	8+	6×	3−
11+		5		4÷				

Challenging +/−/×/÷ 203

8−		1−		40×	4÷	20+		
2÷	35×		8−			2÷		
	14+			24×	315×			48×
2÷		12+						
3÷	7+	14+		315×		2−		28×
		2÷	17+			2÷	15+	
3−								8−
13+		2−	22+		54×			
1−				3+			7+	

204 Challenging +/−/×/÷

7×	4÷		8+	28×		1−		14+
				4÷	13+		15+	
17+		13+			8−			
	8−		11+		3−		1−	
17+	70×			27×	2÷		4×	
	100×	2−	24×		5−		17+	
					10+			448×
6×	2÷	13+		150×		8+		
		8−			4÷			

2÷		4−		8−		2÷	1−	
21×			168×	4÷			14+	
4−			192×	2	3÷			4−
144×	144×				13+	70×		
	11+			4÷		18×		168×
		40×			1−		8−	
42×	3÷	11+	3÷					
			9	17+		22+	32×	
	13+							

206 Challenging +/−/×/÷

17+	14+	160×		2÷		3−	
		7−	8−	2÷	2−	3÷	
		168×				4÷	
3+		10+	17+		12×		35×
24×		162×	15+	3−			
2−		2			14+	8−	
7−	2−	1−					15+
	16+	11+		315×		10+	
		4−			2		

10×	4÷		17+	378×		3÷		12+
	21×				2−	20×		
252×	17+		11+				3−	
	11+				8−	48×	2−	5−
	6+	3÷	196×					
288×					105×		8−	17+
		12+	50×		48×			
3÷	16+					13+		168×
			3÷		7−			

208 Challenging +/−/×/÷

3÷		15×	15+		17+	20+	6−	
1−			12+				2−	
	35+	4−		1	15+		14+	280×
5				3÷				
18×		1−				1−		
		2÷	13+				16+	3÷
			6−					
1−	2÷		4−	3÷		5−	8−	
	5−			35×			24×	

Challenging +/−/×/÷ 209

5−	4÷	13+	3−		3+		405×	5
			23+					
2÷	5−	48×			36×		8+	21×
		6−		27+		5		
7	160×	5−	3+			48×		
				5−	13+	3÷	2−	5−
135×	10+	175×						
			8−		9+	2−	6−	2÷
	8−		2÷					

210 Challenging +/−/×/÷

7	2÷		3−	3+		54×		12+
3+	8−			20×		5−		
	18+		168×	10×		324×		
5−	45×		1		64×			
	3−		17+		210×	6−	3	24×
60×	2÷			8−				
		3÷				17+	280×	
15+	1−	5−	1−	3÷				
				24×		2	4÷	

Challenging +/−/×/÷ 211

17+		144×		1−	40×		5−	
1−			22+			90×		4−
			8−		6×			
3÷	192×		210×				20+	
			20×			19+	22+	
6+		10+	108×					
4−			3−		2	12×		
28×	17+			4−		2÷		30×
		7−		8	18×			

212 Challenging +/−/×/÷

25+		8−	5−		6×		80×	
	5+		1728×					6−
		3	140×	1−		2−		
11+				126×		2−	5−	2÷
4÷	4−	19+			5−			
			3+			9+	15+	
6−	48×		5−				9	
	6		4÷	28×		27+		1−
12+			3÷					

Challenging +/−/×/÷ 213

84×			3+	7−	3÷		19+	
140×	4−				2÷	11+	11+	
	1−	5−	432×	5				
				3÷	8×		2−	12+
54×					3−			
2÷	8−	14+			13+	7−	7−	
		35×		2÷			3÷	
3−		3÷	120×		6−		3−	
1−					2÷		4−	

214 Challenging +/−/×/÷

4−	8−	2−		540×	3+		2÷	
		2÷			16+	240×	28×	
3+	17+		2−				17+	
				2−			1−	
18+			1		4÷	378×	45×	
2−		2÷	2÷	15+				2−
18+					4−	4÷		
9		12+	2÷			3÷	5+	
2−			252×				1−	

Challenging +/−/×/÷ 215

9408×		5	8+	15+		14+		
		8−		63×			144×	
384×				40×		27×		126×
			3÷					
6×	42×		3−		17+			
	27+		23+			12+		
				12×		9+	3−	
		112×		72×	24×		8−	
45×							28×	

216 Challenging +/−/×/÷

17+		15×		8−	21×	48×		
1−		14+				3+		336×
882×		3−	8+		4÷	1	17+	
			7+			240×		
2÷	12×	2−	8−	60×			14×	
						5−		4
14+	3+		378×				20×	
	5−	2÷	5−	6−		45×		15+
				4	1−			

Challenging +/−/×/÷ 217

1−	24×		6−		10+	9+	630×	
	36×		5−					7−
6−		1−		7−	1−	6		
10+		1−				4÷	1−	3÷
7	90×	7−	15×					
24×			30+				56×	
		3÷		15+	5−	4−		
2÷	6−	30×				3÷	21+	
			90×					

218 Challenging +/−/×/÷

405×	1−		1−	1−		9+		
		28×		4−		24×	4÷	1−
24×			8−					
2÷	13+		11+			7	26+	2÷
			15+					
2−	2÷	2−		14+		15+		
		5−			96×	3÷		19+
5−		3÷		15+			2÷	12+
3−		3−						

Challenging +/−/×/÷ 219

21×	2÷		72×			30+		
	80×	2−	10+	8−	4−			120×
					2÷	4÷		
8−		3÷		1512×			2−	
2−	9+				3−		2÷	
	6		4−		3+	3÷		14+
4−	72×			240×		189×		
	3−						6	18×
120×			2÷		1−			

220 Challenging +/−/×/÷

7−		17+	17+		5×	4−		2÷
1−						56×		
5−	1−		8−	10×	108×	20×		
	2÷						16+	
4−	9+	13+		17+			2÷	
		3÷		256×	42×	3+	20×	15+
42×	1−							
	10×			21×	5−		2−	24×
8+		2÷			45×			

Challenging +/−/×/÷ 221

48×			2÷		16+	2−	3÷	2−
2÷		3+						
2÷			63×	1−		11+	6+	2÷
1−		1−		3÷				
60×			56×			24×	13+	
	9	10+	240×					
3+	3−			16+		2−	15+	
		576×			8−		7	
25+						8	1−	

222 Challenging +/−/×/÷

10×	4÷	2÷	1−		18+			9
			5−	1−	8−	8+	2−	
17+	1−	30×					5−	
			9+			15×	8−	
1−		8−		2−			5−	
4−	1−	135×			6	2÷	4−	24×
		56×		7+				
4−		18+	24×			15+	2−	
3÷				2−			2÷	

Challenging +/−/×/÷ 223

48×	18+	4−	7−	4−		1−		16+
				108×		5−	2−	
8−		16+	18×					10+
			1−		19+	1−		
1−		13+	2−			5−	14+	
2÷				6−				
4÷		42×	30+				10×	
15×	189×			64×	5−	1−	54×	
							7−	

224 Challenging +/−/×/÷

5−	6×	3−	1−		8−		3÷	
			8−		26+			
8−		3÷	5−		12+	30×	2÷	2−
13+			7−					
140×		16+		17+		3+	8×	
	32×				21+		441×	
25+			1−				16+	
		12+		17+	40×	10+		
							1−	

Challenging +/−/×/÷ 225

60×			3+		30×	72×	3−	14×
11+		7×	3−	5−				
4÷					2÷	20×		15+
	3÷		9+	1−		4−		
8−	2÷				2÷		15×	
	5+		4	45×		2÷	224×	
13+	1−	30×		7−				3÷
		10×	2÷		10+	2÷		
1−			8−			224×		

226 Challenging +/−/×/÷

12+		2÷	2	320×		4−	5−	63×
6		2−						
4÷	1−	21×	24×		17+		4−	
			16+		3−			11+
10+	13+	15×				2−		
		192×		5−	144×		12+	
	19+				108×		3−	
		8−				2		64×
35+					3÷			

168×	17+		45×		3+	15+		
		3+		17+		12+	5−	
7−			3÷				3÷	
6−	8+			13+	270×	160×		
	3−	3÷	1			7+		48×
80×			36×	2÷		24×		
	3−	10+			126×			1
			17+		11+	8+		2÷
14+			11+			8−		

3÷	2÷		6−		4−	2−	1−	
	2−		72×				14+	8−
2÷		5−	1−	2÷				
4÷	1−			3−		21+		
		210×			7−		3÷	
8+			10+	162×		18+		
3÷	7−	21+			49×	120×		96×
2−			64×			3÷		6

3÷	2−		8−	2÷	56×		12+	
	7+					17+		2÷
2÷		3÷		30×			1344×	
5	3÷		1−	3+				
168×				210×	8−		6×	5−
8−		30×			4	42×		
4÷			36×					5
42×		3+		2÷	13+		6	8−
	7	1−			162×			

230 Challenging +/−/×/÷

210×		4÷		9+	8−	72×	16+	11+
		1−						
2÷		20×		1−				45×
4−	2÷	1134×		2÷		16+		
				1−			16+	3÷
216×				20+				
3−		1−			576×		9+	
2÷	8−		200×			21×		
	1−					378×		

4÷		120×			20+		5+	1470×
21×	12×			2÷	17+			
	16+	20×	1−					
2÷				1−		12+		11+
	15+		5−	8+		21+		
1−		6×		18×				12+
17+	11+		21+	8+		2		
					3−	20+		8×
	7−		2−				4	

232 Challenging +/−/×/÷

168×			8	504×	3−		5−	
30+		9+				3÷	8−	
	4−		3−	6×			2−	
	216×	6−		4−		2−	1−	
			14+				2−	
6+		3÷		1−		98×		19+
	14+		6×		32×		45×	
6×		54×		2−				
15+					10+		4÷	

Challenging +/−/×/÷ 233

42×		9+	2−		2÷		7−	
4−			2−		3÷		336×	
3−		8−	3−	90×		2÷		
10+	48×			48×			2−	4−
		1−				280×		
	7+	30+					48×	3÷
		2÷	13+					
10+			2−		8+	7−		2−
48×			35×				4	

234 Challenging +/−/×/÷

24+			10+				1−	
40×	3÷		54×	3−		7−		378×
	2	168×		2−	12+			
						22+		
9+		14+	12×			3÷		
6×			21+	7	21+	120×		11+
5−				8−			10×	
36×		3÷				42×		
3÷			3−				36×	

Challenging +/−/×/÷ 235

2÷		42×			1−	3−	4−	
14+	2÷	24+					3÷	
		2−		12+	12+		252×	
8+	14+					45×		
	15+	7−		14+	8−	2÷		13+
15×						9+		
	3÷	9+		42×			112×	
11+		28×	4−		14+			
			17+			8	2−	

5	26+	18+		224×		8−		15+
				15+		6×		
10+					5−	294×		
21+		144×					7−	
3−					4−	288×		
	5−	8	10+				105×	
7−		4−	17+			15+		
	36×		8	2−			3÷	
		6−			4÷		9+	

Challenging +/−/×/÷ 237

63×		128×		1−	14+	4÷	45×	
13+								336×
	40×	8−		4	1−		108×	
		3−	14+			2−		
12+			11+					13+
	9+		12+			13+		
216×		2÷		120×	3−			8+
	3−					17+		
	2÷		45×		112×			

238 Challenging +/−/×/÷

45×		4÷		1−	2÷		12+	8−
16+		42×		11+				
27+		54×			20×		20+	
			16+					
	2−			6	17+		5−	
	64×	42×	8−		4	17+	13+	
			135×					
7		15×		5−		1440×		5−
9+		4÷						

Challenging +/−/×/÷ 239

2−	504×			4÷		4÷	11+	2÷
	288×		720×					
		5−		23+		40×	11+	
18+							15+	
		3+		1080×				
40×	28+		8−		23+			144×
				42×	3+			
	5−		4032×			72×		
60×						12×		

240 Challenging +/−/×/÷

13+		4÷	2−		60×	8−		27×
	6−		2÷					
7		3−		672×			3−	15+
8×	36×	1−		16+	17+			
		3−				5	2÷	
13+		8−			36×	3+	1−	12+
	17+	4−						
50×		3÷	2−		6−	10752×		
			15+					

Challenging +/−/×/÷ 241

56×	3÷		16+			2−		8+
		7−	120×			4÷		
3−			19+		8−		21×	
192×		20+				189×	1−	8
4−				3+				4−
	3−	3−	4÷		8+	3÷	17+	
189×				5−				13+
	56×				60×			
	3+		180×			14+		

242 Challenging +/−/×/÷

24×		3+	22+			3−	1575×	
2÷			8−					
3−	20×	3−			21×		9+	3÷
		84×	16+			10+		
6−			3+	30×	1−		2÷	
3÷							3÷	
70×		3−	12×			56×	48×	
2÷			17+					5−
	210×			8	9+			

162×		2−	2÷		1−	32×	8−	5
	1920×		5−					15+
3+			2−		8−			
		11+	7+			1350×	1568×	
7	3+		40×				2÷	
18+					17+			
	21×		3−			3÷	14+	
		5−	8−		18+		21+	
2÷								

244 Challenging +/−/×/÷

30×			8+	28×		17+	24×	8−
18+		2−		4−				
13+					252×		7+	
	4÷		3−		16+		23+	2−
	8−	14+		6				
17+			3+			36×		105×
	5−	17+	210×	2÷				
3					14+	7+	5−	4÷
84×								

Challenging +/−/×/÷ 245

1−	36×	2÷	35×		8−		3÷	
			13+	216×	15×		20+	
6×					20+			
11+		2÷				8+		23+
20+			3+		2÷			
8−		8640×		168×	17+	1−		
2÷							19+	
2÷	13+	35×			17+			
			1−		1		2÷	

246 Challenging +/−/×/÷

2÷		3÷		280×		6×	
16+		7+	216×		4÷	19+	
	3÷		15×			1−	
8−		2−		20×	2÷		2−
	16+	24×			2−	56×	
		28×	3+	3−	4−	22+	
2÷	17+					5+	20×
		22+		6−			
14+					12+		

Challenging +/−/×/÷ 247

63×	14+		140×			3÷		1−
	2÷		432×			1−		
84×		1−	7+	8−		2÷	144×	
	42×			4−	9+		20+	
			6−					5
15+		192×		5		19+	28×	
3−							8−	
5−		12+	4	17+		17+	7+	
1−							1−	

248 Challenging +/−/×/÷

252×		3÷		18+		17+	7+	
		14+	1−		84×		8−	
28×						105×	64×	
	27×	11+						280×
6		17+		22+	3+			
360×					14+		12+	
		2÷	21×	8−				
14+				21×	9	24+	13+	
	5	8×						

Challenging +/−/×/÷   **249**

80×		14+		560×	8−		16+	
8−		270×				192×		
			12×	4÷	35×			
7+						1890×		
21+			126×				96×	
84×		11+	17+			56×		216×
			8−	6+	11+			
3−							3−	
36×		1−		36×			4−	

250 Challenging +/−/×/÷

3÷	4÷		105×			5−		13+
	216×	1−	42×	13+	1−	5−	14+	
4−								10×
		11+	4÷	3÷	3+	2−		
2−	1−						5−	5−
		14+	23+			4÷		
120×			3−		1−		8+	
9+				19+		24+		24×
	8−							

Challenging +/−/×/÷ 251

6×	2−		5−		1−	144×		
	8−		3−			120×	168×	
2−		2÷	2−	1	17+		4÷	
21+	144×			21+				3+
		9+				2÷		
		10+	14×		80×	7×		20+
18+						17+		
4÷			3÷		1−			
	4÷		3÷			16+		

252 Challenging +/−/×/÷

700×		16+	1−	24×	8−	16+	7+	
								7
54×	4÷		60×				2−	3÷
		3+	14+			2−		
1008×			4÷	11+	2÷		360×	
	17+					1−		
	1008×					8−		
3÷	6	112×		63×	72×		180×	
	7+					8×		

Challenging +/−/×/÷ 253

5−		17+		20×		3÷		24×
4−		3−	4÷	252×	22+			
8−					2−		105×	
17+	10+				2016×			4÷
		7	6+			3÷		
6		18+					840×	
2−		5−	4−	17+	8−			
9+					16+			8−
3−		42×		5+		4÷		

254 Challenging +/−/×/÷

2÷	2−		7−		28×			8×
	14+			13+		17+		
14+		84×		9+		4÷	3÷	
17+	288×		17+				45×	
				12+			8−	7
7		14×		19+		2−		15+
8×					280×			
	17+		24×			2−		6×
	3−			19+				

Challenging +/−/×/÷ 255

6−	7+	96×		16+			3−	
				6048×				120×
21+		8−	6×	6×	10+			
12+				56×	2−			
	13+		3+			13+		8−
	324×	56×	1−	5−		3÷		
					4−		3÷	1−
3÷	30×		20+	288×				
				120×			5−	

256 Challenging +/−/×/÷

8−	54×		23+		192×		630×	
	21+	17+						
				5−	20×	64×		
	21×		7+				1512×	
11+			315×	17+				1
672×	2÷			15×	5−		18+	
		3−	2÷					
2−			12+	8−		5040×		
	4−			1−				

Challenging +/−/×/÷ 257

4−		30×	216×	120×	48×		4÷	
17+	9+					3+		15+
					3÷			
19+		24+	7−			270×	120×	13+
2÷								
24×		17+						
4−	56×	8−		6+	17+		108×	
		24×	3÷			1260×		
2÷					3−			

258 Challenging +/−/×/÷

10×	1260×	22+		54×		4÷		3
			4−	5−	3+		3	32×
3−				19+	8−			
	1−		3−				1260×	
8−		5	4÷		1−			
17+	6×		5−		19+			70×
	18+		7+	24×		17+		
2÷		6+			2−			
	2			4−		22+		

7056×			2−		5	8−		24×
20×				2÷		5		
	48×		189×		3+		5−	
378×	10×			3+	672×			
		4÷			19+			9
	17+		24+			42×		
8×	2−				13+		4÷	
	13+			36×		3780×		
8−			20+					

260 Challenging +/−/×/÷

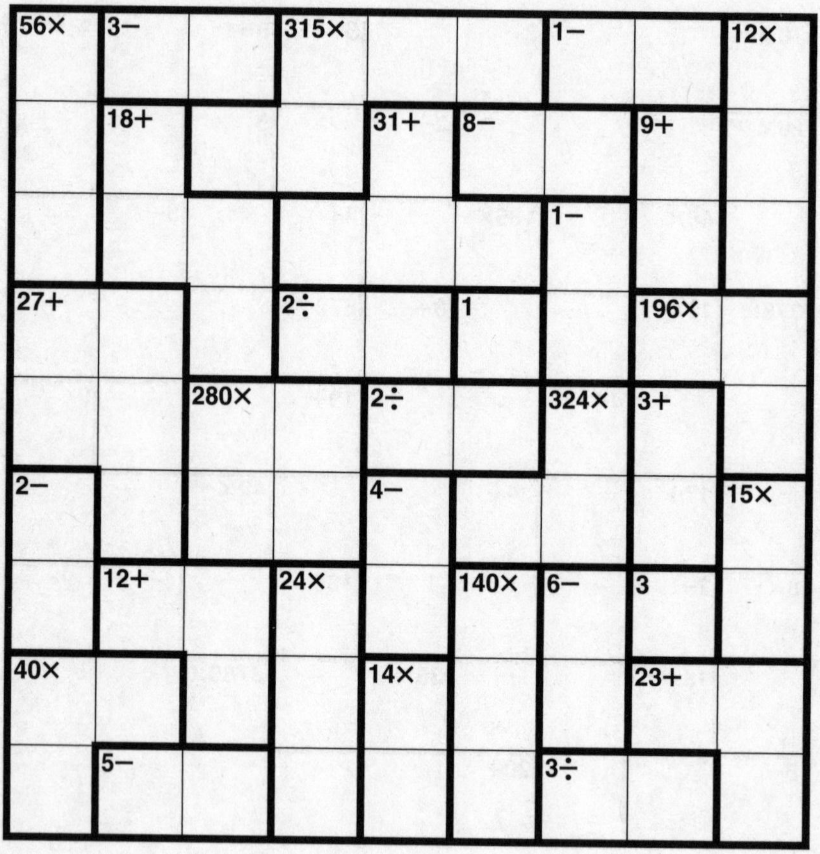
56×
3−
315×
1−
12×
18+
31+
8−
9+
1−
27+
2÷
1
196×
280×
2÷
324×
3+
2−
4−
15×
12+
24×
140×
6−
3
40×
14×
23+
5−
3÷

1−	17+		6×			18+		5−
	42×	7	8−	3÷	90×		160×	
		4−				3+		
2−	5−		8	15×			2÷	1−
		5−			11+			
4÷	10+	2−		36×	15+		20+	3÷
			98×		4÷			
5−	4−					3÷		4÷
	2÷		360×			3−		

262 Challenging +/−/×/÷

60×		3−	5−		4÷		3−	
17+			189×			720×	10+	
	30×				40×			
2016×		20+				1−		18+
2			17+				8−	
		3−		3÷	7			
14+	5	54×				13+		240×
	8−	4÷	12+					
			2÷		63×		3−	

Challenging +/−/×/÷ 263

120×	3+	175×		48×		108×		
			1−			112×		17+
	160×	8−		16+				
126×			2÷		3−	3+		13+
	48×		1−			576×	3	
	3402×		8−					
3÷		6−		315×			120×	3÷
		72×	6−		160×			
8						18×		

2−		2÷		40×	12+		8−	
17+		105×			21+		11+	
	15+	2÷		1−		2÷	54×	
25+			2÷		3÷			21+
		45×		7		72×		
			9+					
3+	1−		8−		24+	5−		2÷
	120×			1−				
2÷		17+			28×		3−	

2÷	3÷		2	2÷	14+	1−	4−	
	180×	8−					19+	48×
		7+	3−					
29+					17+		24×	
	2−		14+		3÷		5−	
		210×				7−		1−
3+		315×	15+		13+	20+		7−
84×				192×				
	4÷						8−	

266 Challenging +/−/×/÷

144×		140×			2÷		7−	
2−		7+		21+		6−	5−	
21+		42×	20×	3−				
16+					17+		6+	
2÷	3−	17+		2−		22+		
		2−	7−	6−				
4	3+				40×	2÷	2−	
20+	63×	8×						
	2÷		18+			1−		

Challenging +/−/×/÷ 267

30×		17+			4÷		3÷	
5−		2160×					6−	
9+		7+	17+		1	20+	1−	
3−							4−	
5	12+		8−	9+	14×	1152×		
17+	2−						3+	1−
		50×	19+			126×		
8−				288×			2÷	
54×						140×		

3+		24×		105×	6−		56×	
840×		24×				45×	192×	
	9+			72×			54×	
		17+			6−			
7−	7+	1−	15×		4÷	1−	1−	4÷
				20+				
11+		12+			2−		8−	
1512×		3÷			9+	6−	315×	
			8−					

Challenging +/−/×/÷ 269

576×				19+				4−
4÷	12+		8−	19+			5−	
	2−			63×	14×			6+
189×		10+					8+	
	21+				8−	96×		4
	8−	56×		2÷				3−
1−		23+	30×		19+		24×	
								4÷
4÷			16+		3÷			

270 Challenging +/−/×/÷

54×	17+		40×			2−		4−
	21+		160×			2−		
4÷			8−		90×	11+	1−	
21×	24×						180×	4−
		36×	23+			3−		
2÷				42×	5−			2−
	19+					8−		
50×			108×	2−	22+		31+	

Challenging +/−/×/÷ 271

1−	8−		3	3÷		3−		2−
	40×	1−	40×			3−	21×	
3+			15×	2016×				29+
	1−			2−				
45×		6−			24+			1
		20+	21×			36×	2÷	
336×			8−		5			12+
	2−	15+		8−		7+	7−	
			126×					

8−		13+	18×		2−		2÷	4÷
3+	1−			17+		17+		
		2−	2−	5−			7−	
84×	14+				7−		13+	4−
		7−		7+		252×		
		4÷	2−	1−				8
3−	21×				10+		10+	
		17+	56×				630×	
15+					2÷			

Challenging +/−/×/÷ 273

40+			2÷	4÷		28×		
			12600×	4−	12+		8−	
4÷	7+				12×			
	24+	126×				45×	13+	
6			2÷	4−				
6×			8−	2−	13+	19+		
	2÷			11+		1−		
16+	8−		3−	17+				
				18+				

274 Challenging +/−/×/÷

13+		50×		1176×		12+	
	5+			3÷		17+	
17+		11+	8−		20×	60×	576×	
1960×							
			17+		6		24×
3÷	13+			8−		2−	
	315×			120×	64×		
8−	2−	5−			3−		1−	12+
		4−			3÷		

Challenging +/−/×/÷ 275

3−		30×	25+			8−	2÷	
10+				50×			8×	
3+	14+	17+			20+	2÷		35×
			2÷					
1−		2−		4	5−		14×	
13+		20×	56×		21+		24+	
			8−	16+				
4−		5−				5−	10+	
36×			42×				2−	

276 Challenging +/−/×/÷

11+	5−		17+	54×	15+		2÷	
	14+	504×				15×		3−
1−					3+			
	315×	4÷		1−		7−		120×
9		3−		2÷		1−		
4÷		21×		2−		7−		
	5+	8+		20×	29+	20+		8−
3÷			140×				6	
	2÷						48×	

Challenging +/−/×/÷ 277

36×	192×			3÷		12+		4÷
	4−		22+			54×		
240×	2−			24+		2÷		63×
	2÷	3				1−		
		22+	2÷	20×		112×	4	
2÷				315×				3−
	3÷	2÷			168×		6+	
10+			9+	1−	4−			1−
	42×					36×		

278 Challenging +/−/×/÷

336×	3+	2−		2÷		9+		9+
		12×		13+			288×	
	945×			8−	3−	5−		
4÷		3÷						14+
	17+	14+	3÷		7	8−		
17+				10+	8−	35×	23+	
	13+							
	13+	6×		56×				27×
		3−		1−		6−		

Mind-Melting +/−/×/÷ 279

1−	324×				12×		21+	
	24+			3−		5−		
1−		1296×			8×	21+		
3÷			13+	8−				432×
	3−				10×	15×		
14+		42×		72×		576×		
72×								3
	18×		12+	24+			192×	
				2−		3		

280 Mind-Melting +/−/×/÷

80×		2÷		2−	4−		7−	
		15+			40×		25+	
3+		2−		27+				
14+	2−		1				14+	
	12+		15×		5−	8−		
20+		144×				10×		
	17+		13+	3+	30×	14+	120×	
	3							
2−		17+			3÷		2÷	

Mind-Melting +/−/×/÷ 281

54×		2÷	20×		18+		4÷	63×
4			2÷		30×			
19+		6+				14+	2−	
	2÷		24+	54×			1−	2−
13+		3−			6+			
	4−			28×			8−	
22+		4−		1−		8+		
		2−	4−	11+			17+	
2−				2÷		7		

282 Mind-Melting +/−/×/÷

4÷	2÷		4−	24×	2−	84×	3−	
	21+							96×
3	15+		24×	14+		14+		
				2−			4−	6−
24+	6+				5−	1−		
	3−		3÷				2−	36×
	1−	2−	5−		20+			
14+			6+				2−	15×
		9	224×					

Mind-Melting +/−/×/÷ 283

60×		4÷		6×	20+	17+		
	18×		2−				224×	
1−	2−	3+		18+				3÷
			5−	4−	11+	10+		
12+						2	10+	
9+	48×			3−		20×		
	9+	2÷	1−		21+			
1−			42×	11+			3−	4−
	11+			6+				

284 Mind-Melting +/−/×/÷

8−		4−		3÷		5760×		
1−	24+	13+	120×		2÷			
			2÷		140×	24+		27×
1−								
	80×	2÷		54×		7	672×	
		5−		6×		12+		
1	162×		11+					
3136×			15+			6−	18+	
				8−				

Mind-Melting +/−/×/÷ 285

24×		8−		1−	6+	3−	28+	
	2÷		5+					
8−		14+		1−	22+	1−		30×
8	24×		6×			2÷		
2−				6+		8×		
		1−			4−	16+	3÷	
120×		1−						2÷
3−		21+	1−		1−	8−	90×	
			5−					

286 Mind-Melting +/−/×/÷

8−		108× 3	4÷		280×		2−	
4−	6+				8	3−		16+
		56×	1−	3−		16×		
2÷	1−			5−			6+	14+
		40×		22+				
4÷	2÷	4−	2−	6+	3−			
						1728×		1−
2÷		19+						
224×			7−		14+			

Mind-Melting +/−/×/÷ 287

3−		4−	4÷	12+	7+	54×	3−	
3−							18×	
2÷		1−			2−		45×	
24+		4÷	24+			4−		4−
			1−	19+		14+		
8−	9+			11+			15+	
	16+				8−	3		
20+	14+					35×	448×	
		1−		2−			1	

288 Mind-Melting +/−/×/÷

126×		2÷	8−	9+		4−		4−
19+				720×		13+	6+	
	18+	5	12+					5−
				16+				
6+				15+		2÷	72×	
16+	2−				6+		3−	
	60×			180×		63×		1−
	126×		7			2−		
		9+			1−		30×	

Mind-Melting +/−/×/÷ 289

90×	3−		96×	3÷		1−	5−	8+
				3÷				
252×	2−		24+			6×	240×	
		14×		24×				3
	96×	3÷			1−		28+	
			2÷		2−			
24×			2−		4÷		19+	
3÷	8+	2−	3−		17+			
			2−			72×		

290 Mind-Melting +/−/×/÷

2−	7−		8×	4÷		2÷		26+
	1−			20+				
8+		18+		3÷			6+	
22+				9+		4÷		3−
2÷		6+	5−	3−				
7−	1			1−	15+	1−	1−	
	16+		4−				24×	
17+				3÷	3÷		90×	
		21×			1−			

Mind-Melting +/−/×/÷ 291

4÷	21×		1−		3÷	1−		54×
		3−		1−		4÷		
3−	4−	2−			24+			
		216×	48×		2−	1−	5−	
2			8−				29+	
4−	2÷			1−		20×		
	3÷		70×	7	8−			
3−	1−			5−	7+	756×		
		2÷						5

292 Mind-Melting +/−/×/÷

4÷		3−	45×	240×				42×
96×	72×			16+		45×		
		1−		5−		6+	2÷	
	14+		4		2÷		8+	8−
		2−	3−					
13+	13+		1−	2÷		3−		5
		1		336×	9+		5−	
5	18+				8−	3−		2÷
2−		12+				4÷		

Mind-Melting +/−/×/÷ 293

36×			19+		8−		14+	
12+		4÷			40×	1−		8−
	42×		10+	2−			5	
22+					168×	2−		1−
	13+	4−	3÷			3÷		
			13+			1	4−	
126×	40×	15+		24+			20×	
				6+			2−	2÷
			17+		2−			

294 Mind-Melting +/−/×/÷

4÷	14+	112×		8−		20+	
				2÷	7	12+	
112×		1152×			3−		2−
	3÷					1−	15×	6−
9+			8−		19+			
1−	8−		1−			18+		
	378×		6+	16+				16+
210×						1−		
			48×		3÷			

Mind-Melting +/−/×/÷ 295

1−	1−	28×		12×		2−	8−	
		4−		30×			1−	
3−	21×				1260×			3÷
	180×		48×			8−		
14+			4÷		288×			
	2÷		1−		9	28×	2÷	40×
	25+		5	135×				
		1−	2−			15+		
1−			24+				1−	

70×			2−		8−		2−	4−
36×		23+	4÷	19+	2÷			
						7×		
2−	4÷		10×		2−			3−
		2÷	16+	6−		3−		
3+				2016×	3÷	3−	4−	
2−		1−					2−	4
11+			8−		14+			4÷
11+						15×		

Mind-Melting +/−/×/÷ 297

4−		4−		60×	8+		2÷	
2÷	162×					504×		
		6+			3−	3024×		10+
90×		9+	2−					
			7−	24+	45×			7+
20+		1−			108×			
8−			1−				14+	
	1−			3−	5−	72×		3−
15+			8					

298 Mind-Melting +/−/×/÷

24+			3−	6×	1−	24×		13+
16+						672×		
15+			864×		3−		18+	
1−								8−
3÷	2÷	18+	84×					
				140×	22+		2÷	
4−		84×				6	14+	
1−	30×	28×			8−		13+	
			8−		4−			

Mind-Melting +/−/×/÷ 299

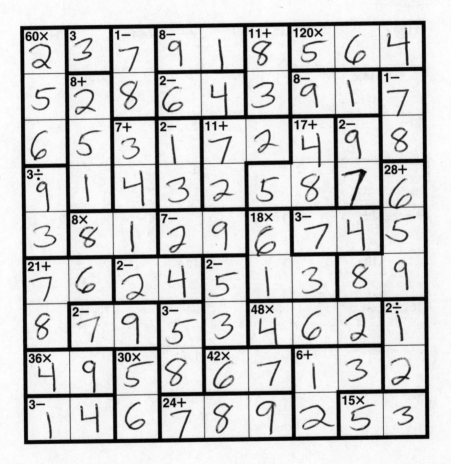

60×2	3 3	1−7	8−9	1	11+8	120×5	6	4
5	8+2	8	2−6	4	3	8−9	1	1−7
6	5	7+3	2−1	11+7	2	17+4	2−9	8
3÷9	1	4	3	2	5	8	7	28+6
3	8×8	1	7−2	9	18×6	3−7	4	5
21+7	6	2−2	4	2−5	1	3	8	9
8	2−7	9	3−5	3	48×4	6	2	2÷1
36×4	9	30×5	8	42×6	7	6+1	3	2
3−1	4	6	24+7	8	9	2	15×5	3

300 Mind-Melting +/−/×/÷

1120×			17+		2−	864×		3+
	14×						8−	
22+		25+			8			3÷
				4−	1−			
3÷	2÷		17+			6−		2−
	19+		14+		12+			
162×			23+		9+		700×	
		17+			135×			
3÷							2÷	

ANSWERS

1

2÷ **2**	**1**	1− **4**	6× **3**
3− **1**	**4**	**3**	**2**
12× **4**	3 **3**	2÷ **2**	**1**
3	3+ **2**	**1**	4 **4**

2

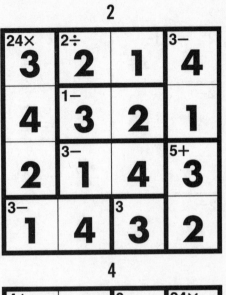

24× **3**	2÷ **2**	**1**	3− **4**
4	1− **3**	**2**	**1**
2	3− **1**	**4**	5+ **3**
3− **1**	**4**	3 **3**	**2**

3

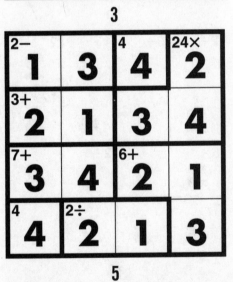

2− **1**	**3**	4 **4**	24× **2**
3+ **2**	**1**	**3**	**4**
7+ **3**	**4**	6+ **2**	**1**
4 **4**	2÷ **2**	**1**	**3**

4

4+ **1**	**3**	3− **4**	24× **2**
2÷ **4**	2 **2**	**1**	**3**
2	3− **1**	6× **3**	**4**
3 **3**	**4**	**2**	**1**

5

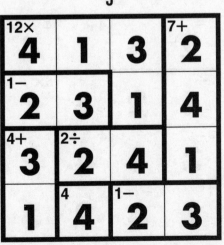

12× **4**	**1**	**3**	7+ **2**
1− **2**	**3**	**1**	**4**
4+ **3**	2÷ **2**	**4**	**1**
1	4 **4**	1− **2**	**3**

6

9+ **4**	**2**	**3**	2− **1**
6+ **2**	12× **4**	**1**	**3**
1	**3**	2÷ **4**	**2**
3	2÷ **1**	**2**	4 **4**

7

2 **2**	1− **4**	3− **1**	6× **3**
2− **1**	**3**	**4**	**2**
3	7+ **1**	**2**	**4**
2÷ **4**	**2**	2− **3**	**1**

8

3− **1**	2÷ **4**	**2**	4+ **3**
4	1− **2**	**3**	**1**
6× **2**	2− **3**	**1**	2÷ **4**
3	**1**	4 **4**	**2**

9

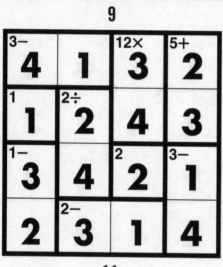

3− **4**	**1**	12× **3**	5+ **2**
1 **1**	2÷ **2**	**4**	**3**
1− **3**	**4**	2 **2**	3− **1**
2	2− **3**	**1**	**4**

10

2÷ **1**	5+ **4**	1− **3**	2 **2**
2	**1**	**4**	12× **3**
6× **3**	**2**	2÷ **1**	**4**
1− **4**	**3**	**2**	**1**

11

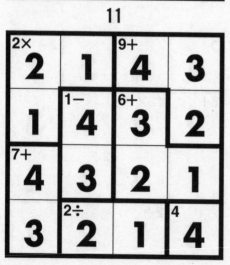

2× **2**	**1**	9+ **4**	**3**
1	1− **4**	6+ **3**	**2**
7+ **4**	**3**	**2**	**1**
3	2÷ **2**	**1**	4 **4**

12

1− **2**	**3**	4+ **1**	4 **4**
2÷ **4**	**2**	**3**	6× **1**
4+ **3**	**1**	4 **4**	**2**
1 **1**	2− **4**	**2**	**3**

13

2− **2**	**4**	3× **1**	**3**
4 **4**	7+ **2**	**3**	**1**
9× **1**	**3**	**2**	2÷ **4**
3	5+ **1**	**4**	**2**

14

2÷ **1**	**2**	3 **3**	1− **4**
6× **2**	1 **1**	2÷ **4**	**3**
3	7+ **4**	**2**	1 **1**
4 **4**	**3**	2÷ **1**	**2**

15

3× **3**	**1**	4 **4**	2÷ **2**
1	9+ **2**	**3**	**4**
2 **2**	**4**	2− **1**	**3**
1− **4**	**3**	2÷ **2**	**1**

16

2÷ **1**	**2**	1− **4**	**3**
10+ **2**	**4**	9× **3**	3+ **1**
4	**3**	**1**	**2**
4+ **3**	**1**	2÷ **2**	**4**

17

8× **2**	7+ **3**	**4**	1 **1**
4	2÷ **2**	**1**	18× **3**
1	3− **4**	**3**	**2**
3 **3**	**1**	2÷ **2**	**4**

18

3 **3**	3− **4**	**1**	2÷ **2**
1− **2**	**3**	12× **4**	**1**
5+ **1**	2 **2**	**3**	7+ **4**
4	3+ **1**	**2**	**3**

19

1¹	**5**⁴⁻	**2**¹⁸ˣ	**3**	**4**²÷
4¹¹⁺	**1**	**3**	**5**⁴⁻	**2**
2	**4**⁴	**5**⁹⁺	**1**	**3**⁹⁺
5	**3**⁸⁺	**4**	**2**⁷⁺	**1**
3	**2**	**1**	**4**	**5**

20

5⁷⁵ˣ	**2**³⁺	**1**	**3**³	**4**¹⁶ˣ
3	**5**	**2**³⁻	**4**	**1**
4¹⁻	**3**	**5**	**1**²÷	**2**
2²÷	**1**⁸⁺	**4**¹¹⁺	**5**	**3**¹⁵ˣ
1	**4**	**3**	**2**	**5**

21

1¹	**2**²÷	**4**	**3**¹⁵ˣ	**5**
4¹⁻	**5**¹⁰⁺	**3**	**2**	**1**²÷
3	**4**⁹⁺	**5**	**1**²⁰ˣ	**2**
5³⁻	**1**³ˣ	**2**²	**4**	**3**¹²ˣ
2	**3**	**1**	**5**	**4**

22

5⁵	**2**²÷	**4**	**1**³ˣ	**3**¹⁻
2⁹⁺	**5**¹⁴⁺	**1**	**3**	**4**
3	**4**	**5**	**2**²÷	**1**
4	**1**¹	**3**⁶⁰ˣ	**5**	**2**¹⁰ˣ
1⁶⁺	**3**	**2**	**4**	**5**

23

2³⁰ˣ	**3**	**4**¹²ˣ	**5**⁵ˣ	**1**
5	**2**²÷	**3**	**1**	**4**⁹⁺
3¹²ˣ	**4**	**1**⁵ˣ	**2**²	**5**
4	**1**	**5**	**3**³⁶ˣ	**2**²
1⁴⁻	**5**	**2**²	**4**	**3**

24

2³⁺	**4**⁴	**1**²⁵ˣ	**5**	**3**²⁴ˣ
1	**3**¹¹⁺	**5**	**2**	**4**
3	**5**	**2**²⁻	**4**³⁻	**1**
5⁹⁺	**1**²÷	**4**	**3**⁷⁺	**2**³⁻
4	**2**	**3**	**1**	**5**

25

2 ^{3−}	3 ^{12×}	4 ^{2÷}	5 ^{5×}	1
5	4	2	1	3 ¹²⁺
1 ³⁺	2	3 ^{2−}	4	5
3 ^{1−}	5 ^{25×}	1	2 ^{2÷}	4
4	1	5	3 ^{1−}	2

(KenKen puzzles — grids 25 through 30)

25
- 2[3−] 3[12×] 4[2÷] 5[5×] 1
- 5 4 2 1 3[12+]
- 1[3+] 2 3[2−] 4 5
- 3[1−] 5[25×] 1 2[2÷] 4
- 4 1 5 3[1−] 2

26
- 3[3] 4[9+] 5 2[40×] 1
- 5[4−] 3[12+] 2[2÷] 1 4
- 1 2 3 4 5
- 4[2÷] 5[4−] 1[3−] 3[18×] 2
- 2 1 4 5[5] 3

27
- 6[5−] 5[4−] 1 2[32×] 4 3[8+]
- 1 3[2÷] 6 4 2[3÷] 5
- 4[5+] 1 3[8+] 5 6 2[3÷]
- 3[1−] 2 4[3−] 1 5[15×] 6
- 5[3−] 4[2−] 2 6[6] 3 1[5+]
- 2 6[11+] 5 3[3÷] 1 4

28
- 4[1−] 3 6[3÷] 2 5[2−] 1[5+]
- 6[2÷] 2[10×] 5 1 3 4
- 3 6[5−] 2[7+] 4 1 5[11+]
- 2[3+] 1 3[12+] 5 4 6
- 1 5[9+] 4 3[3] 6[3÷] 2[5+]
- 5[1−] 4 1[5−] 6 2 3

29
- 3[90×] 1[3+] 2 6[10+] 4 5[15+]
- 6 3[3÷] 1 2[7+] 5 4
- 1 5 3[2÷] 4[1−] 2[3+] 6
- 5[160×] 4 6 3 1 2[3+]
- 2 6[2−] 4 5[8+] 3 1
- 4 2[7+] 5 1[5−] 6 3[3]

30
- 1[2÷] 4[24×] 6 5[3−] 2 3[90×]
- 2 1 5[1−] 4[2÷] 3[3÷] 6
- 6[2÷] 3 4 2 1 5
- 4[12+] 6[2÷] 3 1[4−] 5 2[8×]
- 3 5[3−] 2 6[10+] 4 1
- 5 2[3+] 1 3[3−] 6 4

31

2÷ 4	18× 1	6	3	7+ 2	5
2	11+ 3	10+ 4	6	6+ 5	1
5− 6	2	1	5	2÷ 3	1− 4
1	15+ 4	5	2 (2)	6	3
75× 5	6	2− 3	1	2÷ 4	2
3	5	2÷ 2	4	5− 1	6

32

6+ 5	1	3− 6	3	48× 4	2
1− 3	4	60× 5	3+ 1	2	6
2÷ 4	6	2	11+ 5	9× 1	3
2	60× 5	4	6	3	1 (1)
3+ 1	2	3	480× 4	6	5
3− 6	3	2÷ 1	2	5 (5)	4

33

4− 5	2÷ 6	5− 1	2÷ 4	1− 3	2
1	3	6	2	20× 4	5
7+ 4	6× 2	3	1	11+ 5	5− 6
3	11+ 4	2	5	6	1
3÷ 6	4− 1	1− 5	3− 3	2÷ 2	4
2	5	4	6	3÷ 1	3

34

3÷ 1	3	24× 6	4	7+ 5	2
2− 3	5− 6	6+ 5	1	8× 2	24× 4
5	1	8+ 3	2 (2)	4	6
240× 2	4	1	11+ 5	6	45× 3
4	5	3÷ 2	6	3	1
6	8× 2	4	3÷ 3	1	5

35

5− 1	6	3 (3)	40× 4	5	2
10+ 4	5+ 1	11+ 5	6	5+ 2	12+ 3
6	4	2÷ 2	1	3	5
30× 2	3÷ 3	1	11+ 5	6	4
3	5	2÷ 4	2	5− 1	6
3− 5	2	2÷ 6	3	5+ 4	1

36

6 (6)	3÷ 1	3	3− 2	5	1− 4
3+ 1	2	40× 5	2− 6	4	3
2− 5	3	2	4	5− 1	6
2− 2	4	120× 6	5	3÷ 3	1
72× 3	6	4	3+ 1	2	10× 5
4	4− 5	1	2÷ 3	6	2

37

³3	¹¹⁺5	6	⁴⁸ˣ4	²÷1	2
⁵⁻6	1	4	3	⁸⁺2	5
²⁰ˣ5	4	⁵⁺3	³÷2	6	1
¹⁻4	3	2	¹⁵ˣ1	5	²⁻6
⁴ˣ1	2	¹¹⁺5	6	3	4
2	⁷⁺6	1	⁵5	¹⁻4	3

38

⁶⁰ˣ5	¹⁸ˣ1	6	3	⁴4	³÷2
3	²÷4	2	⁴⁻5	³⁺1	6
4	¹¹⁺6	5	1	2	¹⁵ˣ3
⁵⁻6	²÷2	1	²÷4	²÷3	5
1	²⁻5	3	2	6	²⁰ˣ4
¹⁻2	3	²⁴ˣ4	6	5	1

39

⁴4	¹⁻6	5	⁶ˣ3	1	2
³⁺1	2	²÷6	³⁻5	⁶⁰ˣ4	3
¹⁵⁺6	4	3	2	5	⁵⁻1
5	²÷1	2	¹³⁺4	3	6
³⁰ˣ2	³3	⁵⁺4	⁵⁻1	6	⁴⁰ˣ5
3	5	1	6	2	4

40

⁵⁺1	4	¹¹⁺6	5	⁶ˣ2	3
²⁻5	⁵⁻1	¹¹⁺4	3	³⁰ˣ6	²÷2
3	6	²2	4	5	1
²⁴ˣ6	²⁻3	5	³⁺2	1	²⁰ˣ4
4	²⁰ˣ2	³÷1	⁵⁻6	¹³⁺3	5
2	5	3	1	4	6

41

³⁺2	¹²ˣ4	3	⁶⁺5	1	³⁻6
1	¹⁷⁺2	6	4	5	3
²÷6	3	³⁻2	³÷1	¹⁻4	5
¹⁻4	¹¹⁺6	5	3	³÷2	³⁻1
3	5	⁸ˣ1	2	6	4
⁶⁺5	1	4	⁶6	⁵⁺3	2

42

¹⁶ˣ2	4	³ˣ1	3	¹¹⁺6	¹⁻5
⁹ˣ3	2	³÷6	1	5	4
1	3	2	¹¹⁺5	²⁻4	²÷6
¹⁰⁺4	1	⁹⁰ˣ5	6	2	3
5	6	3	¹⁰⁺4	³÷1	²÷2
¹¹⁺6	5	4	2	3	1

43

10× 5	2	**8+** 3	**3−** 1	**2−** 4	6
3÷ 1	3	2	4	**5−** 6	**20×** 5
3	**5−** 6	**11+** 5	**1−** 2	1	4
2÷ 4	1	6	3	**8+** 5	**2÷** 2
2	**20×** 5	4	**11+** 6	3	1
24× 6	4	1	5	**1−** 2	3

44

6× 2	3	**1−** 5	4	**5−** 1	6
1	**2÷** 2	4	**14+** 6	3	5
1− 4	5	**1−** 3	2	**6** 6	**6×** 1
2÷ 6	**3+** 1	2	**100×** 5	4	3
3	**120×** 4	**5−** 6	**2−** 1	5	2
5	6	1	3	**2÷** 2	4

45

11+ 5	**32×** 4	2	**36×** 6	3	**3÷** 1
6	**3−** 5	4	2	**4−** 1	3
15+ 3	2	**5−** 6	**8+** 1	5	**40×** 4
2	6	1	3	4	5
4	**3×** 1	**8+** 3	5	**14+** 6	2
1	3	**1−** 5	4	2	6

46

2÷ 4	2	**5** 5	**2÷** 6	**9+** 3	1
5+ 2	**14+** 6	**16×** 4	3	**8+** 1	5
3	5	1	4	2	**6** 6
1− 6	3	**2÷** 2	1	5	**12×** 4
5	**5−** 1	6	**40×** 2	4	3
12× 1	4	3	5	**3÷** 6	2

47

36× 6	**10×** 5	2	**3÷** 1	3	**60×** 4
3	**5−** 1	6	**2÷** 4	2	5
2	**3÷** 6	**1−** 4	5	**6+** 1	3
16× 4	2	**2÷** 3	6	5	**12×** 1
1	4	**2−** 5	3	6	2
2− 5	3	**3+** 1	2	**10+** 4	6

48

5− 6	**11+** 5	**9×** 3	1	**8+** 4	2
1	6	**16+** 5	3	2	**4** 4
2÷ 4	**2** 2	6	5	**4−** 1	**2÷** 3
2	**24×** 3	**3−** 1	4	5	6
2− 5	4	2	**48×** 6	**3−** 3	**4−** 1
3	1	4	2	6	5

49

18× 3	6	1− 5	4	4× 2	1
1	12× 3	4	11+ 5	6	2
30× 6	1	6× 2	3	5	4
2÷ 4	5	5− 6	3÷ 2	1 1	90× 3
2	40× 4	1	6	12× 3	5
5	2	3÷ 3	1	4	6

50

3÷ 6	60× 4	3	5	2 2	4− 1
2	8+ 3	10+ 4	3÷ 6	3− 1	5
5+ 1	5	6	2	4	6× 3
4	5− 6	1	15× 3	5	2
8+ 3	7+ 2	5	5− 1	6	10+ 4
5	1− 1	2	7+ 4	3	6

51

12× 4	3	2÷ 2	6	4− 5	1
2− 3	5− 6	1	2	2÷ 4	11+ 5
5	1	8+ 3	5+ 4	2	6
2÷ 2	4	5	1	2÷ 6	3
5− 6	9+ 5	4	9× 3	1	2÷ 2
1	60× 2	6	5	3	4

52

9× 3	1	15+ 5	4	6	2÷ 2
5− 6	3	6+ 1	5	24× 2	4
1	11+ 5	6	3÷ 2	4	3
2÷ 4	5+ 2	3	6	25× 1	5
2	15+ 6	1− 4	3	5	10+ 1
5	4	3+ 2	1	3	6

53

3÷ 2	2− 6	4	4− 1	5	2− 3
6	2− 4	3÷ 1	10× 2	72× 3	5
4 4	2	3	5	6	7+ 1
6+ 1	3÷ 3	11+ 5	6	4	2
5	1	2÷ 6	3	2 2	4
2− 3	5	2÷ 2	4	5− 1	6

54

3÷ 6	2	72× 4	11+ 5	3÷ 3	1
3+ 2	6	3	1	5	1− 4
1	4 4	36× 6	3	2	5
15× 5	3	3+ 2	2÷ 4	5− 1	6
7+ 4	11+ 5	1	2	144× 6	5+ 3
3	1	5	6	4	2

55

4	2÷ 2	11+ 5	6	3÷ 3	1
9× 3	4	1 1	20× 2	1- 6	5
1	3	2	5	4 4	11+ 6
300× 2	5	72× 6	3	1	4
6	5- 1	12× 3	4	3- 5	2
5	6	4	1	6× 2	3

56

1- 4	1- 3	5- 1	6	11+ 5	2- 2
5	2	15× 3	1	6	4
3+ 1	2÷ 4	2	5	2÷ 3	6
2	30× 5	6	60× 3	5+ 4	1
2÷ 6	6× 1	5	4	16× 2	15× 3
3	6	4	2	1	5

57

30× 3	5	3+ 2	1	2- 4	6
2	4- 1	5	2÷ 3	6	2÷ 4
6+ 5	2÷ 3	6	3- 4	1	2
1	48× 2	4	6	45× 3	5
96× 4	5- 6	1	3- 2	5	3
6	4	2- 3	5	2÷ 2	1

58

60× 5	3	3÷ 1	6	5- 4	2- 2
4	16× 2	3	1	14+ 6	5 5
3+ 1	4	2	5	3	10+ 6
2	90× 5	6	3	1 1	4
5- 6	1	9+ 5	2÷ 4	1- 2	3
3- 3	6	4	2	4- 5	1

59

9+ 2	3÷ 1	3	10+ 4	6	25× 5
3	4	3÷ 6	2	5	1
8+ 1	2	20× 4	5	3- 3	6
21+ 6	5	2× 2	1	96× 4	3
5	6	1	3 3	2	4
4	2- 3	5	5- 6	1	2 2

60

2- 3	2÷ 4	3+ 1	2	30× 5	6
1	2	90× 5	2÷ 3	6	9+ 4
2÷ 4	3	6	3+ 1	2	5
2	10+ 5	3	2- 6	4	3÷ 1
11+ 5	5- 6	2	3- 4	1	3
6	1	12+ 4	5	3	2 2

61

105× 3	5	2÷ 2	4	6− 7	1	5− 6
7	14+ 4	11+ 3	6	2	300× 5	1
24× 4	2	5	3÷ 3	1	6	11+ 7
6	3	6− 7	1	5	2	4
5− 1	6	12+ 4	5	3	14× 7	2
7+ 5	6− 7	1	2 2	72× 6	4	15× 3
2	1 1	168× 6	7	4	3	5

62

13+ 7	6	40× 2	4	9+ 5	1	3
2÷ 2	4	5	252× 7	6	3 3	35× 1
2÷ 3	11+ 2	4	6	6− 1	7	5
6	5	3÷ 3	1	2− 2	4	7
60× 5	3	14× 1	2	7	144× 6	4
4	1	7	30× 5	3	2	6
6− 1	7	72× 6	3	4	10× 5	2

63

12× 4	5 5	3÷ 3	1	13+ 6	7	13+ 2
1	3	3÷ 6	10+ 5	2	4	7
1− 5	4	2	7 7	3	5− 1	6
3÷ 6	6− 1	84× 7	3	4	1− 2	20× 5
2	7	240× 5	6	6− 1	3	4
21× 3	3÷ 6	4	2	7	1− 5	3÷ 1
7	2	20× 1	4	5	6	3

64

1− 4	13+ 6	7	1− 5	6× 1	3	2
3	2÷ 2	5+ 1	6	1− 7	3− 5	7+ 4
5 5	1	4	6− 7	6	2	3
3÷ 6	14× 7	2	1	1− 3	4	5 5
2	8+ 5	30× 6	3 3	2÷ 4	5− 1	8+ 7
6− 7	3	5	2÷ 4	2	6	1
1	7+ 4	3	2	210× 5	7	6

65

1− 3	1− 4	5	5− 7	2	1− 6	3+ 1
4	4− 6	5− 1	105× 3	7	5	2
6− 1	2	6	5	13+ 3	4 4	210× 7
7	3+ 1	2	4 4	6	5+ 3	5
17+ 5	7	1− 3	8+ 1	4	2	6
3÷ 2	5	4	6	1	8+ 7	7+ 3
6	10+ 3	7	7+ 2	5	1	4

66

18+ 6	84× 3	4	7	20× 5	1− 2	1
5	3+ 1	10× 2	5− 6	4	14+ 7	2÷ 3
7	2	5	1	3	4	6
24× 4	6	6− 7	2÷ 2	1	8+ 3	5
6× 3	1− 5	1	1− 4	18+ 7	6	5− 2
1	4	14+ 6	3	3÷ 2	5	7
2	7 7	3	5	6	5+ 1	4

67

2÷ 2	4	24× 1	11+ 5	2÷ 6	3	13+ 7
4- 7	3	4	2	6- 1	5 5	6
120× 5	14+ 2	6	4	7	3+ 1	60× 3
6	5	7	3÷ 1	3	2	4
4	6× 1	3	13+ 7	60× 2	6	5
3 3	42× 7	2	6	5	112× 4	2÷ 1
1	6	2- 5	3	4	7	2

68

525× 7	3	5	4- 6	2÷ 4	2	11+ 1
3+ 1	5	17+ 3	2	13+ 7	6	4
2	12+ 1	7	4	3	20× 5	6
15× 5	7	4	3- 3	6	1	9+ 2
3	2 2	12+ 6	5	1	4	7
288× 4	6	2	6- 1	105× 5	7	3
6	5+ 4	1	7	10+ 2	3	5

69

13+ 7	6	105× 3	56× 2	4	1	19+ 5
40× 2	1	5	7	60× 3	4	6
4	105× 3	7	1	5	6	2
5	7	4 4	144× 6	3+ 1	2	11+ 3
2÷ 3	5	3+ 2	4	6	7	1
6	13+ 2	1	150× 5	21× 7	3	3- 4
1	4	6	3	2	5	7

70

90× 3	5	6	2÷ 1	2	3- 7	4
1- 4	2÷ 2	1	18+ 6	7	5	14+ 3
5	21× 3	4 4	7	1	2÷ 2	6
7	1	11+ 2	3	6	4	5
14× 2	7	60× 3	4	5	5- 6	1
120× 6	4	5	3- 2	3 3	6- 1	7
1 1	13+ 6	7	5	24× 4	3	2

71

20× 2	5	144× 6	4	6- 7	3÷ 1	3
10+ 5	2	15× 3	6	1	2- 4	7 7
1	4	5	4- 7	3	6	10× 2
13+ 6	7	1- 4	5	5+ 2	3	1
14+ 4	1 1	6- 7	2÷ 3	6	60× 2	5
7	2÷ 3	1	4× 2	1- 4	5	6
3	6	2	1	5	28× 7	4

72

21× 7	2 2	24× 6	1	4	10+ 5	3
3	6- 7	1	15+ 5	6	4	2
3÷ 2	10+ 5	4	7	1	6× 3	1- 6
6	1	14+ 7	4	3	2	5
20× 4	3÷ 6	2	3	4- 5	1	8+ 7
5	12+ 4	3	2	13+ 7	6	1
3÷ 1	3	3÷ 5	6	2	11+ 7	4

73

7+ 4	13+ 6	3÷ 3	1	3÷ 2	35× 7	5
3	7	120× 4	5	6	6× 2	1
2÷ 2	1	6	13+ 7	15× 5	3	24× 4
3− 7	4	6− 1	6	3	120× 5	2
7+ 5	2	7	9+ 4	1	6	3
5− 1	2− 5	2	3	7	4	6 6
6	3	3− 5	2	4	6− 1	7

74

6− 1	7	12× 3	4	3− 5	2	2− 6
12× 3	10× 5	1	14× 7	2	2÷ 6	4
4	2	12+ 5	1	6	3	14+ 7
28× 7	4	3÷ 6	2	3× 3	1	5
30× 5	3 3	13+ 7	6	1	28× 4	2
6	3+ 1	2	1− 5	4	7	3÷ 3
3÷ 2	6	4 4	15+ 3	7	5	1

75

2− 4	2	6− 1	7	90× 6	5	3
15× 1	5	3	168× 2	13+ 7	6	16+ 4
3÷ 2	3÷ 1	30× 6	4	3	7	5
6	3	5	6× 1	32× 4	2	7
5 5	1176× 7	2	3	1	4	5− 6
7	6	4	210× 5	30× 2	3	1
1− 3	4	7	6	5	1− 1	2

76

10+ 7	56× 2	5 5	7+ 1	6	15× 3	24× 4
3	7	4	2 2	5	1	6
2÷ 6	3	16+ 7	4	2	6+ 5	1
14+ 4	6	3	49× 7	1	60× 2	5
25× 5	4	3+ 1	2÷ 3	7	6	12+ 2
1	5	2	6	4 4	7	3
3+ 2	1	14+ 6	5	3	3− 4	7

77

13+ 7	6	3÷ 1	1− 3	4	210× 5	11+ 2
1− 2	1	3	4 4	6	7	5
3	7	13+ 2	3+ 1	1− 5	6	4
15× 5	3	6	2	5+ 1	4	6− 7
5− 6	20× 4	5	13+ 7	5+ 2	3	1
1	5	28× 4	6	10+ 7	2	2÷ 3
2÷ 4	2	7	2− 5	3	1	6

78

2÷ 2	1	120× 4	5	6	4− 7	3
30× 5	6	49× 7	1	24× 2	3	4
3÷ 3	36× 2	6	7	20× 4	5	6− 1
1	3	7+ 2	4 4	210× 5	6	7
3− 4	5	1− 3	2	7	3+ 1	1− 6
7	4	6+ 1	6	2÷ 3	2	5
13+ 6	7	5	3÷ 3	1	2÷ 4	2

79

18+ 7	6	5	2÷ 1	2	1− 3	4
3÷ 1	7+ 5	36× 6	4− 3	7	1− 4	5− 2
3	2	1	6	22+ 4	5	7
12× 4	3	7	5	6	2÷ 2	1
13+ 2	4− 7	3	2÷ 4	5− 1	6	14+ 5
6	16× 1	4	2	35× 5	7	3
5	4	14× 2	7	3 (3)	1	6

80

2÷ 4	2	140× 7	9× 1	3	11+ 5	6
5− 1	5	4	3	13+ 7	6	5− 2
6	15× 3	1	5	2÷ 4	2	7
1− 3	4	13+ 5	6	2	6− 7	1
9+ 2	756× 7	6	2÷ 4	3× 1	3	1− 5
7	6	3	2	5 (5)	1	4
10× 5	1	2	7	13+ 6	7+ 4	3

81

3÷ 6	2	24× 4	3	1 (1)	13+ 7	70× 5
16+ 4	1− 5	2	3÷ 1	3	6	7
5	6	4− 3	7	5+ 4	1	2
7	3÷ 1	17+ 5	36× 2	6	3	4 (4)
8× 1	3	7	5	2÷ 2	4	10+ 6
2	4	5− 1	1− 6	7	3− 5	3
4− 3	7	6	9+ 4	5	2	1

82

30× 1	8× 4	3− 7	2− 5	6 (6)	3+ 2	11+ 3
5	2	4	3	28× 7	1	6
6	45× 3	6− 1	7	4	1− 5	2
2÷ 4	5	3	3+ 2	1	6	8+ 7
2	126× 6	11+ 5	3− 4	5+ 3	16+ 7	1
3	7	6	1	2	4	5
6− 7	1	60× 2	6	5	12× 3	4

83

6+ 1	5	2÷ 4	2	16+ 7	3	6
2÷ 4	8+ 2	5	3 (3)	36× 6	1	4− 7
2	1	140× 7	4	5	6	3
13+ 6	105× 7	3	5	2÷ 4	2	4− 1
7	14+ 6	6× 2	1	3	112× 4	5
5	3	36× 1	6	10+ 2	7	4
1− 3	4	6	7	1	3− 5	2

84

13+ 6	3	4	2 (2)	13+ 7	5	1
4 (4)	15× 1	30× 2	3	5	13+ 7	3÷ 6
3	5	12+ 7	4	1	6	2
4× 1	2	15× 3	2− 5	2÷ 6	112× 4	7
2	17+ 6	5	7	3	15× 1	4
7	4	1 (1)	36× 6	2÷ 2	3	5
2− 5	7	6	1	4	6× 2	3

85

7 (13+)	6	1 (2×)	5 (15×)	4	3	2 (2÷)
5 (1−)	1	2	3	6 (13+)	7	4
4	2 (10+)	6 (120×)	7 (6−)	1	5 (2−)	3
6 (2÷)	3	5	4 (2÷)	2	1 (6−)	7
3	5	4	2 (14×)	7	6 (11+)	1 (30×)
1 (14×)	4 (84×)	7	6 (5−)	3	2	5
2	7	3	1	5 (1−)	4	6

86

1 (6−)	7	2 (5−)	4 (1−)	5	6 (18+)	3
3 (8+)	1 (3+)	7	6 (3÷)	2	5	4
5	2	4 (3−)	1	7 (84×)	3	6 (60×)
7 (17+)	3 (36×)	6	2	1	4	5
4	5 (1−)	1 (3÷)	3	6 (13+)	7	2
6	4	5 (2−)	7 (14+)	3	2 (2)	1 (7×)
2 (3÷)	6	3	5 (5)	4	1	7

87

6 (13+)	3	5 (40×)	2	4	7 (7×)	1
7 (3−)	4	6 (126×)	3	5 (5)	1	2 (3−)
4	1 (3÷)	3	7	2 (4−)	6	5
1 (2÷)	2	4 (1−)	5	7 (16+)	3	6
3 (4−)	7	2 (2×)	1	6 (108×)	5 (1−)	4
2 (12+)	5	1	6	3	4 (14+)	7
5	6 (168×)	7	4	1 (3+)	2	3

88

1 (3÷)	2 (1−)	3	4 (4)	6 (180×)	5
3	4 (12×)	2 (2÷)	1	5 (3−)	6
5 (10×)	3	1 (5−)	6 (11+)	2	4 (1−)
2	1 (5−)	6	5	4 (7+)	3
4 (10+)	6	5 (3−)	2	3	1 (4+)
6	5 (60×)	4	3	1	2

89

5 (4−)	1	2 (3÷)	6	3 (216×)	4 (4)
1 (5−)	2 (12+)	5	4	6	3
6	5	3 (54×)	2 (3−)	4 (5+)	1
4 (7+)	3	6	5	1 (2÷)	2
3	6 (2−)	4	1 (10×)	2	5 (30×)
2 (2÷)	4	1 (3÷)	3	5	6

90

6 (90×)	1 (4−)	4 (1−)	3	5 (3−)	2 (3÷)
3	5	1 (3÷)	4 (3−)	2	6
5	2 (1−)	3	1	6 (10+)	4 (3−)
2 (3+)	3	5 (11+)	6 (3÷)	4	1
1	4 (96×)	6	2	3 (3÷)	5 (15×)
4	6	2 (3−)	5	1	3

91

16+ 2	5	4	5- 6	1	36× 3
5	2÷ 2	1- 6	3	4	1
5- 6	4	5	5+ 1	1- 3	3- 2
1	5- 6	1- 3	4	2	5
11+ 3	1	2	720× 5	6	4
4	3	1	10× 2	5	6

92

5- 1	6	96× 2	4	3	30× 5
11+ 5	8+ 3	3+ 1	2	4	6
6	1	3 3	3- 5	2	7+ 4
5+ 2	4	720× 6	4- 1	5	3
3	5	4	6	5- 1	2÷ 2
2÷ 4	2	2- 5	3	6	1

93

36× 2	6	3+ 1	12× 3	4	4- 5
11+ 6	3	2	1- 4	5	1
5	12× 2	6	1	12× 3	4
1- 4	10+ 5	3	2	7+ 1	6
3	4× 1	1- 4	11+ 5	6	1- 2
1	4	5	3÷ 6	2	3

94

6× 6	11+ 5	7+ 3	4	16× 1	2
1	6	3- 5	2- 3	2	4
36× 4	3	2	5	5- 6	1
3	3÷ 2	6	3- 1	4	90× 5
10× 2	6+ 4	1	11+ 6	5	3
5	1	4 4	5+ 2	3	6

95

2÷ 4	8+ 1	3	9+ 6	2	2- 5
2	30× 5	4	1	15+ 6	3
2- 3	2	4- 1	5	4	10+ 6
1	3	3÷ 6	2	5	4
2- 6	4	3- 5	1- 3	2÷ 1	2
30× 5	6	2	4	2- 3	1

96

2÷ 6	3	4- 5	1	32× 4	2
2- 2	3- 5	5- 6	3÷ 3	1	4
4	2	1	14+ 5	3	5- 6
2- 5	3- 4	7+ 3	2 2	6	1
3	1	4	3÷ 6	2	75× 5
5- 1	6	2÷ 2	4	5	3

97

3÷ 6	2	5− 1	3÷ 3	100× 4	5
2÷ 2	4	6	1	5	1− 3
8+ 5	11+ 6	6× 3	2	5− 1	4
3	5	2− 2	4	6	3+ 1
3− 4	1	600× 5	6	36× 3	2
2− 1	3	4	5	2	6

98

11+ 6	2− 3	5	10× 2	1	2÷ 4
1	4	3− 3	6	5	2
2 2	2÷ 1	5− 6	1− 5	7+ 4	3
18+ 5	2	1	4	3− 3	6
3	6	3− 4	1	36× 2	4− 5
4	3− 5	2	3	6	1

99

3÷ 2	6+ 1	5	1− 4	3	2÷ 6
6	2− 4	3÷ 1	2÷ 2	15+ 5	3
6+ 5	6	3	1	4	7+ 2
1	3− 2	144× 4	14+ 3	6	5
7+ 3	5	2	6	2÷ 1	3− 4
4	3	6	5	2	1

100

72× 6	5+ 3	1− 4	2÷ 2	4− 1	5
3	2	5	4	3÷ 6	7+ 1
4	15× 5	3	1	2	6
8+ 5	2÷ 1	2	13+ 6	4	1− 3
1	2− 4	5− 6	2− 5	3	2
2	6	1	3	20× 5	4

101

8+ 3	1	30× 5	6	3÷ 2	14+ 4
5+ 1	4	1− 3	2	6	5
4	3− 6	4− 1	5	3	2
4− 2	3	6 6	8× 4	90× 5	1
6	12+ 5	2	1	3− 4	3
5	2	1− 4	3	1	6

102

2÷ 6	3	8× 4	4− 5	1	3− 2
7+ 4	1	2	2÷ 3	6	5
3	2÷ 4	3÷ 6	2	20× 5	5− 1
4− 5	2	3÷ 3	1	4	6
1	11+ 6	5	2÷ 4	2	1− 3
3− 2	5	5− 1	6	3 3	4

103

1-**2**	**3**	3-**1**	11+**6**	60×**4**	**5**
7+**6**	**1**	**4**	**5**	**3**	1-**2**
7+**4**	3÷**2**	4-**5**	**1**	11+**6**	**3**
3	**6**	2÷**2**	**4**	**5**	5+**1**
6+**1**	**5**	3-**6**	1-**3**	9+**2**	**4**
1-**5**	**4**	**3**	**2**	**1**	**6**

104

90×**5**	**6**	3-**1**	**4**	12×**3**	**2**
8×**1**	**3**	2-**4**	4-**5**	**2**	14+**6**
2	**4**	**6**	**1**	**5**	**3**
6+**3**	**1**	**2**	23+**6**	**4**	**5**
2-**4**	2-**5**	**3**	**2**	**6**	3-**1**
6	10×**2**	**5**	3÷**3**	**1**	**4**

105

3÷**6**	4-**5**	**1**	3-**2**	1-**3**	**4**
2	12×**4**	**3**	**5**	2÷**1**	5-**6**
8+**5**	**3**	10+**6**	**4**	**2**	**1**
2÷**1**	**2**	1-**5**	**6**	1-**4**	1-**3**
1-**3**	2-**6**	**4**	3÷**1**	**5**	**2**
4	1-**1**	**2**	**3**	30×**6**	**5**

106

3÷**1**	10×**2**	**5**	2-**6**	1-**4**	2÷**3**
3	6+**1**	**2**	**4**	**5**	**6**
1-**4**	**3**	6+**1**	**5**	3÷**6**	1-**2**
5	14+**6**	1-**4**	**3**	**2**	**1**
4-**6**	**5**	**3**	2÷**2**	3÷**1**	20×**4**
2	10+**4**	**6**	**1**	**3**	**5**

107

6+**5**	**1**	3-**4**	2-**3**	144×**2**	**6**
2÷**6**	3÷**2**	**1**	**5**	**4**	**3**
3	**6**	3+**2**	**1**	1-**5**	**4**
24×**4**	20×**5**	5+**3**	**2**	5-**6**	**1**
1	**4**	1-**5**	11+**6**	10+**3**	**2**
2	**3**	**6**	**4**	**1**	**5**

108

2-**4**	**6**	2÷**3**	20×**5**	2÷**2**	**1**
1-**3**	**2**	**6**	**1**	**4**	2-**5**
4-**6**	1-**4**	3-**5**	**2**	5-**1**	**3**
2	**5**	3÷**1**	**3**	**6**	2÷**4**
4-**5**	**1**	2÷**4**	13+**6**	**3**	**2**
3÷**1**	**3**	**2**	**4**	11+**5**	**6**

109

4 (20×)	**5**	**6** (5−)	**1**	**3** (10+)	**2**
5 (3−)	**4** (1−)	**2** (12+)	**3**	**6**	**1**
2	**3**	**5** (4−)	**6** (10+)	**1**	**4**
3 (2÷)	**6** (5−)	**1**	**4**	**2** (13+)	**5** (2−)
6	**1**	**4**	**2**	**5**	**3**
1 (2÷)	**2**	**3** (8+)	**5**	**4** (2−)	**6**

110

6 (24×)	**1** (60×)	**5**	**4** (2÷)	**2**	**3** (3)
4	**2**	**6**	**3** (2÷)	**5** (9+)	**1** (2÷)
3 (3÷)	**5** (11+)	**1** (3+)	**6**	**4**	**2**
1	**6**	**2**	**5** (7+)	**3** (3÷)	**4** (120×)
5 (3−)	**4** (36×)	**3**	**2**	**1**	**6**
2	**3**	**4** (4)	**1** (5−)	**6**	**5**

111

1 (10×)	**5**	**3** (14+)	**2**	**4** (1−)	**6** (14+)
2	**6**	**5**	**3**	**1** (1)	**4**
3 (72×)	**4**	**2** (16×)	**6** (17+)	**5**	**1**
6	**2**	**4**	**1** (3÷)	**3**	**5**
4 (20×)	**3** (10+)	**1** (4−)	**5**	**6** (12+)	**2** (1−)
5	**1**	**6**	**4**	**2**	**3**

112

3 (1−)	**6** (5−)	**2** (2÷)	**4**	**1** (6+)	**5**
2	**1**	**5** (180×)	**6**	**4** (1−)	**3** (3÷)
5 (1−)	**4** (12×)	**6**	**2** (10×)	**3**	**1**
6	**3**	**1** (8+)	**5**	**2** (4−)	**4** (2÷)
1 (12+)	**5**	**4**	**3**	**6**	**2**
4	**2**	**3** (4+)	**1**	**5** (1−)	**6**

113

3 (60×)	**4**	**5**	**2** (3+)	**1**	**6** (48×)
6 (90×)	**3**	**1**	**5** (1−)	**4**	**2**
1 (1)	**5**	**6** (3−)	**3**	**2** (7+)	**4**
2 (120×)	**6**	**3** (48×)	**4**	**5**	**1** (9+)
5	**2**	**4**	**1** (5−)	**6**	**3**
4 (7+)	**1**	**2**	**6** (2÷)	**3**	**5**

114

1 (4−)	**6** (72×)	**4**	**5** (18+)	**2**	**3**
5	**1** (10+)	**3**	**6**	**4** (1−)	**2**
4	**5**	**2** (12+)	**1**	**3**	**6** (5−)
3 (9+)	**2**	**5**	**4**	**6** (5−)	**1**
2 (3÷)	**4**	**6** (5−)	**3**	**1** (1−)	**5** (14+)
6	**3** (3)	**1**	**2**	**5**	**4**

115

¹⁻3	4	¹⁻5	6	²÷2	1
¹⁻6	5	⁵⁻1	²÷2	¹⁵ˣ3	¹⁻4
³⁻2	³÷1	6	4	5	3
5	3	⁷⁺4	⁴⁻1	⁵⁻6	⁴⁻2
²÷4	2	3	5	1	6
⁵⁻1	6	¹⁻2	3	²⁰ˣ4	5

116

¹⁰⁰ˣ4	5	¹⁰⁺6	1	3	⁵⁺2
5	²⁴ˣ4	³÷2	6	⁸⁺1	3
6	1	¹⁻3	4	2	5
⁶ˣ2	¹¹⁺6	5	¹⁻3	4	¹¹⁺1
1	⁹⁺3	4	⁶⁰ˣ2	5	6
3	2	⁶⁺1	5	6	4

117

²÷1	¹⁸⁰ˣ3	6	2	5	¹⁻4
2	⁶⁺1	3	⁷²ˣ4	6	5
¹⁻5	2	¹³⁺4	¹³⁺6	3	1
6	4	5	3	1	2
²⁻4	6	²÷1	⁶⁺5	¹⁻2	3
¹⁵ˣ3	5	2	1	¹⁰⁺4	6

118

¹⁻4	5	²⁴ˣ1	¹⁰⁺2	²÷6	3
1	4	6	3	5	²2
¹⁰⁸ˣ3	6	⁴4	⁴⁰ˣ5	2	1
6	³⁻2	5	1	²⁻3	4
³⁻5	¹⁻3	2	³⁻4	1	¹¹⁺6
2	³÷1	3	²⁻6	4	5

119

⁶⁰ˣ5	⁶ˣ3	²÷2	4	⁵⁻6	¹1
3	2	¹¹⁺5	6	1	²÷4
4	⁷⁺1	6	¹⁵ˣ5	3	2
¹⁷⁺6	5	³⁻4	³÷1	⁹⁺2	3
⁷⁺2	6	1	3	4	¹⁶⁺5
1	4	⁵⁺3	2	5	6

120

⁴⁻1	5	¹⁵⁺4	6	³⁻3	¹¹⁺2
¹⁻4	3	⁴⁸ˣ2	5	6	1
⁶ˣ2	4	6	⁶⁺1	5	3
3	⁵ˣ1	5	2	¹⁹⁺4	6
¹⁻5	6	1	3	²÷2	4
⁴⁻6	2	¹⁻3	4	1	5

121

3− 4	1	2− 3	2− 6	3− 2	5
12× 2	3	5	4	18× 6	1
90× 5	2	3− 4	3+ 1	3	15+ 6
3	6	1	2	5	4
5− 1	1− 5	2÷ 6	3	3− 4	5+ 2
6	4	7+ 2	5	1	3

122

1− 6	2− 4	10× 5	2	1	18× 3
5	2	6× 3	15+ 4	6	1
3− 4	1	2	6	11+ 3	5 5
3÷ 1	3	5+ 4	5	2	6
1− 2	11+ 6	1	3 3	11+ 5	4
3	5	24× 6	1	4	2

123

4− 1	5	3÷ 3	3÷ 6	2− 4	2
30× 5	6	1	2	9+ 3	4
1− 4	1	8+ 5	3	2	1− 6
3	3÷ 2	6	3− 4	1	5
12+ 2	1− 3	4	11+ 5	6	9+ 1
6	4	2÷ 2	1	5	3

124

2÷ 2	2÷ 3	1− 4	5	3÷ 1	1− 6
4	6	3+ 1	2	3	5
90× 6	15× 1	5	3	2 2	5+ 4
3	3÷ 2	6	1− 4	5	1
1	3− 5	2	10+ 6	4	6× 3
5	1− 4	3	5− 1	6	2

125

2− 1	2÷ 6	3	3− 2	5	2− 4
3	25× 5	5+ 1	4	24× 2	6
240× 6	1	5	3	4	7+ 2
4	2	11+ 6	5	1	3
5	4 4	12+ 2	6	14+ 3	1
1− 2	3	4	1 1	6	5

126

1− 3	4	8+ 1	13+ 5	3÷ 2	6
3− 4	1	3	6	3− 5	2
12+ 6	5	4	2	9× 3	1
1	3− 2	5	2− 4	6	3
30× 5	3÷ 6	2	3÷ 3	1	80× 4
2	3	5− 6	1	4	5

127

2÷ 1	2	7+ 6	10× 5	1− 4	3
9+ 4	5	1	2	2÷ 3	6
90× 5	3	2÷ 4	2− 6	2× 2	1
11+ 3	6	2	4	1	11+ 5
6	20× 4	3÷ 3	1	90× 5	2
2	1	5	3	6	4

128

1− 3	2	2÷ 4	30× 5	1	6
1− 5	11+ 6	2	5+ 4	3÷ 3	1
4	5	7+ 6	1	10+ 2	3
3+ 2	1− 4	1	3− 3	6 6	5
1	3	2− 5	6	2÷ 4	2
5− 6	1	3	40× 2	5	4

129

30× 3	2	5	11+ 1	4	6
8+ 1	6	5+ 2	3	11+ 5	4 4
11+ 5	1	2÷ 4	2	6	1− 3
6	1− 4	4− 1	5	3÷ 3	2
2÷ 2	3	10+ 6	4	1	4− 5
4	15× 5	3	3÷ 6	2	1

130

4− 6	2− 4	10× 2	5	7+ 3	6+ 1
2	6	5+ 1	3− 3	4	5
1− 5	2− 3	4	6	3+ 1	5+ 2
4	5	5− 6	1	2	3
3÷ 1	1− 2	2− 3	40× 4	5	144× 6
3	1	5	2	6	4

131

5− 1	12× 4	17+ 2	6	2− 5	3
6	3	4	5	2÷ 2	1
1− 4	1− 2	3	5− 1	6	10× 5
5	5− 6	1	1− 4	3	2
1− 3	6+ 1	13+ 5	2	2− 4	6
2	5	6	3 3	5+ 1	4

132

1− 5	48× 6	4	8+ 3	2 2	5− 1
4	30× 3	2	5	30× 1	6
3÷ 3	2	5− 6	1	5	2÷ 4
1	5	7+ 3	4	6	2
48× 6	4	6+ 1	2	3	12+ 5
2	1	1− 5	6	4	3

133

12× 4	1	3÷ 2	6	8+ 3	5
3	1- 5	4	2÷ 2	6× 6	1
2- 5	3	1- 6	4	1	6× 2
3÷ 2	6	5	2- 1	13+ 4	3
11+ 6	2÷ 2	1	3	5	4
1	4	15× 3	5	3÷ 2	6

134

11+ 6	5	4× 2	1	1- 3	3- 4
2- 3	11+ 6	5	2	4	1
5	3÷ 1	1- 3	2÷ 4	2	3÷ 6
3+ 1	3	4	11+ 5	6	2
2	3- 4	1	15+ 6	4- 5	8+ 3
2- 4	2	6	3	1	5

135

5- 7	20× 5	4	1	3÷ 2	6	2÷ 3
2	16+ 7	5	3- 4	1	42× 3	6
24× 6	4	22+ 1	5	3 3	2	7
4	2÷ 6	3	7	18+ 5	1- 1	2
1	6× 3	7	2	6	13+ 5	4
2- 3	1	2	3- 6	7	4	4- 5
5	3÷ 2	6	3	3- 4	7	1

136

2- 7	2- 6	4	90× 3	5	8× 1	2
5	1- 7	6	1	2	3	4
13+ 4	2	7	14+ 5	2÷ 3	6	10+ 1
10+ 6	4	5 5	2	6- 1	7	3
6+ 2	3	1	7	1- 4	5	6
3÷ 3	2÷ 1	2	1008× 6	7	4	14+ 5
1	12+ 5	3	4	6	2	7

137

4- 3	3÷ 6	12+ 4	5- 7	2	30× 5	3- 1
7	2	5	3	1	6	4
30× 6	5	1- 3	2	17+ 4	6- 1	7
1- 5	4	6- 7	1	6	2	3 3
6× 2	3	3- 1	4	5	1- 7	6
3- 4	6- 1	3÷ 6	5 5	84× 7	3	7+ 2
1	7	2	2÷ 6	3	4	5

138

3+ 1	1- 4	126× 6	3	7	60× 2	1- 5
2	3	6- 7	1	6	5	4
2- 7	3+ 2	12+ 5	4	3	2- 6	7+ 1
5	1	3 3	5- 7	2	4	6
13+ 3	7	4	30× 6	4- 5	1	12+ 2
4	3÷ 6	2	5	6- 1	7	3
6	4- 5	1	2 2	4	1- 3	7

139

6−**1**	**7**	13+**6**	1−**3**	2÷**4**	**2**	20×**5**
3−**6**	5+**1**	**7**	**2**	75×**3**	**5**	**4**
3	**4**	7+**1**	13+**7**	**5**	2÷**6**	4−**2**
2−**7**	**5**	**4**	**1**	2**2**	**3**	**6**
2÷**4**	3−**6**	**2**	**5**	28×**7**	2−**1**	**3**
2	**3**	2−**5**	2−**6**	**1**	**4**	6−**7**
3−**5**	**2**	**3**	13+**4**	**6**	**7**	**1**

140

3÷**3**	140×**7**	**5**	2÷**2**	**1**	**4**	2÷**6**
1	**4**	25+**7**	**5**	**6**	**2**	**3**
11+**5**	6×**2**	2−**6**	**4**	**7**	10+**3**	5+**1**
6	**1**	**3**	6−**7**	**2**	**5**	**4**
12+**2**	**6**	**4**	**1**	15+**3**	**7**	**5**
28×**7**	4−**5**	**1**	2÷**3**	2−**4**	**6**	5−**2**
4	1−**3**	**2**	**6**	4−**5**	**1**	**7**

141

2−**4**	35×**5**	3+**1**	**2**	3**3**	13+**7**	2−**6**
2	**7**	12+**5**	**3**	3+**1**	**6**	**4**
24×**6**	**1**	**4**	7**7**	**2**	30×**3**	**5**
6−**7**	**4**	2÷**6**	3−**1**	35×**5**	**2**	1−**3**
1	14+**6**	**3**	**4**	**7**	35×**5**	**2**
5	**3**	12+**2**	**6**	**4**	**1**	**7**
1−**3**	**2**	210×**7**	**5**	**6**	3−**4**	**1**

142

24×**4**	11+**5**	**1**	1−**6**	**7**	**2**	1−**3**
1	**6**	**5**	2÷**2**	1−**3**	**4**	840×**7**
36×**2**	252×**3**	7**7**	**1**	**4**	**6**	**5**
6	**7**	**3**	5**5**	2÷**2**	3−**1**	**4**
3	**4**	168×**6**	**7**	**1**	60×**5**	**2**
6−**7**	**1**	80×**2**	**4**	2−**5**	**3**	**6**
5	**2**	**4**	2÷**3**	**6**	6−**7**	**1**

143

2÷**4**	72×**3**	1−**7**	**6**	70×**2**	**5**	10×**1**
2	**6**	**4**	1−**3**	**7**	6−**1**	**5**
17+**6**	4−**1**	**5**	**4**	13+**3**	**7**	**2**
1	**5**	9+**2**	**7**	**4**	2÷**6**	**3**
5	6−**7**	**1**	3+**2**	**6**	1−**3**	168×**4**
4−**3**	2−**4**	6**6**	**1**	20×**5**	**2**	**7**
7	**2**	2−**3**	**5**	**1**	**4**	**6**

144

2÷**4**	300×**2**	**5**	6−**7**	**1**	2÷**6**	**3**
2	4**4**	**6**	**5**	15+**7**	120×**3**	4−**1**
294×**7**	3÷**1**	**3**	**6**	**2**	**4**	**5**
6	**7**	2**2**	8+**3**	**5**	**1**	3−**4**
15×**1**	1−**3**	**4**	2**2**	10+**6**	**5**	**7**
3	20+**5**	**7**	**1**	**4**	**2**	84×**6**
5	**6**	**1**	1−**4**	**3**	**7**	**2**

145

6− 1	2÷ 4	2	1− 7	6	2− 5	3
7	40× 5	4	2	2÷ 3	6	8+ 1
13+ 2	1 1	14× 6	12× 4	2− 5	3	7
6	2÷ 3	7	1	4 4	3− 2	5
5	6	1	3	3− 7	4	2÷ 2
12× 3	18+ 7	5	6	2÷ 2	1	4
4	5+ 2	3	4− 5	1	7	1− 6

146

3÷ 6	2	72× 3	35× 7	28× 4	4− 5	1
8+ 2	4	6	5	7	1	13+ 3
5	1	15+ 4	6	2	3	7
13+ 7	6	2 2	3	20× 1	4	5
20× 1	12+ 3	5	4	13+ 6	7	10+ 2
4	5	21× 7	1	3	2	6
4− 3	7	8+ 1	2	5	10+ 6	4

147

1− 3	40× 2	13+ 6	7	16+ 1	5	3− 4
2	4	5	30× 6	7	3	1
6− 1	1− 3	4	5	3÷ 2	6	2− 7
7	4− 6	2	2− 3	5+ 4	1	5
84× 4	7	3	1	2− 5	3÷ 2	6
11+ 6	5	1	2÷ 4	3	5− 7	2
5 5	6− 1	7	2	13+ 6	4	3

148

30× 2	5	42× 6	4	2÷ 3	1	14× 7
6− 1	3	7	5	6	2	1− 4
7	7+ 2	5	1	10+ 4	6	3
12× 6	1	2	36× 3	16+ 7	4	5
4− 3	7	11+ 4	2	10+ 1	11+ 5	6
15+ 5	4	3	6	2	7	6+ 1
4	6	6− 1	7	5 5	3	2

149

6− 1	13+ 6	2	4− 7	2− 4	10+ 5	6× 3
7	6+ 1	5	3	6	4	2
3	2	2− 6	4	105× 5	1	17+ 7
16+ 6	5	6− 7	2÷ 1	3	2 2	4
5	12× 4	1	2	7	16+ 3	6
672× 2	3	4	1− 6	1− 1	7	6+ 5
4	7	3	5	2	6	1

150

3÷ 3	15+ 5	2÷ 2	4	14+ 1	6	7
1	3	7 7	14+ 5	6	240× 2	4
16+ 4	7	3+ 1	2	3	5	6
7	3÷ 1	3	3÷ 6	2	40× 4	5
5	3÷ 6	12× 4	3	23+ 7	3× 1	2
4− 6	2	5	7	4	3	1
2	24× 4	6	1	105× 5	7	3

151

2÷ 3	6	13+ 5	2÷ 2	4	4− 7	12× 1
10× 5	2	6	11+ 7	6− 1	3	4
2	6+ 5	1	4	7	720× 6	3
7 7	6+ 1	2	3	60× 5	4	6
5+ 1	7+ 3	4	11+ 6	2	5	14+ 7
4	17+ 7	3	5	6	2÷ 1	2
2− 6	4	7	3÷ 1	3	2	5

152

6× 6	1	252× 3	3− 5	2	16× 4	12+ 7
4− 3	7	2	72× 6	4	1	5
8+ 1	6	7	3	10× 5	2	9+ 4
5	3÷ 3	1	4	13+ 6	7	2
2	140× 4	15+ 6	1− 1	2− 7	5	3
7	5	4	2	18× 1	3	6 6
2− 4	2	5	21× 7	3	6	1

153

140× 5	4	7	3+ 1	2	2÷ 3	6
6− 1	1− 5	2− 2	2− 6	4	7 7	3÷ 3
7	6	4	14× 3	180× 5	3+ 2	1
9+ 4	2	3	7	6	1	5 5
36× 2	3÷ 3	30× 5	4	1	6	9+ 7
3	1	6	16+ 5	7	4	2
6	6− 7	1	1− 2	3	1− 5	4

154

2÷ 3	6	13+ 5	2÷ 2	4	4− 7	12× 1
10× 5	2	6	11+ 7	6− 1	3	4
2	6+ 5	1	4	7	720× 6	3
7 7	6+ 1	2	3	60× 5	4	6
5+ 1	7+ 3	4	11+ 6	2	5	14+ 7
4	17+ 7	3	5	6	2÷ 1	2
2− 6	4	7	3÷ 1	3	2	5

155

14× 2	7	8+ 4	1	3	11+ 5	6
2÷ 1	2	90× 3	6	5	28× 7	4
16+ 7	6+ 3	2	5 5	13+ 6	4	8+ 1
4	1	1− 6	1− 2	6− 7	3	5
5	4 4	7	3	1	48× 6	2
2÷ 6	5	6− 1	7	4	2	4− 3
3	6	40× 5	4	2	1	7

156

5+ 4	3+ 1	13+ 3	2	5	1− 6	42× 7
1	2	19+ 7	3	4	5	6
2− 7	2÷ 6	1	4	3	5− 2	1− 5
5	3	4− 6	1	6− 2	3+ 7	4
15+ 6	21+ 5	2	7	1	72× 4	6× 3
2	7	4	5	6	3	1
3	4	18+ 5	6	7	1	2

157

3+ 1	2	2− 3	5	4	6	210× 7
21× 3	2÷ 1	2	40× 4	1− 6	7	5
7	480× 4	1	2	5	24× 3	6
35× 5	7	6	3 3	2÷ 2	4	2− 1
3÷ 6	5	4	1− 7	1	2	3
2	2− 3	5	6	6− 7	1	2÷ 4
2− 4	6	6− 7	1	15× 3	5	2

158

6× 2	2− 6	4	3− 5	6− 7	1	12× 3
3	35× 7	5	2	36× 1	6	4
120× 4	9+ 2	23+ 7	3	6	4− 5	1
6	3	3+ 2	1	5	4	7
5	4	1	7	8+ 3	3÷ 2	6
6− 7	5− 1	6	672× 4	2	3	3− 5
1	5	2− 3	6	4	7	2

159

1− 4	3+ 1	2− 3	5	13+ 6	7	9+ 2
5	2	15+ 6	14+ 3	4	6× 1	7
11+ 2	5	4	7	1	6	9+ 3
6	2− 4	2	1 1	4− 7	3	5
3	245× 7	5	24× 6	80× 2	4	1
8+ 1	2÷ 3	7	4	5	2	10+ 6
7	6	2÷ 1	2	2− 3	5	4

160

2− 3	980× 4	7	5	36× 6	1	3+ 2
5	7	9+ 3	2	4	6	1
1− 7	11+ 2	4	4− 3	9+ 1	5	2− 6
6	4− 1	5	7	3	28× 2	4
7+ 1	5	10+ 6	4	2	7	105× 3
2	2÷ 3	14+ 1	6	7	12× 4	5
4	6	8+ 2	1	5	3	7

161

6× 6	1	75× 5	16+ 7	96× 4	3	9+ 2
1	5	3	6	2	4	7
5− 7	2	20+ 1	3	5	2− 6	4
15+ 5	3	2	4	6	6− 7	1
3	24+ 7	4	2	300× 1	5	6
4	6	7	3÷ 1	3	2	5
2÷ 2	4	18+ 6	5	7	3÷ 1	3

162

1− 4	1− 3	2	4× 1	17+ 5	7	1− 6
3	3÷ 2	6	4	1	5	7
2− 5	12+ 7	72× 3	2	6	3÷ 1	3− 4
7	1	4	3	2	252× 6	5 5
1 1	4	11+ 5	6	7	2	3
3÷ 6	4− 5	1	140× 7	4	36× 3	2÷ 2
2	1− 6	7	5	3	4	1

163

20× 5	12+ 2	3÷ 3	1	26+ 6	7	4
1	3	7	28× 2	4	5	17+ 6
4	1	2	7	9× 3	6	5
210× 7	5	6	3	1	2- 4	2
252× 6	2- 4	10× 1	5	2	1- 3	6- 7
3	6	9+ 5	24× 4	12+ 7	2	1
2	7	4	6	5	2- 1	3

164

3- 4	1- 7	6	18+ 5	1- 2	3	6+ 1
1	6+ 3	4- 7	6	4	48× 2	5
2	1	3	7	5	6	4
21+ 3	2÷ 2	4	3× 1	22+ 6	5	7
7	5	10× 2	3	1	4	2÷ 6
6	15+ 4	5	2÷ 2	4- 7	6- 1	3
5	6	1	4	3	7	2, 2

165

12+ 5	14+ 7	6	1- 2	4	3	2÷ 1
7	144× 6	1	3	5	16× 4	2
2	3	27+ 5	6	7	1	4
4	2÷ 1	3	140× 7	6	60× 2	5
15× 3	2	4	5	1	6	20+ 7
1	5	11+ 2	4	3	7	6
2- 6	4	6- 7	1	2	8+ 5	3

166

3÷ 6	2	420× 5	3	4	7	8+ 1
11+ 2	5	1	36× 6	7	12× 4	3
17+ 3	4	42× 2	1	6	5	42× 7
5	3	7	1- 4	3+ 2	1	6
6- 7	6	3	5	1	13+ 2	9+ 4
1	6- 7	9+ 4	2	3	6	5
4	1	210× 6	7	5	3	2

167

7+ 2	2÷ 3	6	5- 1	3- 7	4	90× 5
4	2- 7	5	6	2÷ 2	1	3
1	10+ 2	12+ 3	4	5	14+ 7	6
3	1	4	13+ 7	6	5	2
13+ 7	7+ 5	2	9× 3	1	11+ 6	4
6	15+ 4	2- 7	5	3	42× 2	1
5	6	7+ 1	2	4	3	7

168

2÷ 4	42× 6	7	16+ 5	2÷ 2	1	3÷ 3
2	75× 5	3	7	4	13+ 6	1
3÷ 3	1	5	432× 4	6	7	40× 2
56× 7	4	2	6	6- 1	3, 3	5
3÷ 6	2	3- 1	3	7	10× 5	4
13+ 5	7	4	6+ 1	3	2	1- 6
1	2÷ 3	6	2	20× 5	4	7

169

20× 5	4	3+ 1	120× 6	42× 2	7	3
3÷ 6	23+ 7	2	4	5	7+ 3	6- 1
2	6	5	3 · 3	15+ 1	4	7
4 · 4	5	6- 7	1	3	4- 2	6
21× 7	6× 2	3	5	6	6+ 1	2÷ 4
3	1	2- 6	56× 7	4	5	2
2- 1	3	4	2	13+ 7	6	5 · 5

170

4- 1	13+ 7	10× 5	2	5+ 3	14+ 4	6
5	6	4- 3	7	2	2÷ 1	4
14+ 4	6- 1	7	30× 5	13+ 6	2	150× 3
3	24× 4	6	1	7	5	2
7	2÷ 2	4	6	10+ 1	2÷ 3	5
3÷ 2	15× 5	3÷ 1	3	4	6	49× 7
6	3	2÷ 2	4	5	7	1

171

14+ 7	24× 2	3	4	30× 5	6	1- 1
3	12+ 4	30× 5	13+ 6	3+ 1	6- 7	2
4	5	6	7	2	1	3 · 3
3÷ 6	3	8× 1	2	4	12+ 5	12+ 7
2	6- 7	56× 4	1	126× 6	3	5
30× 5	1	2	15× 3	7	4	48× 6
1	6	7	5	3	2	4

172

192× 4	2	6- 7	2÷ 3	6	4- 5	1
6- 7	6	1	6× 2	3	9+ 4	5
1	4	720× 6	5	5- 7	2	3 · 3
4- 5	1	2÷ 4	6	6× 2	3	13+ 7
1- 3	630× 5	2	4	6- 1	7	6
2	7	2- 3	6+ 1	5	6	2- 4
6	3	5	3- 7	4	2÷ 1	2

173

14× 2	7	2÷ 1	18+ 6	5	7+ 4	3
6- 1	3÷ 3	2	1- 5	7	48× 6	4
7	1	13+ 6	4	72× 3	2	5 · 5
10× 5	2	7	14× 1	4	3 · 3	3÷ 6
7+ 4	90× 5	3	7	6	35× 1	2
3	6	60× 4	2	2÷ 1	5	7
2- 6	4	5	3	2	8+ 7	1

174

36× 4	3	3÷ 2	6	10+ 1	210× 7	5
3	14× 2	7	2÷ 1	4	5	6
17+ 7	6	4	2	14+ 5	3÷ 1	3
3÷ 6	3÷ 1	3	5 · 5	2	4	6- 7
2	2- 7	5	3- 4	3	108× 6	1
25× 5	5+ 4	1	7	6	3	16× 2
1	5	16+ 6	3	7	2	4

175

⁵⁻7	³⁻4	⁴⁻2	6	³3	³÷1	¹⁻5
2	7	²⁻4	¹⁻5	⁶⁻1	3	6
²÷3	⁷⁵ˣ5	6	4	7	¹³⁺2	³⁺1
6	3	5	¹1	4	7	2
³⁺1	2	⁶⁻7	¹⁰⁺3	⁴⁻6	²⁰ˣ5	4
²⁰ˣ5	³⁶ˣ6	1	7	2	⁴4	⁴⁻3
4	1	3	2	¹¹⁺5	6	7

176

¹²⁶ˣ1	3	6	³⁺2	²⁻7	5	¹²ˣ4
²¹⁰ˣ6	7	⁷⁵ˣ5	1	⁴⁸ˣ2	⁴4	3
7	5	3	6	4	1	¹³⁺2
5	⁶⁻1	7	⁷⁺4	¹⁻3	2	6
²÷4	³÷6	2	3	1	7	5
2	³²ˣ4	1	¹²⁺5	²÷6	3	⁶⁻7
³3	2	4	7	5	6	1

177

²⁻4	6	⁶⁻1	7	¹⁴⁴ˣ2	3	²¹⁰ˣ5
¹⁰⁵ˣ5	³⁺1	2	¹¹⁺3	4	6	7
7	¹⁴⁰ˣ4	3	5	6	²÷2	1
3	7	⁵5	²÷2	1	¹⁰⁺4	6
³÷2	5	7	¹³⁺6	⁵²⁵ˣ3	³⁻1	4
6	²⁻2	4	¹1	5	7	3
³÷1	3	²⁴ˣ6	4	7	5	2

178

³²ˣ1	8	4	¹⁻2	²⁻3	¹⁸⁺5	7	6
²÷4	⁷⁺2	¹⁻7	3	5	³÷1	¹⁰⁺6	²⁸⁰ˣ8
2	5	6	⁹⁺8	1	3	4	7
²÷3	⁸⁺1	²÷2	4	¹⁻6	7	¹³⁺8	5
6	7	8	⁷⁻1	2	²÷4	5	⁶⁺3
²⁻7	²⁻4	¹⁵ˣ5	²⁻6	8	⁴÷2	³÷3	1
5	6	3	¹³⁺7	³⁻4	8	1	2
⁵⁻8	3	1	5	7	¹²⁺6	2	4

179

⁶6	⁴⁻5	⁴²ˣ7	1	²÷8	4	¹¹²ˣ2	¹⁰⁺3
³⁻4	1	6	²⁻3	5	8	7	2
7	¹⁷⁺3	4	²¹⁺8	³÷2	6	⁵5	1
⁴⁻5	2	8	7	6	²⁻1	3	4
1	¹⁶⁸ˣ7	3	¹⁴⁺6	4	⁴÷2	8	¹⁶⁸⁰ˣ5
¹³⁺3	8	²2	4	³⁰ˣ1	5	6	7
2	²⁻6	⁸⁺1	²⁻5	7	⁸⁺3	4	8
8	4	5	2	⁴⁻3	7	1	6

180

⁷⁻8	1	¹⁹⁺3	7	¹⁵⁺5	2	⁴⁸ˣ6	4
²÷3	6	⁴²ˣ7	1	8	¹²⁺5	4	2
⁶⁺1	5	6	8	²÷2	4	3	¹⁻7
¹⁵⁺7	2	³⁻5	3	¹²ˣ4	²⁵⁶ˣ4	1	6
6	¹⁶⁺7	2	4	³÷1	3	8	¹⁶⁸⁰ˣ5
5	4	²÷8	⁶⁰ˣ2	6	⁷⁺1	7	3
⁴÷2	8	4	6	¹²⁶ˣ3	¹²⁺7	5	1
⁷⁺4	3	1	5	7	6	2	8

181

15+ 7	6− 1	192× 4	8	4− 2	6	1− 5	6+ 3
8	7	3	2	140× 4	5	6	1
15× 5	3	96× 6	24× 4	7	56× 8	1	2
1	2	8	6	4− 5	7	1− 3	4
40× 2	1− 6	5	3÷ 3	1	84× 4	8	7
4	5	2² 2	1	36× 6	3	7	240× 8
2÷ 6	2÷ 8	20+ 1	7	3	2	2÷ 4	5
3	4	7	5	9+ 8	1	2	6

182

4÷ 8	15+ 2	7	3÷ 1	3	210× 6	5	1− 4
2	6	9+ 5	4	7− 1	8	7	3
15+ 4	6× 1	6	14+ 5	17+ 8	3	2	23+ 7
5	5− 3	1	2	7	4	8	6
6	8	84× 4	7	60× 5	1	3	2
11+ 1	11+ 5	2	3	4	1− 7	6	40× 8
7	4	11+ 3	8	3÷ 6	2	1 5	5
3	336× 7	8	6	40× 2	5	4	1

183

5− 8	3	1− 5	6	7+ 1	4	7	9+ 2
2− 6	2− 5	3	4	2	9+ 8	1	7
4	7	1− 8	2÷ 3	6	5 5	2÷ 2	1
2− 5	2÷ 8	4	14× 2	7	36× 1	6	3 3
7	2÷ 1	2	5	3	6	2÷ 4	8
3+ 1	5− 2	7	15+ 8	4	3	1− 5	6
2	2− 4	6	40× 1	8	4− 7	3	9+ 5
2÷ 3	6	6− 1	7	5	4÷ 2	8	4

184

8+ 1	5	1− 7	36× 3	2− 6	8	9+ 2	2÷ 4
5 5	2	6	1	3	4	7	8
48× 6	4	2	11+ 5	1	15+ 7	8	3÷ 3
9+ 2	7	1− 4	8	20+ 5	216× 6	3	1
2− 3	1	5	4	8	2	6	2− 7
21+ 7	6	8	2÷ 2	4	3÷ 3	1	5
23+ 8	3	4410× 1	6	7	5	1− 4	4− 2
4	8	3	7	3+ 2	1	5	6

185

10+ 3	1	6	8+ 2	15+ 5	7	1792× 4	8
2− 6	4	2÷ 2	5	1	3	8	7
10× 2	3− 3	1	21+ 7	6	8	10+ 5	4
5	6	1− 4	3	4÷ 8	2	1− 7	1
7− 1	5− 2	1− 7	8	1− 3	4	6	7+ 5
8	7	24× 3	120× 6	4	5	1	2
2− 7	5	8	7+ 4	2	1	108× 3	6
17+ 4	8	5	1	1− 7	6	2	3

186

7− 8	1	3÷ 3	1− 6	7	40× 5	2	4
1− 7	96× 2	1	420× 3	4	6	5	32× 8
6	3	2	5	1− 8	7	4	1
10+ 3	8	1− 5	7	4÷ 1	4	2− 6	3− 2
4	22+ 7	6	7− 1	6× 2	3	8	5
2	6	4	8	4− 5	1	13+ 3	7
1	5	1− 8	2− 4	6	14× 2	7	3
20× 5	4	7	5+ 2	3	15+ 8	1	6

187

3−4	6−7	1	6+5	6−8	3	1−2	48×6
7	2÷3	6	1	2	20×4	5	8
1−5	4	2−8	6	6−1	7	5+3	2
3÷6	2	20×4	12+7	5	7+1	5−8	3
7−8	1	5	1−2	3	6	3−7	4
2÷3	6	5−2	1−4	13+7	3−8	4−1	5
80×2	8	7	3	6	5	18+4	1
1	5	11+3	8	2÷4	2	6	7

188

2−6	42×1	7	1−4	5	3	4−8	4÷2
4	6	6+1	3	2	7	3−5	8
7	15+5	6	2	8	1	10+4	7+3
5−3	8	2	1−7	6	5	1	4
2−5	3	18+8	7+6	1	32×4	3÷2	12+7
16×8	7	3	1	4	2	6	5
2	32×4	280×5	8	7	6	2−3	3÷1
1	2	4	5	8+3	8	13+7	6

189

4−1	5	2÷4	2−3	6×2	11+7	21+6	8
2−5	7	2	1	3	4	8	24×6
2−6	18+3	8	2	5	1−1	7	4
4	7−8	1	1−7	6	2	10×5	3÷3
4−7	2÷6	3	4−8	4	40×5	2	1
3	14+2	5	6	1	8	8+4	70×7
2÷2	1	1−7	1−4	15+8	2÷6	3	5
4−8	4	6	5	7	3	1	2

190

26+7	1−6	5	56×8	8×1	4	6×2	3
6	13+8	3	7	2	16+5	6+1	7+4
8	10+3	2	16×6	4	7	5	1
5	7	6	4	2÷3	3÷1	21+8	2
24×2	20×5	6−7	1	6	3	4	280×8
1	4	13+8	2	21+7	6	3	5
4	2	1	15×3	15×5	8	6	7
3	4÷1	4	5	8	2	13+7	6

191

4−5	3÷6	2	24×8	3	3−4	7	6−1
1	2÷3	6	15+4	35×5	4÷8	2	7
56×2	24×8	3	5	7	24×1	6	4
4	7	1−5	6	1	2÷3	4÷8	2
35×7	5	4	1−3	3÷2	6	7−1	8
2÷3	1	23+8	2	6	14×7	60×4	5
6	64×4	7	7−1	8	2	14+5	3
8	2	1	7	1−4	5	3	6

192

60×4	5	784×7	8	2	9	1	8−3	10+6
240×6	3	17+5	7	7−8	48×2	4	72×9	1
5	8	3	9	1	6	2	4	27+7
36×3	2	6	3+1	2−5	7	17+9	8	4
8−9	2−6	8	2	12×3	4	8+7	1	5
1	2÷4	2	17+3	6	8	2−5	7	9
17+8	7	16×1	4	16+9	9×3	19+6	5	2
2	17+9	4	24+5	7	1	3	6	24×8
7	1	9	6	4	13+5	8	2	3

193

3	4	9	8	6	5	1	7	2
7	5	1	6	2	8	3	4	9
8	1	5	4	7	3	2	9	6
5	6	2	7	4	9	8	3	1
9	7	4	2	8	1	5	6	3
2	9	3	1	5	4	6	8	7
4	2	6	3	1	7	9	5	8
1	8	7	9	3	6	4	2	5
6	3	8	5	9	2	7	1	4

194

6	3	7	5	4	8	1	9	2
7	8	5	4	9	3	6	2	1
9	1	4	2	5	7	8	6	3
4	6	2	7	1	5	3	8	9
1	9	3	6	2	4	7	5	8
8	2	6	9	7	1	4	3	5
2	5	1	8	3	6	9	7	4
5	4	8	3	6	9	2	1	7
3	7	9	1	8	2	5	4	6

195

3	9	2	6	7	5	4	8	1
7	4	8	5	1	6	3	2	9
8	3	4	2	9	7	5	1	6
2	1	3	8	5	4	9	6	7
5	8	1	7	3	9	6	4	2
6	2	7	4	8	3	1	9	5
4	7	9	3	6	1	2	5	8
9	6	5	1	2	8	7	3	4
1	5	6	9	4	2	8	7	3

196

2	6	1	7	5	8	9	4	3
7	8	4	2	9	5	6	3	1
9	5	6	3	2	7	8	1	4
8	9	5	1	3	6	4	2	7
5	4	2	6	1	9	3	7	8
4	2	9	5	7	3	1	8	6
1	7	3	9	8	4	5	6	2
3	1	8	4	6	2	7	5	9
6	3	7	8	4	1	2	9	5

197

3	5	1	2	9	8	6	4	7
6	1	2	3	7	4	9	8	5
4	9	3	1	2	5	7	6	8
1	2	7	9	5	6	8	3	4
9	8	6	7	3	2	4	5	1
7	6	5	8	4	9	2	1	3
8	3	9	4	1	7	5	2	6
2	4	8	5	6	1	3	7	9
5	7	4	6	8	3	1	9	2

198

1	4	6	3	5	8	2	9	7
7	8	3	2	9	5	6	1	4
9	6	8	4	2	7	5	3	1
8	9	1	5	6	4	7	2	3
3	7	2	1	4	9	8	6	5
6	1	7	9	8	3	4	5	2
5	3	9	6	7	2	1	4	8
4	2	5	8	3	1	9	7	6
2	5	4	7	1	6	3	8	9

199

²⁸⁸ˣ 4	9	8	¹⁶⁺ 5	2	²÷ 6	3	⁷ 7	⁵ˣ 1
⁴⁻ 7	3	¹⁻ 6	9	¹⁴⁺ 8	4	2	1	5
¹⁰⁺ 2	5	7	⁶⁷²ˣ 6	²÷ 3	1	8	²³⁺ 9	4
3	³⁻ 7	4	8	6	¹⁸⁹ˣ 9	¹²⁺ 1	¹⁷⁺ 5	2
⁸⁻ 9	¹⁰ˣ 2	5	7	¹ 1	3	6	4	8
1	²⁹⁺ 6	9	2	⁵⁻ 4	7	5	8	¹³⁺ 3
6	8	²÷ 2	1	9	¹⁻ 5	4	3	7
⁹⁺ 5	4	1	⁶⁰ˣ 3	²⁴ˣ 7	8	9	²³⁺ 2	6
¹²⁺ 8	1	3	4	5	⁵⁻ 2	7	6	9

200

²¹⁰ˣ 6	5	8	2	¹⁵⁺ 3	7	¹⁸⁹ˣ 1	9	⁸⁻ 4
7	⁵⁻ 1	¹⁻ 4	5	9	6	²⁻ 8	2	¹⁷⁺ 3
⁸⁻ 1	6	5	¹⁴⁺ 3	¹⁸⁰ˣ 4	9	7	8	²⁴⁺ 2
9	¹³⁺ 4	3	8	5	¹⁵ˣ 1	⁵⁻ 2	7	6
⁵ 5	2	²²⁺ 9	6	7	3	⁴÷ 4	1	8
⁵⁻ 8	7	6	¹⁹⁺ 4	2	²⁴ˣ 5	9	³÷ 3	1
3	¹⁷⁺ 8	³⁺ 1	9	6	2	5	¹⁵⁺ 4	7
⁹⁺ 4	9	2	⁴⁹ˣ 7	¹³⁺ 1	8	¹¹⁺ 3	6	²⁵⁺ 5
2	3	7	1	8	4	6	5	9

201

⁴⁸ˣ 8	2	¹⁻ 4	²⁴ˣ 9	¹⁰⁺ 1	¹⁵⁺ 6	⁴⁻ 3	¹⁶⁺ 7	5
¹⁻ 6	3	5	8	9	4	7	1	2
5	²⁸⁸ˣ 8	⁸⁻ 9	7	3	2	¹⁴⁺ 6	¹²⁺ 4	1
9	4	1	⁸⁴ˣ 6	2	7	8	5	3
⁷ˣ 1	¹⁸⁺ 7	3	¹⁹⁺ 5	6	8	¹⁶ˣ 4	2	⁴⁸⁶ˣ 9
7	1	8	⁶⁺ 3	⁶⁰ˣ 4	5	2	9	6
⁷⁺ 3	⁵⁴ˣ 9	6	2	¹⁵⁺ 7	1	¹³⁺ 5	8	³⁻ 4
4	⁷⁺ 5	2	1	8	3	⁵⁴ˣ 9	6	7
³÷ 2	6	¹⁶⁺ 7	4	5	⁸⁻ 9	1	²⁴ˣ 3	8

202

²÷ 6	3	1	7	⁸⁺ 8	2	⁴⁸ˣ 4	³⁺ 9	¹⁸⁰ˣ 5
⁴ 4	²⁷⁰ˣ 9	⁵⁻ 7	⁷⁺ 3	6	1	⁸⁰ˣ 2	5	8
5	6	2	4	⁴⁻ 3	7	¹⁷⁺ 9	8	⁴÷ 1
1	³⁺ 2	²÷ 6	¹⁷⁺ 8	9	¹⁵ˣ 3	²¹⁰ˣ 5	7	4
¹⁴ˣ 7	1	3	¹⁸⁰ˣ 9	4	5	8	⁸ 6	²⁴ˣ 2
2	7	¹⁶⁺ 9	¹⁷⁺ 1	⁶⁺ 5	8	⁴⁸ˣ 6	4	3
¹⁷⁺ 9	4	8	5	2	⁹⁺ 6	²÷ 3	1	⁶⁻ 7
8	5	¹²⁺ 4	2	7	⁹ 9	1	⁸⁺ 3	⁶ˣ 6 ³⁻
¹¹⁺ 3	8	⁵ 5	6	⁴÷ 1	4	7	2	9

203

⁸⁻ 1	9	¹⁻ 3	4	⁴⁰ˣ 8	⁴÷ 2	²⁰⁺ 6	7	5
²÷ 4	³⁵ˣ 5	7	⁸⁻ 9	1	8	²÷ 3	6	2
8	¹⁴⁺ 3	2	1	5	²⁴ˣ 4	³¹⁵ˣ 7	9	⁴⁸ˣ 6
²÷ 2	4	9	¹²⁺ 7	3	6	5	1	8
³÷ 9	⁷⁺ 6	¹⁴⁺ 8	2	³¹⁵ˣ 7	5	²⁻ 1	3	²⁸ˣ 4
3	1	5	²÷ 6	¹⁷⁺ 4	9	²÷ 8	¹⁵⁺ 2	7
³⁻ 5	2	1	3	6	7	4	8	⁸⁻ 9
¹³⁺ 6	7	²⁻ 4	²²⁺ 8	9	⁵⁴ˣ 3	2	5	1
¹⁻ 7	8	6	5	³⁺ 2	1	9	⁷⁺ 4	3

204

⁷ˣ 1	⁴÷ 8	2	3	⁸⁺ 7	²⁸ˣ 4	6	¹⁻ 5	¹⁴⁺ 9
7	1	3	2	⁴÷ 8	¹³⁺ 9	4	¹⁵⁺ 6	5
¹⁷⁺ 4	7	¹³⁺ 5	8	2	1	⁸⁻ 9	3	6
6	⁸⁻ 9	1	¹¹⁺ 7	4	³⁻ 8	5	¹⁻ 2	3
¹⁷⁺ 8	⁷⁰ˣ 2	7	5	²⁷ˣ 9	²÷ 6	3	⁴ˣ 1	4
9	¹⁰⁰ˣ 5	²⁻ 6	²⁴ˣ 4	3	⁵⁻ 7	2	¹⁷⁺ 8	1
5	4	8	6	1	¹⁰⁺ 3	7	9	⁴⁴⁸ˣ 2
⁶ˣ 2	²÷ 3	¹³⁺ 4	9	¹⁵⁰ˣ 6	5	⁸⁺ 1	7	8
3	6	⁸⁻ 9	1	5	⁴÷ 2	8	4	7

205

(2÷)4	2	(4−)3	7	(8−)9	1	(2÷)8	(1−)6	5
(21×)3	7	1	(168×)6	(4÷)2	8	4	(14+)5	9
(4−)5	1	7	4	(192×)8	(2)2	9	(3÷)3	(4−)6
(144×)8	(144×)4	9	1	3	(13+)6	(70×)5	7	2
9	(11+)5	4	8	(4÷)1	7	6	(18×)2	(168×)3
2	6	(40×)8	5	4	(1−)3	1	(8−)9	7
(42×)7	(3÷)9	(11+)5	(3÷)2	6	4	3	1	8
1	3	6	(9)9	(17+)7	5	(22+)2	(32×)8	4
6	(13+)8	2	3	5	9	7	4	1

206

(17+)3	(14+)7	(160×)4	8	5	(2÷)2	1	(3−)6	9
5	4	(7−)8	(8−)1	9	(2÷)3	7	(2−)2	(3÷)6
9	3	1	(168×)7	4	6	5	(4÷)8	2
(3+)2	1	(10+)5	6	(17+)8	9	(12×)3	4	(35×)7
(24×)4	6	2	(162×)9	3	7	(15+)8	(3−)5	1
(2−)7	9	3	2	6	8	(14+)4	1	(8−)5
(7−)1	5	(2−)7	3	2	4	6	9	(15+)8
8	(16+)2	(11+)6	4	1	(315×)5	9	(10+)7	3
6	8	(4−)9	5	7	1	(2)2	3	4

207

(10×)5	(4÷)4	1	(17+)8	(378×)9	7	(3÷)2	6	(12+)3
2	(21×)3	7	9	6	(2−)4	(20×)5	8	1
(252×)7	(17+)8	9	(11+)3	1	6	4	(3−)2	5
4	(11+)2	8	1	3	(8−)9	(48×)6	(2−)5	(5−)7
9	(6+)5	(3÷)6	(196×)7	4	1	8	3	2
(288×)6	1	2	4	7	(105×)5	3	(8−)9	(17+)8
8	6	(12+)4	(50×)2	5	(48×)3	7	1	9
(3÷)1	(16+)7	3	5	8	2	(13+)9	4	(168×)6
3	9	5	(3÷)6	2	(7−)8	1	7	4

208

(3÷)6	2	(15×)5	(15+)3	4	(17+)8	(20+)9	1	(6−)7
(1−)7	3	1	(12+)2	8	9	5	(2−)4	6
8	(35+)9	(4−)7	4	(1)1	3	(15+)6	5	(280×)2
(5)5	7	3	6	(3÷)9	2	1	8	4
(18×)2	6	(1−)9	8	3	1	(1−)4	7	5
1	8	(2÷)4	(13+)7	6	5	3	(16+)2	(3÷)9
9	5	2	(6−)1	7	4	8	6	3
(1−)3	(2÷)4	8	(4−)5	(3÷)2	6	(5−)7	(8−)9	1
(5−)4	1	6	9	(35×)5	7	2	(24×)3	8

209

(5−)6	(4÷)8	(13+)3	(3−)7	4	(3+)1	2	(405×)9	(5)5
1	2	6	4	(23+)8	3	7	5	9
(2÷)2	1	(48×)8	6	5	(36×)4	9	(8+)7	(21×)3
4	6	(6−)2	8	(27+)3	9	(5)5	1	7
(7)7	(160×)5	(5−)4	(3+)1	9	6	(48×)8	3	2
8	4	9	2	(5−)7	(13+)5	(3÷)3	(2−)6	(5−)1
(135×)9	(10+)3	(175×)7	5	2	8	1	4	6
3	7	5	(8−)9	1	2	(9+)6	(2−)8	(6−)4
5	(8−)9	1	(2÷)3	6	7	4	2	8

210

(7)7	(2÷)4	8	(3−)3	(3+)2	1	(54×)6	9	(12+)5
(3+)2	(8−)1	9	6	(20×)5	4	(5−)3	8	7
1	(18+)8	3	7	(168×)4	(10×)2	5	6	(324×)9
(5−)3	(45×)9	5	(1)1	7	(64×)8	4	2	6
8	(3−)7	4	9	(17+)6	5	(210×)1	(6−)3	(24×)2
(60×)5	(2÷)2	1	8	9	6	7	4	3
4	3	(3÷)6	2	1	7	(17+)9	(280×)5	8
(15+)6	(1−)5	2	(1−)4	(3÷)3	9	8	7	1
9	6	7	5	(24×)8	(2)3	2	(4÷)1	4

211

8	9	6	4	3	1	5	7	2
3	6	1	7	2	8	9	5	4
4	7	5	3	1	9	6	2	8
2	3	4	6	5	7	1	8	9
6	2	8	1	4	5	7	9	3
5	1	3	2	9	4	8	6	7
9	5	7	8	6	2	4	3	1
1	8	9	5	7	3	2	4	6
7	4	2	9	8	6	3	1	5

212

4	7	9	6	1	3	2	5	8
5	3	1	9	6	8	4	2	7
9	2	3	7	5	4	6	8	1
3	8	4	5	9	2	7	1	6
2	9	8	4	7	1	5	6	3
8	5	7	1	2	6	3	4	9
7	4	6	3	8	5	1	9	2
1	6	2	8	4	7	9	3	5
6	1	5	2	3	9	8	7	4

213

2	7	6	1	8	9	3	5	4
7	4	8	2	1	6	5	3	9
4	2	7	9	5	3	6	8	1
5	3	2	6	9	1	8	4	7
1	6	9	8	3	4	7	2	5
6	9	4	3	7	5	2	1	8
3	1	5	7	4	8	9	6	2
8	5	3	4	2	7	1	9	6
9	8	1	5	6	2	4	7	3

214

7	9	3	5	6	1	2	8	4
3	1	8	9	2	6	5	4	7
1	3	4	2	5	7	6	9	8
2	5	9	4	1	3	8	7	6
8	4	6	1	3	2	7	5	9
4	2	1	3	7	8	9	6	5
5	7	2	6	8	9	4	1	3
9	6	7	8	4	5	1	3	2
6	8	5	7	9	4	3	2	1

215

7	8	5	1	9	6	4	2	3
6	4	1	2	7	9	5	3	8
4	7	9	5	1	8	3	6	2
8	3	4	6	2	5	9	1	7
1	2	3	8	5	7	6	4	9
3	9	7	4	8	2	1	5	6
2	1	6	9	3	4	7	8	5
5	6	8	7	4	3	2	9	1
9	5	2	3	6	1	8	7	4

216

9	8	3	5	1	7	4	6	2
4	5	6	8	9	3	2	1	7
7	9	2	3	5	4	1	8	6
2	7	5	4	3	1	6	9	8
3	4	7	9	6	8	5	2	1
6	3	9	1	2	5	8	7	4
8	2	1	6	7	9	3	4	5
1	6	4	7	8	2	9	5	3
5	1	8	2	4	6	7	3	9

217

6	8	3	7	1	4	2	9	5
5	4	9	3	8	6	7	2	1
9	3	4	5	2	1	6	7	8
4	6	7	8	9	2	1	5	3
7	2	8	1	3	5	4	6	9
3	5	1	9	6	7	8	4	2
8	9	2	6	4	3	5	1	7
2	1	5	4	7	8	9	3	6
1	7	6	2	5	9	3	8	4

218

9	7	8	3	4	5	2	6	1
5	9	4	2	3	7	1	8	6
3	8	7	9	1	4	6	2	5
4	5	1	6	2	3	7	9	8
2	1	6	8	7	9	5	3	4
6	3	5	7	8	1	9	4	2
8	6	9	4	5	2	3	1	7
7	2	3	1	6	8	4	5	9
1	4	2	5	9	6	8	7	3

219

7	2	1	6	4	3	5	9	8
3	5	9	7	1	6	2	8	4
2	8	7	3	9	4	1	5	6
9	1	6	2	3	8	4	7	5
6	4	3	9	7	5	8	2	1
4	6	2	5	8	1	9	3	7
5	9	8	1	6	2	7	4	3
1	7	4	8	5	9	3	6	2
8	3	5	4	2	7	6	1	9

220

2	9	8	5	6	1	7	3	4
4	3	9	6	1	5	8	7	2
8	6	7	9	2	3	4	1	5
3	8	4	1	5	2	6	9	7
5	4	6	7	9	8	3	2	1
9	5	1	3	8	7	2	4	6
7	2	3	8	4	6	1	5	9
6	1	5	2	7	4	9	8	3
1	7	2	4	3	9	5	6	8

221

8	1	6	2	4	5	7	3	9
4	8	1	3	2	6	5	9	7
6	3	2	7	5	4	9	1	8
7	6	8	9	1	3	2	5	4
5	4	9	1	7	8	3	6	2
3	9	7	6	8	2	1	4	5
1	2	3	5	9	7	4	8	6
2	5	4	8	3	9	6	7	1
9	7	5	4	6	1	8	2	3

222

2	1	4	6	5	7	8	3	9
5	4	2	7	3	9	1	6	8
9	6	5	2	4	1	7	8	3
8	7	6	4	2	3	5	9	1
4	5	9	1	6	8	3	2	7
7	8	3	5	9	6	2	1	4
3	9	7	8	1	2	4	5	6
6	2	1	3	8	4	9	7	5
1	3	8	9	7	5	6	4	2

223

8	7	5	1	6	2	3	4	9
6	5	1	8	9	4	2	3	7
1	6	8	9	2	3	7	5	4
9	2	6	4	3	5	8	7	1
7	8	4	3	5	9	1	6	2
2	4	9	5	1	7	6	8	3
4	1	3	6	7	8	9	2	5
5	3	2	7	8	1	4	9	6
3	9	7	2	4	6	5	1	8

224

8	3	7	5	4	1	9	6	2
3	2	4	1	9	7	8	5	6
1	9	3	7	2	4	6	8	5
7	6	9	8	1	2	5	4	3
4	7	5	9	3	6	2	1	8
5	4	2	6	8	3	1	7	9
6	1	8	2	5	9	4	3	7
2	8	1	3	6	5	7	9	4
9	5	6	4	7	8	3	2	1

225

3	5	4	1	2	6	8	9	7
4	7	1	3	8	5	9	6	2
2	1	7	6	3	8	4	5	9
8	3	9	2	7	4	5	1	6
9	4	8	7	6	1	2	3	5
1	2	3	4	5	9	6	7	8
7	8	6	5	9	2	3	4	1
6	9	5	8	4	7	1	2	3
5	6	2	9	1	3	7	8	4

226

3	6	4	2	8	5	1	9	7
6	3	2	7	9	8	5	4	1
2	1	7	8	3	6	4	5	9
8	2	3	9	5	4	7	1	6
4	9	1	3	2	7	6	8	5
1	4	8	5	6	2	9	7	3
5	7	6	4	1	9	8	3	2
7	5	9	1	4	3	2	6	8
9	8	5	6	7	1	3	2	4

227

4	9	8	5	3	1	6	2	7
7	6	1	3	8	2	5	4	9
1	8	2	6	5	4	7	9	3
3	1	7	2	6	9	4	8	5
9	4	3	1	7	6	2	5	8
2	7	9	4	1	5	8	3	6
8	5	4	9	2	7	3	6	1
5	2	6	8	9	3	1	7	4
6	3	5	7	4	8	9	1	2

228

2	6	3	7	1	8	9	4	5
6	3	5	9	8	4	7	2	1
8	4	1	2	6	3	5	7	9
1	7	6	3	2	5	8	9	4
4	8	7	6	5	9	2	1	3
5	1	2	4	9	6	3	8	7
9	2	4	1	3	7	6	5	8
3	9	8	5	7	1	4	6	2
7	5	9	8	4	2	1	3	6

229

```
3÷      2-          8-      2÷      56×             12+
 1   6   8   9   3   2   4   5   7
     7+                      17+            2÷
 3   5   2   1   6   7   9   8   4
2÷      3÷          30×                 1344×
 4   8   9   3   1   5   6   7   2
 5   3÷  3   1-  3+
 5   9   3   7   2   1   8   4   6
168×                210×    8-          6×      5-
 6   4   7   8   5   9   1   2   3
8-      30×                 4       42×
 9   1   5   6   7   4   2   3   8
4÷          36×                         5
 8   2   6   4   9   3   7   1   5
42×     3+          2÷      13+         6       8-
 7   3   1   2   4   8   5   6   9
     7       1-                 162×
 2   7   4   5   8   6   3   9   1
```

230

```
210×        4÷          9+      8-      72×     16+     11+
 6   1   8   2   7   9   4   5   3
             1-
 5   7   4   3   2   1   6   9   8
2÷          20×         1-                      45×
 4   8   5   1   6   7   3   2   9
4-      2÷  1134×       2÷          16+
 3   6   9   4   1   2   8   7   5
216×                20+
 7   3   2   9   4   5   1   8   6
                                        16+     3÷
 9   4   6   7   3   8   5   1   2
3-          1-              576×         9+
 8   5   7   6   9   3   2   4   1
2÷      8-      200×             21×
 2   9   1   8   5   6   7   3   4
         1-                 378×
 1   2   3   5   8   4   9   6   7
```

231

```
4÷          120×            20+         5+      1470×
 1   4   8   3   5   6   9   2   7
21×     12×         2÷      17+
 7   1   2   6   8   9   4   3   5
        16+     20×     1-
 3   9   5   2   4   8   1   7   6
2÷                      1-          12+         11+
 8   7   4   1   2   3   5   6   9
            15+         5-      8+      21×
 4   8   7   9   3   5   6   1   2
1-          6×          18×                     12+
 5   6   1   4   9   2   7   8   3
17+     11+         21×     8+      2
 9   3   6   8   1   7   2   5   4
                                3-      20+         8×
 2   5   3   7   6   4   8   9   1
        7-          2-                  4
 6   2   9   5   7   1   3   4   8
```

232

```
168×                8       504×    3-          5-
 4   7   3   8   9   2   5   6   1
30+         9+          3÷      8-
 6   2   4   5   8   7   3   1   9
        4-          3-      6×              2-
 8   1   5   7   2   3   9   4   6
        216×    6-          4-          2-      1-
 7   9   8   4   1   5   6   2   3
                    14+                 2-
 9   4   2   1   7   6   8   3   5
6+          3÷          1-          98×         19+
 1   6   9   3   5   4   2   7   8
        14+         6×          32×     45×
 5   8   6   2   3   1   7   9   4
6×          54×         2-
 2   3   1   9   6   8   4   5   7
15+                         10+         4÷
 3   5   7   6   4   9   1   8   2
```

233

```
42×         9+      2-              7-
 6   7   5   3   1   8   4   9   2
4-              2-          3÷      336×
 5   9   4   6   8   3   1   2   7
3-          8-      3-      90×         2÷
 7   4   9   1   2   5   6   3   8
10+     48×         48×              2-      4-
 2   8   1   4   6   9   3   7   5
        1-                      280×
 3   6   8   9   4   2   7   5   1
    7+      30+                     48×     3÷
 4   2   7   8   9   6   5   1   3
        2÷      13+
 1   5   3   2   7   4   8   6   9
10+             2-          8+      7-          2-
 9   1   6   5   3   7   2   8   4
48×             35×                 4
 8   3   2   7   5   1   9   4   6
```

234

```
24+             10+                         1-
 7   9   8   4   2   1   3   6   5
40×     3÷      54×     3-          7-          378×
 5   3   9   2   4   7   8   1   6
        2   168×         2-      12+
 8   2   4   3   5   6   1   7   9
                            22+
 1   7   6   9   3   5   4   8   2
9+          14+     12×             3÷
 4   5   7   1   6   2   9   3   8
6×              21+     7   21+     120×         11+
 6   1   2   8   7   9   5   4   3
5-              8-              10×
 3   8   5   7   9   4   6   2   1
36×         3÷              42×
 9   4   3   6   1   8   2   5   7
3÷          3-                      36×
 2   6   1   5   8   3   7   9   4
```

235

2÷ 4	8	42× 7	6	1	3	1− 2	3− 9	4− 5
14+ 6	2÷ 2	24+ 9	8	7	4	5	3÷ 3	1
8	1	2− 3	5	12+ 2	6	252× 4	7	9
8+ 1	14+ 6	8	7	3	2	45× 9	5	4
7	15+ 5	7− 2	9	14+ 4	8− 1	2÷ 3	6	13+ 8
15× 5	4	6	2	8	9	9+ 7	1	3
3	3÷ 9	9+ 5	4	42× 6	7	1	112× 8	2
11+ 9	3	28× 4	4− 1	5	14+ 8	6	2	7
2	7	1	17+ 3	9	5	8	2− 4	6

236

5	26+ 3	18+ 6	7	224× 8	4	8− 9	1	15+ 2
6	8	9	5	15+ 1	7	6× 3	2	4
10+ 2	1	3	4	5	5− 8	294× 6	7	9
21+ 9	5	144× 4	2	6	3	7	7− 8	1
3− 4	7	2	9	3	4− 5	1	288× 6	8
7	5− 9	8	10+ 3	4	1	2	105× 5	6
7− 8	4	4− 1	6	17+ 2	9	5	15+ 3	7
1	2	36× 5	8	8 7	2− 6	4	3÷ 9	3
3	6	7	6− 1	9	2	4÷ 8	4	9+ 5

237

63× 1	7	128× 2	1− 8	14+ 6	9	4÷ 4	45× 5	3
13+ 8	9	4	2	7	5	1	3	336× 6
3	40× 5	8− 9	1	4 4	1− 7	6	108× 2	8
2	8	3− 5	14+ 4	1	6	2− 3	9	7
12+ 7	1	8	11+ 9	2	3	5	6	13+ 4
5	9+ 6	1	12+ 7	3	2	13+ 8	4	9
216× 9	2	2÷ 3	6	120× 8	3− 4	7	1	8+ 5
6	3− 4	7	3	5	1	17+ 9	8	2
4	2÷ 3	6	45× 5	9	112× 8	2	7	1

238

45× 5	9	4÷ 8	2	7	1− 6	2÷ 3	12+ 4	8− 1
16+ 4	1	42× 7	6	8	11+ 2	5	3	9
27+ 8	6	54× 9	3	2	7	20× 1	5	20+ 4
6	5	2	16+ 8	3	1	4	9	7
1	2− 3	5	4	6 6	17+ 8	9	5− 7	2
3	64× 8	42× 6	8− 9	1	4 4	17+ 7	13+ 2	5
9	4	1	135× 7	5	3	2	8	6
7 7	2	15× 3	5	5− 4	9	1440× 6	1	5− 8
9+ 2	7	4÷ 4	1	9	5	8	6	3

239

2− 9	504× 7	3	6	4÷ 2	8	4÷ 4	11+ 5	2÷ 1
7	288× 9	4	720× 5	8	3	1	6	2
8	4	5− 7	1	23+ 3	6	40× 5	11+ 2	9
18+ 1	6	2	7	4	9	8	15+ 3	5
3	8	3+ 1	2	1080× 5	4	6	9	7
40× 2	28+ 3	8	8− 9	1	23+ 5	7	4	144× 6
4	5	9	3	42× 6	3+ 1	2	7	8
5	5− 1	6	4032× 4	7	2	72× 9	8	3
60× 6	2	5	8	9	7	12× 3	1	4

240

13+ 6	4	4÷ 8	2− 7	5	60× 2	8− 9	1	27+ 3
3	6− 7	2	2÷ 8	4	5	6	9	1
7 7	1	5	672× 2	3	4	8	3− 6	15+ 9
8× 8	36× 2	1− 4	5	1	16+ 9	17+ 7	3	6
1	3	3− 6	9	7	8	5 5	2÷ 2	4
13+ 4	6	8− 9	1	8	36× 3	3+ 2	1− 5	12+ 7
9	17+ 8	4− 7	3	2	6	1	4	5
50× 5	9	3÷ 1	2− 4	6	6− 7	10752× 3	8	2
2	5	3	15+ 6	9	1	4	7	8

241

56× 4	3÷ 9	3	16+ 8	6	2	2− 7	5	8+ 1
2	7	7− 9	120× 3	5	8	4÷ 4	1	6
3− 8	5	2	19+ 6	4	9	8− 1	21× 7	3
192× 6	4	5	20+ 2	7	1	189× 9	1− 3	8 8
4− 1	8	6	9	3+ 2	7	3	4	4− 5
5	3− 6	3− 7	4÷ 4	1	3	8+ 2	3÷ 8	17+ 9
189× 7	3	4	1	5− 8	5	6	9	13+ 2
9	56× 1	8	7	3	60× 6	5	2	4
3	3+ 2	1	180× 5	9	4	14+ 8	6	7

242

24× 8	3	3+ 1	22+ 4	7	2	6	3− 9	1575× 5
2÷ 4	8	2	6	8− 1	3	9	5	7
3− 6	20× 4	3− 8	5	9	21× 7	3	9+ 2	3÷ 1
9	5	84× 4	16+ 8	2	6	10+ 1	7	3
6− 7	1	3	3+ 2	30× 6	9	5	2÷ 4	8
3÷ 3	9	7	1	5	8	4	3÷ 6	2
70× 5	2	9	3	12× 4	1	56× 7	48× 8	6
2÷ 2	7	6	17+ 9	3	5	8	1	5− 4
1	210× 6	5	7	8 8	9+ 4	2	3	9

243

162× 6	9	2− 7	2÷ 4	2	3	32× 8	8− 1	5 5
3	1920× 8	5	5− 2	7	4	1	9	15+ 6
3+ 2	5	8	2− 7	9	8− 1	4	6	3
1	6	11+ 2	7+ 3	4	9	1350× 5	1568× 7	8
7 7	3+ 1	3	40× 8	6	5	9	2÷ 2	4
18+ 9	2	6	1	5	8	3	4	7
4	21× 7	1	3− 5	8	6	3÷ 2	14+ 3	9
5	3	5− 4	8− 9	1	7	18+ 6	8	21+ 2
2÷ 8	4	9	6	3	2	7	5	1

244

30× 1	5	6	8+ 4	28× 2	7	17+ 8	24× 3	8− 9
18+ 4	6	2− 5	3	4− 7	2	9	8	1
13+ 6	8	7	1	3	252× 9	4	7+ 2	5
2	4÷ 4	1	8	3− 5	3	16+ 7	23+ 9	2− 6
5	1	8− 2	9	6	8	3	7	4
17+ 8	9	3	3+ 2	1	5	36× 6	4	105× 7
9	5− 2	17+ 8	210× 7	2÷ 4	6	1	5	3
3 3	7	9	6	8	14+ 4	7+ 5	5− 1	4÷ 2
84× 7	3	4	5	9	1	2	6	8

245

1− 8	36× 4	2÷ 3	35× 7	5	8− 9	1	3÷ 6	2
7	9	6	13+ 8	216× 4	15× 3	5	20+ 2	1
6× 2	3	1	4	6	20+ 5	7	8	9
11+ 4	7	2÷ 2	1	9	8	8+ 3	5	23+ 6
20+ 5	6	9	3+ 2	1	4	2÷ 8	7	3
8− 9	1	8640× 4	5	168× 8	17+ 6	1− 2	3	7
2÷ 1	2	8	6	3	7	4	19+ 9	5
2÷ 3	13+ 8	35× 5	9	7	17+ 2	6	1	4
6	5	7	1− 3	2	1	9	2÷ 4	8

246

2÷ 2	4	3÷ 3	9	280× 7	8	5	6× 6	1
16+ 8	1	5	7+ 6	216× 9	4	4÷ 2	19+ 7	3
7	3÷ 6	2	15× 5	1	3	8	1− 4	9
8− 1	2	2− 9	7	20× 4	2÷ 6	3	5	2− 8
9	16+ 7	24× 8	3	5	2− 2	4	56× 1	6
4	5	28× 1	3+ 2	3	3− 9	4− 6	22+ 8	7
2÷ 3	8	7	1	6	5	9	5+ 2	20× 4
6	9	4	22+ 8	2	1	6− 7	3	5
14+ 5	3	6	4	8	7	12+ 1	9	2

247

[63×]9	[14+]8	6	[140×]7	4	5	[3÷]1	3	[1-]2
7	[2÷]2	1	[432×]6	9	8	4	5	3
[84×]3	7	[1-]4	[7+]5	[8-]1	9	6	[2÷]2	8
4	[42×]1	5	2	[4-]7	[9+]6	3	[20+]8	9
1	6	7	[6-]9	3	2	8	4	[5]5
[15+]6	9	[192×]8	3	[5]5	1	[19+]2	[28×]7	4
[3-]2	5	3	8	6	4	7	[8-]9	1
[5-]8	3	[12+]9	[4]4	[17+]2	7	5	[7+]1	6
[1-]5	4	2	1	8	3	9	6	7

248

[252×]7	6	[3÷]3	1	[18+]8	4	[17+]9	[7+]2	5
3	2	[14+]5	[1-]4	6	[84×]7	8	[8-]9	1
[28×]4	7	9	5	2	6	[105×]3	[64×]1	8
1	[27×]9	[11+]6	2	3	5	7	8	[280×]4
[6]6	3	[17+]8	9	[22+]4	[3+]2	1	5	7
[360×]9	1	7	6	5	[14+]8	4	3	[12+]2
5	8	[2÷]4	[21×]7	[8-]9	1	2	6	3
[14+]8	4	2	3	[21×]1	[9]9	[24+]5	[13+]7	6
2	[5]5	[8×]1	8	7	3	6	4	9

249

[80×]5	2	[14+]8	6	[560×]4	1	9	[16+]3	7
[8-]1	8	[270×]9	5	7	4	[192×]3	6	2
9	5	6	[12×]3	[4÷]2	[35×]7	4	1	8
[7+]2	1	3	4	8	5	[1890×]6	7	9
[21+]8	6	1	[126×]7	9	2	5	[96×]4	3
[84×]3	7	[11+]5	[17+]2	6	9	1	8	[216×]4
7	4	2	1	[8-]5	[6+]3	[11+]8	9	6
[3-]6	3	4	9	1	8	7	[3-]2	5
[36×]4	9	[1-]7	8	[36×]3	6	2	[4-]5	1

250

[3÷]1	[4÷]2	8	[105×]3	7	5	[5-]4	9	[13+]6
3	9	[216×]2	6	[1-]5	8	[42×...]1	[14+]4	7
[4-]5	4	1	7	8	9	6	3	[10×]2
9	6	[11+]4	[4÷]8	[3÷]1	2	[2-]3	7	5
[2-]4	8	7	2	3	1	5	[5-]6	[5-]9
6	7	[14+]5	[23+]9	2	3	[4÷]8	1	4
[120×]8	3	6	4	9	7	2	[8+]5	1
[9+]7	5	3	1	[19+]4	6	9	2	8
2	1	9	5	6	4	7	8	3

251

[6×]3	[2-]5	7	[5-]1	6	4	[144×]2	9	8
2	1	[8-]9	[3-]8	5	3	[120×]6	[168×]4	7
[2-]9	7	[2÷]4	[2-]3	[1]1	[17+]8	5	[4÷]2	6
[21+]6	[144×]3	2	5	7	9	4	8	[3+]1
7	8	[9+]5	4	9	1	[2÷]3	6	2
8	6	[10+]3	[14×]2	4	5	[80×]1	[7×]7	[20+]9
[18+]5	4	6	7	8	2	[17+]9	1	3
[4÷]4	9	1	[3÷]6	2	7	8	3	5
1	[4÷]2	8	[3÷]9	3	6	7	5	4

252

[700×]5	7	[16+]6	[1-]8	[24×]3	9	[16+]2	[7+]4	1
4	5	3	9	8	1	6	2	[7]7
[54×]6	[4÷]1	7	[60×]3	4	5	8	[2-]9	[3÷]2
9	4	[3+]2	[14+]5	1	8	3	7	6
[1008×]7	9	1	[4÷]4	[11+]6	[2÷]2	5	[360×]3	8
2	[17+]8	9	1	5	4	7	[1-]6	3
8	[1008×]3	4	6	2	7	[8-]9	1	5
[3÷]1	[6]6	[112×]8	2	[63×]7	[72×]3	4	[180×]5	9
3	[7+]2	5	7	9	6	[8×]1	8	4

253

5− 7	2	17+ 9	8	20× 4	5	3÷ 3	1	24× 6
4− 3	7	3− 2	4÷ 1	252× 6	22+ 8	5	9	4
8− 1	9	5	4	2	2− 6	8	105× 3	7
17+ 8	10+ 6	1	3	7	2016× 9	4	5	4÷ 2
9	3	7− 7	6+ 5	1	4	3÷ 6	2	8
6 6	1	18+ 4	9	5	7	2	840× 8	3
2− 2	4	5− 3	4− 6	17+ 8	1	9	7	5
9+ 4	5	8	2	9	16+ 3	7	6	8− 1
3− 5	8	42× 6	7	5+ 3	2	4÷ 1	4	9

254

2÷ 6	2− 3	5	7− 9	2	28× 4	1	7	8× 8
3	14+ 7	2	5	13+ 4	6	17+ 9	8	1
14+ 5	9	84× 4	7	1	3	4÷ 8	3÷ 2	6
17+ 8	288× 4	3	17+ 6	7	1	2	45× 5	9
9	2	6	8	12+ 3	5	4	8− 1	7
7 7	6	14× 1	3	19+ 8	2	2− 5	9	15+ 4
8× 4	1	7	2	9	280× 8	3	6	5
2	17+ 8	9	24× 1	5	7	2− 6	4	6× 3
1	3− 5	8	4	6	19+ 9	7	3	2

255

6− 7	7+ 2	96× 3	4	16+ 9	1	6	5	3− 8
1	3	2	8	6048× 7	6	4	9	120× 5
21+ 8	5	8− 9	6× 2	6× 1	10+ 3	7	4	6
12+ 5	8	1	3	6	56× 2	9	7	4
3	13+ 7	6	3+ 1	2	4	13+ 5	8	8− 9
4	324× 9	56× 8	1− 5	5− 3	7	3÷ 2	6	1
9	4	7	6	8	4− 5	1	3÷ 3	1− 2
3÷ 2	30× 6	5	20+ 7	288× 4	9	8	1	3
6	1	4	9	120× 5	8	3	5− 2	7

256

8− 1	54× 9	6	23+ 8	5	192× 4	2	630× 3	7
9	21+ 7	17+ 8	1	4	6	3	2	5
5	1	9	3	6	5− 7	20× 4	64× 8	2
8	21× 3	7	7+ 6	1	2	5	1512× 9	4
11+ 2	6	3	315× 5	17+ 8	9	7	4	1 1
672× 3	2÷ 2	4	9	7	15× 5	5− 1	6	18+ 8
7	8	3− 5	2÷ 4	2	3	6	1	9
2− 6	4	2	12+ 7	8− 9	1	5040× 8	5	3
4	4− 5	1	2	3	8	9	7	6

257

4− 7	3	30× 5	216× 9	120× 4	48× 6	1	4÷ 2	8
17+ 9	9+ 4	6	3	5	8	3+ 2	1	15+ 7
8	5	2	4	6	3÷ 9	3	7	1
19+ 2	9	7	24+ 5	7− 8	1	270× 6	120× 3	13+ 4
2÷ 4	2	1	7	9	3	5	8	6
24× 6	1	4	17+ 8	7	2	9	5	3
4− 5	56× 7	8− 9	1	6+ 3	17+ 4	8	108× 6	2
1	8	24× 3	3÷ 6	2	5	1260× 7	4	9
2÷ 3	6	8	2	1	7	3− 4	9	5

258

10× 2	1260× 5	22+ 8	7	54× 9	6	4÷ 1	4	3 3
5	6	7	4− 9	5− 8	3+ 1	2	3 3	32× 4
3− 4	7	6	5	3	19+ 2	8− 9	1	8
7	1− 4	3	3− 2	5	9	8	1260× 6	1
8− 1	9	5 5	4÷ 8	2	4	3	7	6
17+ 9	6× 3	2	5− 6	1	8	19+ 4	5	70× 7
8	18+ 1	9	7+ 3	24× 4	7	6	17+ 2	5
2÷ 3	8	6+ 1	4	6	2− 5	7	9	2
6	2 2	4	1	4− 7	3	22+ 5	8	9

259

2	4	7	6	8	5	9	1	3
4	7	9	2	3	6	5	8	1
5	8	6	3	7	1	2	9	4
6	2	5	9	1	3	8	4	7
7	3	1	4	2	8	6	5	9
3	9	8	5	4	2	1	7	6
1	5	3	7	6	9	4	2	8
8	6	2	1	9	4	7	3	5
9	1	4	8	5	7	3	6	2

260

4	6	9	5	1	3	7	8	2
2	5	3	7	8	9	1	4	6
7	3	2	9	6	8	4	5	1
9	2	8	6	3	1	5	7	4
3	9	5	8	4	2	6	1	7
8	4	7	1	5	6	9	2	3
6	7	1	2	9	4	8	3	5
1	8	4	3	7	5	2	6	9
5	1	6	4	2	7	3	9	8

261

5	8	9	3	1	2	7	6	4
4	2	7	1	6	3	5	8	9
3	7	8	9	2	6	1	4	5
7	9	4	8	3	5	2	1	6
9	4	1	6	5	8	3	2	7
2	3	6	4	9	7	8	5	1
8	5	2	7	4	1	6	9	3
6	1	5	2	7	4	9	3	8
1	6	3	5	8	9	4	7	2

262

5	3	9	6	1	8	2	7	4
8	4	6	9	7	3	5	2	1
9	2	1	5	3	4	6	8	7
6	8	7	1	2	5	4	3	9
2	7	5	4	8	9	3	1	6
1	6	4	8	5	2	7	9	3
7	5	3	2	9	6	1	4	8
3	9	2	7	4	1	8	6	5
4	1	8	3	6	7	9	5	2

263

6	2	7	5	8	1	3	9	4
4	1	5	3	2	6	8	7	9
5	4	1	9	6	3	7	2	8
9	5	8	6	3	4	2	1	7
2	8	6	4	5	7	9	3	1
7	6	3	1	9	2	4	8	5
1	3	2	8	7	9	5	4	6
3	9	4	7	1	8	6	5	2
8	7	9	2	4	5	1	6	3

264

4	2	6	3	8	7	5	1	9
9	1	3	7	5	8	4	2	6
7	8	2	5	4	9	1	6	3
5	7	4	8	3	6	2	9	1
3	9	1	4	7	2	6	8	5
8	5	9	2	6	1	3	4	7
2	6	7	1	9	5	8	3	4
1	4	5	6	2	3	9	7	8
6	3	8	9	1	4	7	5	2

265

²ⷌ÷6	³÷9	3	²2	²÷4	¹⁴⁺7	¹⁻8	⁴⁻1	5
3	¹⁸⁰ˣ4	⁸ˣ9	1	2	5	7	¹⁹⁺8	⁴⁸ˣ6
9	5	⁷⁺1	³⁻6	3	2	4	7	8
²⁹⁺5	7	2	3	1	¹⁷⁺8	9	²⁴ˣ6	4
8	²⁻6	4	¹⁴⁺5	9	³÷1	3	⁵⁻2	7
1	8	²¹⁰ˣ6	7	5	⁷⁻9	2	4	3
³⁺2	1	³¹⁵ˣ5	¹⁵⁺8	7	¹³⁺4	²⁰⁺6	3	⁷⁻9
⁸⁴ˣ4	3	7	9	¹⁹²ˣ8	6	1	5	2
7	⁴÷2	8	4	6	3	5	⁸⁻9	1

266

¹⁴⁴ˣ1	8	¹⁴⁰ˣ5	4	7	²÷6	3	⁷⁻2	9
9	²⁻5	3	⁷⁺1	6	²¹⁺8	4	⁶⁻7	⁵⁻2
2	²¹⁺3	8	⁴²ˣ6	²⁰ˣ4	³⁻5	9	1	7
¹⁶⁺3	6	4	7	5	2	¹⁷⁺8	9	⁶⁺1
7	²÷2	³⁻6	¹⁷⁺9	8	²⁻3	1	²²⁺4	5
6	4	9	²⁻5	2	⁶⁻1	7	8	3
⁴4	³⁺1	2	3	9	7	⁴⁰ˣ5	²÷6	²⁻8
²⁰⁺5	⁶³ˣ9	7	⁸ˣ8	1	4	2	3	6
8	7	²÷1	2	¹⁸⁺3	9	6	⁵5	¹⁻4

267

³⁰ˣ6	5	¹⁷⁺8	2	7	⁴÷4	1	³÷3	9
⁵⁻3	8	²¹⁶⁰ˣ6	4	2	5	9	⁶⁻7	1
⁹⁺7	2	⁷⁺3	¹⁷⁺8	9	¹1	²⁰⁺4	5	¹⁻6
³⁻4	7	1	3	8	6	2	⁴⁻9	5
⁵5	¹²⁺1	7	⁸⁻9	⁹⁺4	2	¹⁴ˣ3	¹¹⁵²ˣ6	8
¹⁷⁺9	²⁻6	4	1	5	7	8	³⁺2	¹⁻3
8	4	⁵⁰ˣ5	¹⁹⁺7	3	9	¹²⁶ˣ6	1	2
⁸⁻1	9	2	5	²⁸⁸ˣ6	3	7	²÷8	4
⁵⁴ˣ2	3	9	6	1	8	¹⁴⁰ˣ5	4	7

268

³⁺1	2	²⁴ˣ4	6	¹⁰⁵ˣ5	⁶⁻9	3	⁵⁶ˣ8	7
⁸⁴⁰ˣ5	8	²⁴ˣ1	4	7	3	⁴⁵ˣ9	¹⁹²ˣ2	6
7	⁹⁺4	3	2	⁷²ˣ6	1	5	⁵⁴ˣ9	8
3	5	¹⁷⁺9	8	4	⁶⁻7	1	6	2
⁷⁻9	6	8	¹⁵ˣ5	3	⁴÷2	7	¹⁻4	⁴÷1
2	1	7	3	²⁰⁺9	8	6	5	4
¹¹⁺8	3	¹²⁺5	7	2	6	²⁻4	1	⁸⁻9
¹⁵¹²ˣ4	9	³÷6	1	8	⁹⁺5	2	⁶⁻7	³¹⁵ˣ3
6	7	2	⁸⁻9	1	4	8	3	5

269

⁵⁷⁶ˣ4	2	9	8	¹⁹⁺1	5	6	7	⁴÷3
⁴÷2	¹²⁺3	4	⁸⁻1	¹⁹⁺6	8	5	⁵⁻9	7
8	²⁻6	5	9	⁶³ˣ3	¹⁴ˣ2	7	4	⁶⁺1
¹⁸⁹ˣ9	8	¹⁰⁺6	4	7	3	1	⁸⁺2	5
7	²¹⁺5	2	6	8	⁸⁻9	⁹⁶ˣ3	1	⁴4
3	⁸⁻9	⁵⁶ˣ8	7	²÷2	1	4	5	³⁻6
¹⁻5	1	²³⁺7	³⁰ˣ2	4	¹⁹⁺6	8	3	²⁴ˣ9
6	7	1	3	5	4	9	8	⁴÷2
⁴÷1	4	3	5	¹⁶⁺9	7	³÷2	6	8

270

⁵⁴ˣ6	¹⁷⁺9	8	⁴⁰ˣ2	5	4	²⁻1	3	⁴⁻7
9	²¹⁺7	6	¹⁶⁰ˣ5	8	1	²⁻4	2	3
⁴÷2	8	1	9	4	⁹⁰ˣ5	¹¹⁺3	7	¹⁻6
²¹ˣ3	²⁴ˣ6	7	1	2	9	8	¹⁸⁰ˣ4	⁴⁻5
7	4	³⁶ˣ3	²³⁺8	9	6	³⁻2	5	1
²÷8	1	2	6	⁴²ˣ7	3	⁵⁻5	9	²⁻4
4	¹⁹⁺3	5	7	6	8	⁸⁻9	1	2
⁵⁰ˣ5	2	4	¹⁰⁸ˣ3	1	²⁻7	6	²²⁺8	³¹⁺9
1	5	9	4	3	2	7	6	8

271

4	9	1	3	2	6	8	5	7
3	8	6	4	5	2	1	7	9
2	5	7	1	8	9	4	3	6
1	2	3	5	6	4	7	9	8
5	3	2	8	4	7	9	6	1
9	1	5	7	3	8	6	4	2
6	7	8	9	1	5	3	2	4
7	6	4	2	9	1	5	8	3
8	4	9	6	7	3	2	1	5

272

9	1	6	2	3	5	7	8	4
2	5	7	3	8	9	6	4	1
1	6	5	7	4	3	8	9	2
4	2	3	5	9	8	1	6	7
7	8	2	9	1	6	4	5	3
3	4	1	6	5	7	9	2	8
5	7	4	8	6	2	3	1	9
8	3	9	4	2	1	5	7	6
6	9	8	1	7	4	2	3	5

273

9	6	5	3	2	8	1	7	4
7	5	8	6	9	3	4	2	1
1	3	4	8	5	7	2	6	9
4	8	3	5	7	1	6	9	2
6	9	7	2	1	4	8	5	3
2	7	6	9	4	5	3	1	8
3	4	2	1	6	9	5	8	7
5	1	9	4	8	2	7	3	6
8	2	1	7	3	6	9	4	5

274

4	6	5	2	7	8	3	1	9
3	1	4	5	6	7	8	9	2
8	9	7	1	2	5	6	3	4
7	3	8	9	4	1	5	2	6
5	7	1	8	9	6	2	4	3
2	3	6	4	1	9	7	5	8
6	5	9	7	3	2	4	8	1
9	2	8	3	5	4	1	6	7
1	4	2	6	8	3	9	7	5

275

6	3	5	2	9	7	1	4	8
3	7	6	4	2	5	9	8	1
1	6	8	3	5	9	4	2	7
2	8	9	6	3	4	7	1	5
8	9	3	5	4	1	6	7	2
4	2	1	8	7	3	5	9	6
7	5	4	1	6	8	2	3	9
5	1	7	9	8	2	3	6	4
9	4	2	7	1	6	8	5	3

276

7	1	6	8	9	5	3	4	2
4	6	8	9	2	1	5	3	7
5	8	9	7	3	6	1	2	4
6	5	4	1	8	7	2	9	3
9	7	3	6	1	2	4	5	8
2	9	7	3	6	4	8	1	5
8	3	5	2	4	9	6	7	1
3	2	1	4	5	8	7	6	9
1	4	2	5	7	3	9	8	6

277

³⁶ˣ9	¹⁹²ˣ8	6	4	³÷3	1	¹²⁺5	7	⁴÷2
4	⁴⁻5	1	²²⁺7	2	3	⁵⁴ˣ9	6	8
²⁴⁰ˣ5	²⁻7	9	2	²⁴⁺4	8	²÷6	3	⁶³ˣ1
8	²÷4	³3	5	6	9	¹⁻1	2	7
6	2	²²⁺8	²÷3	²⁰ˣ1	5	¹¹²ˣ7	⁴4	9
²÷1	9	5	6	³¹⁵ˣ7	4	2	8	³⁻3
2	³÷3	²÷4	9	5	¹⁶⁸ˣ7	8	⁶⁺1	6
¹⁰⁺7	1	2	⁹⁺8	¹⁻9	6	⁴⁻3	5	¹⁻4
3	⁴²ˣ6	7	1	8	2	³⁶ˣ4	9	5

278

³³⁶ˣ8	³⁺2	²⁻9	7	²÷3	6	⁹⁺4	5	⁹⁺1
7	1	¹²ˣ4	3	¹³⁺5	2	6	²⁸⁸ˣ9	8
6	⁹⁴⁵ˣ7	5	9	1	8	⁸⁻3	2	4
⁴÷1	3	³÷2	6	9	5	8	4	¹⁴⁺7
4	¹⁷⁺8	¹⁴⁺3	³÷2	6	7	⁷9	⁸⁻1	5
¹⁷⁺3	9	7	4	¹⁰⁺8	1	³⁵ˣ5	²³⁺6	2
5	¹³⁺4	1	8	2	9	7	3	6
9	¹³⁺5	⁶ˣ6	1	⁵⁶ˣ7	4	2	8	²⁷ˣ3
2	6	³⁻8	5	¹⁻4	3	⁶⁻1	7	9

279

¹⁻5	³²⁴ˣ9	2	3	6	¹²ˣ4	1	²¹⁺8	7
4	²⁴⁺8	7	9	³⁻2	3	⁵⁻6	1	5
¹⁻3	4	¹²⁹⁶ˣ9	6	5	⁸ˣ8	²¹⁺2	7	1
³÷2	3	8	¹³⁺4	⁸⁻9	1	7	5	⁴³²ˣ6
6	³⁻7	4	8	1	¹⁰ˣ2	¹⁵ˣ5	3	9
¹⁴⁺7	2	⁴²ˣ6	1	⁷²ˣ3	5	⁵⁷⁶ˣ4	9	8
⁷²ˣ9	5	1	7	4	6	8	2	³3
1	¹⁸ˣ6	3	¹²⁺5	²⁴⁺8	7	9	¹⁹²ˣ4	2
8	1	5	2	²⁻7	9	³3	6	4

280

⁸⁰ˣ5	1	²÷4	8	6	⁴⁻7	3	⁷⁻2	9
2	8	¹⁵⁺6	9	4	⁴⁰ˣ1	5	²⁵⁺7	3
³⁺1	2	5	3	²⁷⁺7	8	4	9	6
¹⁴⁺6	²⁻7	9	¹1	5	3	8	¹⁴⁺4	2
8	¹²⁺6	2	¹⁵ˣ5	3	4	⁵⁻9	⁸⁻1	7
²⁰⁺7	4	¹⁴⁴ˣ3	6	8	9	¹⁰ˣ2	5	1
4	¹⁷⁺9	8	2	¹³⁺1	³⁺6	³⁰ˣ7	¹⁴⁺3	¹²⁰ˣ5
9	³3	7	4	2	5	1	6	8
²⁻3	5	¹⁷⁺1	7	9	2	³÷6	²÷8	4

281

⁵⁴ˣ1	6	²÷3	²⁰ˣ4	5	¹⁸⁺7	8	⁴÷2	⁶³ˣ9
⁴4	9	6	²÷2	1	³⁰ˣ5	3	8	7
¹⁹⁺8	4	⁶⁺1	3	2	6	¹⁴⁺9	²⁻7	5
7	²÷2	4	²⁴⁺9	⁵⁴ˣ6	1	5	¹⁻3	²⁻8
¹³⁺2	5	³⁻8	7	9	⁶⁺3	1	4	6
6	⁴⁻3	5	8	²⁸ˣ7	4	2	⁸⁻9	1
²²⁺5	7	⁴⁻2	6	¹⁻8	9	⁸⁺4	1	3
9	8	²⁻7	⁴⁻1	¹¹⁺3	2	6	¹⁷⁺5	4
²⁻3	1	9	5	²÷4	8	7	6	2

282

⁴÷4	²÷2	1	⁴⁻5	²⁴ˣ8	²⁻3	⁸⁴ˣ7	9	³⁻6
1	²¹⁺7	4	9	3	5	6	2	⁹⁶ˣ8
³3	¹⁵⁺1	7	²⁴ˣ4	¹⁴⁺5	9	¹⁴⁺8	6	2
5	9	3	6	²⁻7	4	2	⁴⁻8	⁶⁻1
²⁴⁺8	⁶⁺3	2	1	9	6	⁵⁻5	4	7
7	8	³⁻5	³÷2	6	1	4	²⁻3	³⁶ˣ9
9	¹⁻5	²⁻6	⁵⁻7	2	8	²⁰⁺3	1	4
¹⁴⁺6	4	8	⁶⁺3	1	2	9	²⁻7	¹⁵ˣ5
2	6	⁹9	²²⁴ˣ8	4	7	1	5	3

283

60× 3	5	4÷ 4	1	6× 6	9	17+ 7	2	8
4	18× 2	9	2- 3	1	5	6	224× 8	7
1- 6	2- 9	3+ 1	5	18+ 3	7	8	4	3÷ 2
5	7	2	5- 4	4- 8	11+ 3	10+ 9	1	6
12+ 1	6	5	9	4	8	2 2	10+ 7	3
9+ 7	48× 3	8	2	9	6	3- 1	20× 5	4
2	9+ 1	2÷ 6	1- 8	7	21+ 4	5	3	9
1- 9	8	3	42× 7	11+ 5	2	4	3- 6	4- 1
8	11+ 4	7	6	6+ 2	1	3	9	5

284

8- 9	1	3	7	3÷ 6	2	5760× 5	4	8
1- 3	24+ 7	13+ 6	120× 5	8	2÷ 1	2	9	4
4	8	2	2÷ 1	3	140× 5	24+ 6	7	27× 9
1- 6	9	5	2	7	4	8	3	1
5	80× 2	2÷ 8	4	54× 9	6	7 7	672× 1	3
8	5	5- 4	9	6× 2	3	12+ 1	6	7
1 1	162× 3	9	11+ 6	5	7	4	8	2
3136× 7	6	1	3	15+ 4	8	6- 9	18+ 2	5
2	4	7	8	8- 1	9	3	5	6

285

24× 3	2	8- 1	9	1- 6	6+ 5	3- 8	28+ 4	7
4	2÷ 6	3	5+ 2	7	1	5	9	8
8- 1	9	14+ 2	3	1- 4	22+ 6	1- 7	8	30× 5
8 8	24× 3	7	6× 1	5	9	2÷ 4	2	6
2- 9	8	5	6	6+ 3	7	8× 2	1	4
7	1	1- 4	5	2	4- 8	16+ 6	3÷ 3	9
120× 6	5	1- 9	8	1	4	3	7	2÷ 2
3- 2	4	21+ 6	1- 7	8	1- 3	8- 9	90× 5	1
5	7	8	5- 4	9	2	1	6	3

286

8- 1	9	108× 3	4÷ 8	2	7	280× 5	6	2- 4
4- 5	6+ 1	6	2	3	8	3- 4	7	16+ 9
9	5	56× 2	1- 4	6	3	16× 1	8	7
2÷ 6	1- 8	7	3	5- 4	9	2	6+ 1	14+ 5
3	7	4	40× 5	8	22+ 6	9	2	1
4÷ 2	2÷ 6	4- 5	2- 9	6+ 1	4	3- 7	3	8
8	3	9	7	5	1	1728× 6	4	1- 2
2÷ 4	2	19+ 1	6	7	5	8	9	3
224× 7	4	8	1	7- 9	2	14+ 3	5	6

287

3- 8	5	4- 7	4÷ 4	12+ 1	7+ 2	54× 9	3- 6	3
3- 4	7	3	1	8	5	6	18× 2	9
2÷ 2	1	1- 8	7	3	2- 6	4	45× 9	5
24+ 3	6	4÷ 4	24+ 9	7	8	4- 1	5	4- 2
7	8	1	1- 5	19+ 9	3	14+ 2	4	6
8- 9	9+ 4	5	6	11+ 2	7	8	15+ 3	1
1	16+ 2	6	8	5	8- 9	3 3	7	4
20+ 6	14+ 3	9	2	4	1	35× 5	448× 8	7
5	9	1- 2	3	2- 6	4	7	1 1	8

288

126× 7	3	2÷ 4	8- 9	9+ 1	8	4- 2	6	4- 5
19+ 4	6	8	1	720× 2	5	13+ 7	6+ 3	9
6	18+ 4	5 5	12+ 3	8	9	1	2	5- 7
9	8	6	4	16+ 3	7	5	1	2
6+ 1	2	3	5	15+ 7	6	2÷ 4	72× 9	8
16+ 5	2- 9	7	2	6	6+ 3	8	3- 4	1
8	60× 5	2	6	180× 4	1	63× 9	7	1- 3
3	126× 1	9	7 7	5	2	2- 6	8	4
2	7	9+ 1	8	9	4	1- 3	30× 5	6

289

2	8	5	4	9	3	7	6	1
5	9	4	3	6	2	8	1	7
4	3	2	7	8	9	1	5	6
9	5	7	2	4	1	6	8	3
7	2	3	6	1	4	5	9	8
8	6	9	1	2	5	3	7	4
6	4	1	9	7	8	2	3	5
3	1	6	8	5	7	4	2	9
1	7	8	5	3	6	9	4	2

290

5	2	9	8	4	1	3	6	7
3	5	6	1	2	4	9	7	8
1	7	8	6	9	3	5	2	4
8	9	5	4	7	2	1	3	6
6	3	2	7	8	5	4	1	9
9	1	3	2	6	8	7	4	5
2	4	1	9	5	7	6	8	3
7	8	4	5	3	6	2	9	1
4	6	7	3	1	9	8	5	2

291

4	7	1	8	9	2	6	5	3
1	3	7	4	5	6	8	2	9
6	1	5	3	4	8	7	9	2
9	5	4	2	8	7	3	6	1
2	6	9	1	3	5	4	8	7
7	4	8	9	2	3	5	1	6
3	2	6	5	7	9	1	4	8
5	8	2	7	6	1	9	3	4
8	9	3	6	1	4	2	7	5

292

1	4	7	9	2	3	5	8	6
2	8	4	1	3	6	9	5	7
8	9	2	5	4	7	1	6	3
6	5	3	4	9	8	2	7	1
7	2	6	8	5	4	3	1	9
4	7	8	3	1	2	6	9	5
9	6	1	2	7	5	4	3	8
5	3	9	6	8	1	7	4	2
3	1	5	7	6	9	8	2	4

293

2	6	3	7	5	1	9	8	4
1	7	8	4	3	5	6	2	9
4	3	2	9	6	8	7	5	1
9	2	7	1	4	6	5	3	8
8	9	5	6	2	4	3	1	7
5	4	9	3	8	7	1	6	2
3	1	6	2	7	9	8	4	5
7	8	4	5	1	3	2	9	6
6	5	1	8	9	2	4	7	3

294

4	5	8	7	9	1	2	6	3
1	4	5	2	6	7	3	8	9
2	8	9	4	3	6	1	7	5
7	6	2	8	4	9	5	3	1
3	2	4	9	1	8	6	5	7
8	9	1	3	2	5	7	4	6
9	3	6	5	7	2	4	1	8
6	7	3	1	5	4	8	9	2
5	1	7	6	8	3	9	2	4

295

3	8	7	4	2	6	5	1	9
4	9	2	6	5	1	3	8	7
8	7	1	2	3	4	9	5	6
5	4	3	8	6	7	1	9	2
7	5	9	1	4	2	8	6	3
1	3	6	7	8	9	4	2	5
6	2	8	5	9	3	7	4	1
9	6	4	3	1	5	2	7	8
2	1	5	9	7	8	6	3	4

296

5	7	2	4	6	9	1	8	3
1	9	5	8	3	4	2	6	7
4	6	9	2	5	8	3	7	1
7	8	3	5	2	6	4	1	9
9	2	4	3	1	7	8	5	6
2	1	8	7	4	3	6	9	5
3	5	7	6	8	1	9	2	4
8	3	6	1	9	5	7	4	2
6	4	1	9	7	2	5	3	8

297

6	2	9	5	3	7	1	4	8
2	3	6	1	5	4	7	8	9
4	9	1	3	2	5	8	6	7
5	1	2	4	6	8	9	7	3
3	6	7	2	8	9	5	1	4
8	4	5	9	7	3	6	2	1
1	8	4	7	9	2	3	5	6
9	7	8	6	4	1	2	3	5
7	5	3	8	1	6	4	9	2

298

9	7	8	5	2	3	1	4	6
2	9	5	8	1	4	3	6	7
6	8	1	9	3	2	4	7	5
4	3	2	6	8	5	7	1	9
3	4	9	2	6	7	8	5	1
1	2	6	3	7	9	5	8	4
5	1	3	7	4	8	6	9	2
8	6	7	4	5	1	9	2	3
7	5	4	1	9	6	2	3	8

299

2	3	7	9	1	8	5	6	4
5	2	8	6	4	3	9	1	7
6	5	3	1	7	2	4	9	8
9	1	4	3	2	5	8	7	6
3	8	1	2	9	6	7	4	5
7	6	2	4	5	1	3	8	9
8	7	9	5	3	4	6	2	1
4	9	5	8	6	7	1	3	2
1	4	6	7	8	9	2	5	3

300

7	8	5	3	6	4	9	2	1
4	7	1	5	3	6	8	9	2
5	2	3	7	4	8	6	1	9
8	9	4	2	5	1	7	6	3
3	4	2	9	8	5	1	7	6
1	5	6	4	9	7	2	3	8
9	3	8	6	1	2	4	5	7
6	1	7	8	2	9	3	4	5
2	6	9	1	7	3	5	8	4